Anti-Blackness and Human Monstrosity in
Black American Horror Fiction

NEW SUNS: RACE, GENDER, AND

SEXUALITY IN THE SPECULATIVE

Susana M. Morris and Kinitra D. Brooks, Series Editors

Anti-Blackness and Human Monstrosity in Black American Horror Fiction

Jerry Rafiki Jenkins

THE OHIO STATE UNIVERSITY PRESS
COLUMBUS

Library of Congress Cataloging-in-Publication Data

Names: Jenkins, Rafiki, 1967– author.

Title: Anti-Blackness and human monstrosity in Black American horror fiction / Jerry Rafiki Jenkins.

Other titles: New suns: race, gender, and sexuality in the speculative.

Description: Columbus : The Ohio State University Press, [2024] | Series: New suns: race, gender, and sexuality in the speculative | Includes bibliographical references and index. | Summary: "Examines the human monsters—those of White rage, respectability, not-ness, and serial killing—that frequently appear in Black American horror fiction, including works by Tananarive Due, Brandon Massey, Nnedi Okorafor, Victor LaValle, and others, to argue that these monsters represent specific ideologies of American anti-Blackness"—Provided by publisher.

Identifiers: LCCN 2023052235 | ISBN 9780814215364 (hardback) | ISBN 081421536X (hardback) | ISBN 9780814283417 (ebook) | ISBN 0814283411 (ebook)

Subjects: LCSH: Due, Tananarive, 1966—Criticism and interpretation. | Massey, Brandon, 1973—Criticism and interpretation. | Okorafor, Nnedi—Criticism and interpretation. | LaValle, Victor, 1972—Criticism and interpretation. | Racism against Black people. | Racism in literature. | Horror tales, American—History and criticism. | American fiction—African American authors—History and criticism.

Classification: LCC PS374.B635 J46 2024 | DDC 813.609896073—dc23/eng/20240208

LC record available at https://lccn.loc.gov/2023052235

Other identifiers: ISBN 9780814259054 (paperback) | ISBN 0814259057 (paperback)

Cover design by Larry Nozik
Text composition by Stuart Rodriguez
Type set in Palatino Linotype

Dedicated to Beatrice Woodard and Jerry Michael Jenkins
(1946–2001)

CONTENTS

ACKNOWLEDGMENTS

I want to give a big thank you to all the staff and editors at New Suns, especially Ana M. Jimenez-Moreno, for their patience and belief in this project. I also want to thank the anonymous reviewers, whose insightful comments helped make this book better than what it started as. To Black Kirby, the artist collaborative composed of John Jennings and Stacey Robinson, thank you for producing a cover that captures the horrors discussed in this book. In addition to these wonderful people, I would like to acknowledge those folks who took time out of their lives to comment on various chapter drafts of this book: Jim Bradford, Lemuel "C-Cubed" Cabrera, Aaron Chizhik, Carlton Floyd, Martin Japtok, Yader Lanuza, and Glen "G-Dub" Wilson. I also want to acknowledge friends and family members who have provided valuable insights on the topics covered in this book: Cheka Jenkins, Umayma Alexander, Andrew Jenkins, Adrian Jenkins, Allan Jenkins, Michael Jenkins, Majesty Mathews, Emperess Guy, Jason Alexander, JaLiah Alexander, Moses Maddox, Amber Hartgens, Adrian Arancibia, Teahoen "Buu" Aaron, Amilcar Aaron, Shango Aaron, Brian "B-Smoov" Starr, Stephanie Sciurba, Leonard Thomas, Phillip Serrato, Melanie Marotta, Rick Fabes, Carol Martin, Raed Good, Naim Martin, John Isaac Watts Jr., Kiedra Taylor, John Gavin White, and the members of Palomar's Black Faculty and Staff Association.

I am also indebted to Palomar College's sabbatical committee for allowing me the time to revise this evolving project and to San Diego State University's Department of English and Comparative Literature for allowing me to create a course on Black horror. I would like to send a special thanks to Clairesa Clay (founder of Blerd City and Blerd City Con) and to the students who enrolled in my African American Horror fiction course (CLT-584: Topics in Comparative Horror Stories) at SDSU during the Spring 2022 and Spring 2023 semesters—our insightful and lively class discussions helped to shape the final draft of this book:

Spring 2022: Jesse Elkinton, Ren Evenson, Kailey Fabian, Sarah Fisher, Angelina Garcia, Donika Housh, Moroan Laz, Ali Loeza, Ayleen Maldonado, Emily McClelland, Sonia Morris, Nico Mullins, Sophia Nunez, Julia Nuti, Bonnie Palos, Melissa Perez, Raine Porath, Anisa Prom, Tania Romero, Hannah Sowers, Jacob Suarez, Mackenna Teeman, Kassandra Tejeda, Jaclyn Trejo, and Eryca Worthen.

Spring 2023: Monica Arreola, Bryan Beltran, Alexis Dyson, Brisa Fermin, Erica Hill, Joseph King, Sara King, Dharma Leon, Marrion Llanes, Allan Marin, Cecilia Medina, Maximiliano Morales, Jesse Munyoki, Lizzie O'Keeffe, Jimmy Palis, Miranda Roman, Evan Rose, Isabella Rubio, Martha Santana-Garcia, CJ Villegas, and Nina Vindiola.

Finally, and most importantly, I want to thank my sons—Isa, Ras, and Nyo—for their beingness and Katie Sciurba, my wife, partner, and intellectual teammate, who is always on point.

Barely Humans, Black Horror, and American Anti-Blackness

L. D. Peaslee's "A Human Monstrosity" (1913) and Jewelle Gomez's *The Gilda Stories* (1991) are the two texts that inspired the subject of this book. Peaslee's text, published in *Science,* is a short description of whom he considers a human monster: "On May 1, 1912, at Fayette, Missouri, was born a female child (colored) having two heads and three arms. The monstrosity was still-born, but had apparently completed its intra-uterine development" (982). Peaslee's description of the Black female child is noteworthy because it appears not to racialize human monstrosity. For instance, while the "most striking feature" of the child is her two heads, Peaslee notes that "there is no abnormality of any sort in connection with these heads except for the position" (982). Peaslee's decision not to link the girl's abnormalities to her Blackness or to make an argument for race realism—the belief that presumes that "racial differences exist," that racial hierarchies are "real," and that we should, therefore, "accept inequality as a biological fact" (Saini 80–85)—is itself striking because, as Jeffrey Jerome Cohen notes, "from the classical period into the twentieth century, race has been almost as powerful a catalyst to the creation of monsters [in the Western world] as culture, gender, and sexuality" (10). Indeed, although what "race" meant in the classical

1

period is different from how we imagine it today,[1] the lack of race realism in Peaslee's conception of human monstrosity is notable because it is one that emerged after the myth of the Monstrous Races lost its hold on the European imagination during the sixteenth century,[2] when the transatlantic slave trade and European colonialism were in full swing. For example, Peaslee's seemingly raceless depiction of human monstrosity is similar to the 1789 description of Peruntaloo, a thirteen-year-old boy of India's Gentoo cast, in *Philosophical Transactions of the Royal Society of London*. Although the drawings of Peruntaloo, whom the authors refer to as "a Monster of the human Species" (J. Anderson et al. 157), depict him as very brown-skinned, his skin color is not mentioned in the written description of him, nor is it claimed that skin color explains his "monstrosity."

Peaslee's decision to put "colored" in parenthesis after "female child" also implies that the sex of a human monster might be more important than its race. For instance, an 1887 article on a "human cyclopian monster" in *The Transactions of the Royal Irish Academy* claims that "cyclopia occurs with much greater frequency in the female than in the male" (Cunningham and Bennett 101). Although we know that the cyclopian baby under study is female, we do not discover that the baby is White until the end of the article, where she is depicted in a drawing. Similarly, in "A Quantitative Study in Human Teratology" (1930), Charles H. Mead informs readers about the sex of the "simple" (male) and "double" (female) human monsters under examination, but he does not identify the race(s) of these so-called monsters, and the drawings are not racially clear, though one could assume that they

---

1. For an insightful discussion of the difference between today's "caste racism" and the "racial prejudice" that existed in the pre-fifteenth-century world, see Martin Bernal's "Race in History."

2. Alexa Wright notes that the idea of human monstrosity in the West has its roots in the myth of the Monstrous Races, which dates to the publication of Ctesias's treatise on India in fourth century BCE (176). According to Wright, between fifth century BCE and sixteenth century CE, "[Monstrous Races] were popularly characterized throughout Europe as real creatures that could not be considered fully human because of their remote existence, far from 'civilized' human society" (174). Although the "appeal" of the Monstrous Races shifted to the literary and cinematic genres of science fiction, fantasy, and horror toward the end of the nineteenth century (Weinstock 17), the century when "European anti-Semitism and American racism towards black Americans [became] Gothic discourses given over to the making monstrous of particular kinds of bodies" (Halberstam 4), the Monstrous Races are reminders that "even when it is physically located elsewhere, human monstrosity is a construct that is intimately related to the social and moral values of the observer" (A. Wright 179–80).

are White (1–2). While the articles above provide drawings of their human monsters, their written descriptions of these monsters, unlike Peaslee's, are absent of overt racial categorization. I make this point not to prove that Peaslee or his predecessors and contemporaries were or were not racists— though it would not be surprising if they were, given that their publications cover the periods from eighteenth-century racialism (e.g., the works by David Hume, Immanuel Kant, Georges Leopold Cuvier, Johann Friedrich Blumenbach, and Thomas Jefferson) to the eugenics movement of the early decades of the twentieth century that spread to various parts of the world (e.g., Japan, China, India, the US, as well as Europe) after Francis Galton coined the term in 1883—but to point out that their assumptions about normal and abnormal humans are grounded in the same type of thinking as race realism. Indeed, human monstrosity in the articles above, like race, is defined by how one looks instead of what one does and thinks precisely because it is presumed that how one looks explains one's thoughts, actions, and place in the social universe.

In contrast to Peaslee and the scholars of human monstrosity discussed above, Gomez proposes in *The Gilda Stories*, "the first vampire novel with a black protagonist and the first vampire novel written by an African American author" (Nevins 189), that human monstrosity is not a question of biology but ideology. Gilda, a Black lesbian who is born into slavery and becomes a vampire after escaping enslavement, learned very early in life that White men "wearing the clothes of an overseer" are signs of "danger" (Gomez, *Gilda* 9). That danger, as Gilda recalls before she kills the slave catcher who is attempting to rape her, is theorized through her mother's explanation of why White people cannot differentiate butter from lard: "They ain't been here long 'nough. They just barely human. Maybe not even. They suck up the world, don't taste it" (11). While Gilda's mother swears that White people are "not fully human" (10), Gilda learns after she becomes a vampire that one's racialized body does not determine if one is or will be a human monster. For instance, Gilda refers to the White slave catcher, the Black pimp in Boston named Fox, and the twenty-first-century bounty hunters who are paid by the rich to capture vampires to rob them of their blood as "beasts on two legs" (67). Indeed, Gilda's confrontations with the beasts on two legs suggest that the "real" monsters in the novel and in America are, as Miriam Jones puts it, the "racists," "rapists," "pimps," and "power-hungry rich" who "literally feed off others" (166–67). While Gilda's conception of the human monster reminds us that, as

Natalie Wilson puts it, "interrogations of the monster are inevitably bound up with attempts to define the human" (9), it also proposes that theorizing human monstrosity has been part of Black American horror fiction since its inception.[3]

Linda Addison, the first Black American recipient of the Horror Writers Association's Bram Stoker Award, poses a question in "Genesis—The First Black Horror Writers/Storytellers" (2016) that alludes to the role that the human monster has played in Black American horror fiction: "Who were the first Black horror writers in a country that made enslaved Africans' everyday life horrific?" (12). Addison's question suggests that we should not be surprised that Black Americans were telling horror stories during the days of slavery because American slavery itself was an institution of horror and its monsters were very real. As Jess Nevins notes in *Horror Fiction in the 20th Century* (2020), "Horror, in the form of slavery, was a part of the African American experience from the beginning. Unsurprisingly, horror became a part of African American narratives from the first as well. The folklore, legends, and myths brought over from Africa during the Middle Passage and turned into oral literature by the slaves were significant elements in pre-twentieth century African American horror literature" (184). For example, Maisha L. Wester demonstrates in *African American Gothic* (2012) that "slave narratives are wrought with descriptions of screams heard for miles, wicked masters who derive pleasure from the sound, and blood-soaked soil tilled by ruined hands" (40). Indeed, the authors of slave narratives, in their dual experiences as slave and writer, marked themselves as "the Enlightenment ideal of intellectually based being" and the "wicked masters" as human monsters: "Amid gothic plots and landscapes, two ideologies haunt gothic discourse: the rhetoric of the unspoken and the grotesque. Can/should/how does the black writer speak as, of, and about a soul tortured in the horrors

---

3. While I focus exclusively on horror fiction authored by Black Americans, the scholarship on horror films written, produced, and/or directed by Black Americans suggest that an examination of human monstrosity in Black horror films would be beneficial for horror film studies. See, for example, Dawn Keetley's *Jordan Peele's* Get Out: *Political Horror* (2020), Brooks E. Hefner's "Rethinking *Blacula*: Ideological Critique at the Intersection of Genres" (2012), Robin R. Means Coleman's *Horror Noire: Blacks in American Horror Films from the 1890s to Present* (2011), my "*Blacula* and the Question of Blackness" (2005), Harry Benshoff's "Blaxploitation Horror Films: Generic Reappropriation or Reinscription?" (2000), Leerom Medovoi's "Theorizing Historicity, or the Many Meanings of *Blacula*" (1998), and Manthia Diawara and Phyllis Klotman's "*Ganja and Hess*: Vampires, Sex, and Addictions" (1990).

of slavery? Publicly marking pro-slavery 'beings' as monstrous yet members of humankind, how does the black writer imagine his own being?" (36).[4]

While theorizing the human monster continues to be an intellectual and artistic concern in postslavery Black American horror fiction, we do not know much about that theorization partly because, as some Black American horror writers have noted, many readers and gatekeeping institutions assume that Black people do not read or write horror. For example, although Alice Walker's "The Child Who Favored Daughter" (1973); Joseph Nazel's *The Black Exorcist* (1974), a "blaxploitation version" of William Blatty's *The Exorcist* (1971); Octavia E. Butler's "Bloodchild" (1984); and Toni Morrison's *Beloved* (1988) are some of the Black American horror fiction published during the paperback horror wave, which occurred between the 1960s and 1980s (Nevins 187–89),[5] Tananarive Due noted in a 2002 interview that the assumption that "trained" writers, especially "trained" Black writers, do not and should not read or produce horror fiction was shared by her peers in the writing program that she was enrolled in and by the program itself:

> I was basically "trained" in a literary writing program at Northwestern University, where speculative fiction was not a part of our course of study. . . . I remember telling my class that my favorite authors were Toni Morrison and Stephen King. I got looks of approval when I mentioned Toni Morrison, and

---

4. In one sense, Wester's observations about how the Black writers of slave narratives marked themselves and proslavery White people remind us of Julia Kristeva's argument in *Powers of Horror* (1980) that literature is the "privileged signifier" of horror: "Because it occupies its place, because it hence decks itself out in the sacred power of horror, literature may also involve not an ultimate resistance to but an unveiling of the abject: an elaboration, a discharge, and a hollowing out of abjection through the Crisis of the Word" (208). According to Kristeva, by treating literature as an "unveiling" of the horror that accompanies humanity's attempt to deal with that which "disturbs identity, system, order" or "does not respect borders, positions, rules" (4), we find that it is also a byproduct of humanity's attempt to deal with "the hell of naming," that is, the hell of "signifiable identity" (207). As Wester suggests, the "hell of naming" is integral to the works of slave authors, since "a fundamental gothic attribute of the slave narratives" is the conflict between "the desire to transition into European being and the desire to mark a distance/difference from their masters" (36). Indeed, how do we define ourselves when we desire to be and are repulsed by our monstrous others?

5. The paperback horror wave, like the wave of pulp horror stories published in the 1920s and 1930s, contains several novels written by authors about whom there was little information. Indeed, as Nevins puts it, "Some or perhaps many of these authors could have been men or women of color" (187).

incredulous looks when I mentioned Stephen King. So I figured out right
away that I would have to keep my love of horror to myself. (Glave 696)

Given that Due's peers, not Due, put Morrison and King in different literary
categories, the "looks of approval" and "incredulous looks" she received are
examples of not only the pervasiveness of the assumption that horror is not
a Black genre, but also the ways in which that assumption attempts to police
the Black literary community.[6]

Whereas some university writing programs are unwilling to train their
Black students to be horror writers, Robert Fleming asserts in the introduction to his *Havoc After Dark: Tales of Terror* (2004), which he describes as a
"collection of horror stories written by a black writer," that the publishing
industry is reluctant to publish Black horror fiction. According to Fleming, *Havoc After Dark* is a "first of sorts" because the mainstream publishing industry has "frowned on African-American writers taking a shot at the
[horror] genre" (Introduction xiii). Despite the commercial success of Due's
work and the fact that Black readers support the horror fiction of non-Black
writers such as Stephen King, Dean Koontz, Clive Barker, and John Saul,
Fleming notes that "the door for both the short and long forms of horror
fiction remains relatively closed to black writers" (Introduction xiii). According to Brandon Massey, one of the reasons why that door continues to be
closed is partly due to what readers of Black American–authored fiction are
demanding. While Massey states in his introduction to *Dark Dreams: A Collection of Horror and Suspense by Black Writers* (2004) that this text is a "piece
of history" because it is the "first collection of original horror and suspense
stories written exclusively by black writers ever to be released by a major

---

6. Gomez experienced the ramifications of such thinking when she was searching
for a publisher for *The Gilda Stories*. Gomez has stated that she was told in her rejection letters from publishers that her "main character was unsellable because she was
a woman of color, a lesbian, and a vampire" ("Second Law" 349). In "Speculative Fiction and Black Lesbians" (1993), Gomez notes that it is not just the publishing industry
and academia that is responsible for the anti-Black horror sentiment; it is also those
of the Black American literary community who adhere to the "utilitarian approach" to
Black American literature. According to this approach, Black American literature must
be "serious" and "serve a higher purpose"; therefore, Black American writers should not
produce speculative fiction such as horror because that fiction is "fun," "trivial," and an
"indulgence" ("Speculative" 950–51). One of the problems with the utilitarian approach,
as I have noted elsewhere, is that it assumes that *real* Black American literature cannot
be "utilitarian" and "fun" at the same time, "an assumption that defines speculative fiction as a 'white thing' and labels African American writers who produce such works as
literary race traitors" ("Race" 314).

publisher," he admits that such an anthology could have been published before 2004 precisely because he is not "the originator of the concept" (ix). Moreover, Massey was hesitant about pursuing this project, and the reason for his hesitancy might explain why others before him did not follow up on the idea of publishing an anthology on Black-authored horror:

> I'd chatted with my agent many times about this project, but always set it aside, worried that the timing wasn't right and that no one would be receptive to such a book. Relationship-driven novels and urban books dominated the African-American commercial fiction lists, and I knew from my own publishing experiences how much of a challenge it could be to turn people on to something new. (Introduction, *Dark* ix)

As Massey points out, the commercial demand for specific types of Black American literature, not the lack of Black horror writers, is what delayed his pursuit to get a book like *Dark Dreams* published.

In addition to the myth held by some readers and gatekeeping institutions that horror is not a Black genre, another reason why we know little about the theorization of human monstrosity in Black American horror fiction is the ways in which scholars have addressed the horror-gothic relationship. For instance, Noël Carroll argues in his seminal work, *The Philosophy of Horror, or Paradoxes of the Heart* (1990), that gothic and horror are different genres. For Carroll, the "real harbinger of the horror genre" is the end of Matthew Lewis's *The Monk* (1797), when the priest is impaled and a demon appears (4). The presence of monsters is what distinguishes the horror genre, what Carroll calls "art-horror," from the tale of terror or "Gothic exercises" (15). In other words, a text's ability to create a feeling of dread, fear, or terror is not enough to make it a horror text; indeed, it must use monsters to create such feelings to be considered art-horror. Unlike Carroll, Xavier Aldana Reyes proposes that a horror text does not need a monster to produce the effects it seeks to elicit: "horror fiction may be best understood as the literature that actively, and predominantly, seeks to create a pervasive feeling of unease and which, consistently, although not necessarily always successfully, attempts to arouse the emotions and sensations we would normally ascribe to feeling under threat" (3). Following Reyes's line of thought, Nevins treats the gothic text as a type of horror text precisely because it creates, intentionally or unintentionally, a feeling of dread, fear, or terror in its readers (xv). As Nevins sees it, gothic is a descendant of the Restoration horror plays of the 1670s, whose authors sought to "horrify and shock" viewers rather than "titillate and edify them,"[7] and the graveyard poetry of the eighteenth century in which poets used a vocabulary of death and the supernatural that would lay the groundwork for the gothic genre (xvi–xvii). Thus, while there appears to be agreement that, as Nevins puts it, a "significant break" from the gothic occurred in the nineteenth century, Carroll believes that break represents the birth of the horror genre, whereas Nevins believes that break represents the horror genre's liberation from gothic's "nebulous geographical and a-historical settings" by "emplac[ing] it solidly in our world" (xvii). Indeed, what might separate gothic horror fiction from other horror genres is the role that setting plays in gothic horror, where an archaic and barbarous past or the return of repressed or forgotten deeds in the present is the issuing source of horror in the text (see Wester and Reyes 3).

My decision to use "horror" instead of "gothic" to describe the fiction examined in *Anti-Blackness and Human Monstrosity in Black American Horror Fiction* aligns with Nevins's placement of gothic in horror's history and is inspired by Kinitra D. Brooks's discussion of why Black feminist scholars have historically devalued horror studies as a critical framework for examining Black women's creative works (54). In *Searching for Sycorax: Black Women's Hauntings of Contemporary Horror* (2018), Brooks notes that since horror has historically held a "ghettoized status" in the literary arts, as evidenced by how works of horror included in the literary canon have been "ameliorated" as Gothic literature, Black feminist scholars "actively ignored" horror as a research possibility because they were "wrestling with the vagaries of demanding that academic institutions include black woman-authored literature; they did not need the added taint of horror" (55). I use "Black American horror," instead of "Black American gothic," to emphasize, as Brooks

---

7. While I agree with Nevin's view of gothic in horror's modern history, it is important to note, as he does, that horror's history is much older than the Restoration plays, possibly dating back to the "Epic of Gilgamesh" (xvi). For example, in his critique of John Clute's view that horror is, in part, "a subversive response to the falseness of that Enlightenment ambition to totalize knowledge and the world into an imperial harmony," Nevins calls for a definition of horror literature that is not "predicated on a Western historical orientation" precisely because "there was, and still is, a substantial amount of horror published outside the West that did not rely upon the Enlightenment for its conception and execution" (xv). Moreover, since "horror literature is an international phenomenon" (57), limiting the origin of horror storytelling to a particular time or group of people is problematic because horror storytelling, as suggested by Kristeva's view of literature, is intrinsic to the human experience. Paul Santilli makes this point in "Culture, Evil, and Horror" (2007), where he argues that we should think of horror as a "phenomenon of being" in which "horror is not only a peculiar emotion arising from time to time in response to a possible monstrosity, but it is an enduring feature of our being in the world. It is a basic mood and orientation, or *Stimmung*, with respect to existence" (179). As suggested by Kristeva, Nevins, and Santilli, horror has an origin problem because all human cultures have horror stories precisely because being human is, in part, a horror story.

does, the usefulness of horror studies in the analysis of Black American literature and to acknowledge, as Nevins notes, that gothic literature is part
of, not separate from, the horror genre. This means that all Black American
gothic is horror, but not all Black American horror is gothic. As Martin Japtok argues, "Monstrosity, horror, and terror, none of which are automatically gothic, are better terms for an analysis of African American literature;
they lend themselves to traveling across time, cultures, and genres, in part
because they point to something real, as do slave narratives and protest
novels" (9). I believe that treating Black American gothic as a subgenre of
Black American horror emphasizes the diversity of Black American horror
and, therefore, resists the practice of (mis)reading Black American horror fiction as only gothic or as something else besides horror, as in the case of the
"oft-misplaced line of critical inquiry that reads black women's supernatural
writings as magical realism" (Brooks 100).

In addition to its understanding of the gothic-horror relationship, *Anti-
Blackness and Human Monstrosity* questions Carroll's restrictive conception
of the horror monster. According to Carroll, the monsters of horror, unlike
stories with monsters in them such as fairytales, "breach the norms of ontological propriety presumed by the positive human characters in the story";
that is, the monster in a horror story is "an extraordinary character in our
ordinary world," whereas the monster in fairytales is "an ordinary creature
in an extraordinary world" (16). In addition to being viewed by the humans
in the story as "abnormal," the monsters of horror are also "lethal" and
"disgusting" (22). As Carroll explains, if the monster were "only evaluated
as potentially threatening, the emotion would be fear; if only potentially
impure, the emotion would be disgust. Art-horror requires evaluation of
both in terms of threat and disgust" (28). Furthermore, unlike the humans
who commit horrific acts in tales of terror or gothic tales, the monster of art-
horror "refers to any being not believed to exist now according to contemporary science" (27). Thus, Carroll offers what he refers to as an "entity-based"
conception of horror in which monsters—beings who are lethal, disgusting,
and not accounted for by contemporary science—are central to the genre
(41). Given Carroll's entity-based notion of horror, stories featuring lethal
and disgusting humans are either tales of "natural horror," horrifying narratives about the everyday world (12), or tales of terror, fiction rooted in
"abnormal psychologies" (15).

The problem with Carroll's conception of the horror monster, as demonstrated by the entity-based horror fiction examined herein, is that it excludes
human monsters, those humans who become lethal and disgusting because
of their ideologically inspired actions. As Stephen Asma notes in *On Monsters*
(2009), "The term *monster* is often applied to human beings who have, by

their own horrific actions, abdicated their humanity" (8). Thus, what limits Carroll's understanding of art-horror is that it excludes what Philip J. Nickel refers to as "'realistic' monsters," creatures who show that "the threats that horror presents are not always fictional but can bleed into the actual world" (15). This point is captured in Wester's recounting of a discussion she had with Black hair stylists about teaching Morrison's *Beloved* and why they found Morrison's story so horrifying: "For those black women, the monsters and ghosts that make up the text's (hi)story could intrude upon their lives in ways other gothic ghosts never could or would" (1). I emphasize throughout *Anti-Blackness and Human Monstrosity* that the human monsters of Black American horror fiction are, in some ways, more threatening and disgusting than the nonhuman ones precisely because the human monsters exist in everyday life. Indeed, if one of the goals of horror is to remind us that our view of everyday life is mostly fabrication and, therefore, not trustworthy, then what makes the human monsters of horror frightening and disturbing is that they remind us that our reliance on others to not harm us in certain spaces, which is required for us to have an everyday life, is never secure, since the people we tend to rely on the most (e.g., friends, family, and lovers) might be monsters (see Nickel 27–30). This means that while the human monsters discussed in this project do not have bodies that are interstitial, incomplete, or formless, their actions and thinking make them, like all monsters, "threats to common knowledge," threats that are so dangerous and repulsive that they can "render those who encounter them insane, mad, deranged, and so on" (Carroll 34).

While I examine some pre-1960 horror fiction, my focus is the Black horror fiction published after 1960, when, according to W. Scott Poole, a "new American monster" was born (148). Inspired by the "circumstances" of Ed Gein and his horrific crimes,[8] which ushered in "the age of the maniac murderer in American popular culture" (Poole 154), Robert Bloch's *Psycho* (1959) introduces American culture to the most popular representation of the murdering maniac during the final third of the twentieth century and in postmillennial American horror—the serial killer. According to Bernice M. Murphy, "Bloch's novel, in which the supernatural was decisively superseded by human horrors, was immensely influential, primarily thanks to the impact of Alfred Hitchcock's 1960 film adaptation" (117). In contrast to

---

8. When police discovered the grisly murders committed by Ed Gein in Plainfield, Wisconsin, during the winter of 1957, Bloch was living in nearby Weyauwega, Wisconsin. However, as Paula Guran notes, Bloch's *Psycho* is based on "the *circumstances* of the Gein case, not the murderer himself . . . or any specifics of the case" (par. 10). In fact, since Bloch knew relatively little about the Gein case, he stated some years later that he was a bit surprised to discover "how closely the imaginary character I'd created resembled the real Ed Gein both in overt act and apparent motivation" (qtd. in Guran par. 10).

Carroll, who argues that Hitchcock's adaptation is not a horror film because "[Norman] Bates is not a monster," but "a schizophrenic, a type of being that science countenances" (38), Poole contends that Bates is a monster depicted as murdering maniac, "a creature not born from the supernatural shadows or cobbled together in a lab, but coming to deadly life in the midst of American family structures" (148). While the serial killer "spoke to the social upheavals of the 1960s and 1970s" (176), the current conception of this human monster as "a distinct category of pop-culture villain and real-life threat" began in the 1980s (Murphy 119). By 1984, for example, "the cinema's metaphysical gothic Beast . . . had given way to a more visceral, . . . more 'real' form of the monstrous. The American serial killer . . . had come to occupy the symbolic space of monstrosity in the public imagination" (Nixon 219).

The serial killing monster also became a fixture of White-authored American horror fiction, as seen in Bret Easton Ellis's *American Psycho* (1991) and in Stephen King's "Big Driver" and "A Good Marriage," which are part of his short story collection *Full Dark, No Stars* (2011). While Patrick Bateman, the protagonist of Ellis's novel, is a "corporate-ladder-climbing monster" who represents Bates transformed into a "1980s American yuppie turned (maybe) into a serial killer" (Poole 171), Big Driver, a tow-truck driver who rapes and kills women with the help of his mother, and Bob Anderson, King's fictional depiction of Dennis Radar (the BTK killer), are human monsters shaped and protected by American family structures and values similar to the ones that produced Bates. Thus, the murdering maniac, who is responsible for the rise of the slasher horror genre, is a modern version of the human monster that has its origin in nineteenth-century Western thought when the term "teratology," which refers to the study of abnormal physiological development, was introduced (Weinstock 5). While both are viewed as "monstrous births,"[9]

---

9. According to Jeffrey Andrew Weinstock, the theory of "maternal impression"—the idea that the development and appearance of the embryo can be shaped by what a woman sees or ponders during conception and pregnancy—"gained traction" in Europe during the seventeenth and eighteenth centuries as a popular explanation for the existence of human monsters or monstrous births (11). As Martin Japtok and Winfried Schleiner argue in their examination of Shakespeare's late sixteenth-century play *The Merchant of Venice*, "the notion of imagination over inheritance" in Shylock's "'scientific' discourse" about the biblical story of Jacob's stratagem with ewes and lambs is grounded in Renaissance notions about the powerful role that the woman's imagination plays in the nature and condition of the child she bears (156–61). In fact, the theory of maternal impression dates to antiquity. Referencing Marie-Hélène Huet's *Monstrous Imagination* and Josef Warkany's "History of Teratology," Weinstock notes that maternal impression is evidenced in "the theory, attributed to Empedocles, that 'progeny can be modified by the statues and paintings that the mother gazes upon during her pregnancy'" and in the writings of Pliny, who wrote that "both maternal and paternal thoughts during conception can shape the child" (11).

the human monsters of teratology are defined by physiological abnormalities that only threatened their lives, whereas the monstrous abnormalities of Bates and his serial killing descendants (e.g., Buffalo Bill, Hannibal Lecter, and Dexter) are in the mind, hidden from those whom they might harm or kill. Indeed, what makes some serial killers terrifying is that they could be part of our everyday world and we would not know it because their monstrosity is concealed by their *normal* bodies and their performances of the *normal* (Poole 175). As Poole sees it, the serial killer is a human monster who "represents two warring discourses in the same terrifying figure." While the serial killer's "insanity suggests a severe mental disability, one that could perhaps receive and respond to various therapies," the horrors committed by serial killers are "beyond the ken of human experience," making them monsters, beings who "cannot be treated and rehabilitated, only destroyed" (158).

In *Anti-Blackness and Human Monstrosity*, I build upon Poole's discussion of human monstrosity during the age of the murdering maniac by including the human monsters of Black American horror fiction into that discussion. Such inclusion, on the one hand, shows that these human monsters support Poole's claim that monsters are more than "fantastical metaphors" for humanity's dark side—they also represent specific national histories. As Poole puts it, monsters are "part of the genetic code of American history, ciphers that reveal disturbing truths about everything from colonial settlement to the enslavement of African people, from anti-immigrant movements to the rise of religious fundamentalism in the twentieth century" (18). Leila Taylor makes a similar point about the relationship between monsters and American history in her answer to the following question: if America had a national monster, what would it look like? That monster, according to Taylor, would not have scales, fur, or fangs; instead, it would look like The Blob or The Thing because "America's boogeyman changes depending on the latest threat, be they Black or Muslim or Latino or gay or trans. Be it feminism or democratic socialism. Our American Blob can shape-shift at a moment's notice" (68–69). On the other hand, examining human monstrosity in Black American horror fiction not only acknowledges that Black folks have been writing horror stories with human monsters before the age of the murdering maniac, but it also insists that understanding how specific ideologies of Americanness produce human monsters requires severing the link between insanity and human monstrosity associated with the murdering maniac. As we shall see, the virtual absence of murdering maniacs in Black American horror fiction is shaped by the idea that what makes the human monster a terrifying figure is its sanity. Indeed, the fact that sane people can become monsters reminds us of a terrifying truth, a truth that must be repressed for us to have an everyday life—all humans are potential monsters precisely because human monsters are produced by ideas, not by abnormal bodies or mental illnesses.

My goal in *Anti-Blackness and Human Monstrosity* is not to provide an exhaustive list of the types of human monsters that appear in Black American horror fiction; instead, I seek to discuss the human monsters that one is most likely to encounter when reading Black horror fiction. I argue that these monsters can be grouped into four categories—the monsters of White rage, respectability, not-ness, and serial killing—and can be read as personifications of American anti-Blackness, ideologies of Americanness that have been used to devalue the Black body and, consequently, America's Blackness. More specifically, these human monsters represent the ways in which concepts such as the American Dream, American womanhood, American manhood, and the American serial killer have been used to justify the production and consumption of Black bodies in pain. Thus, as João H. Costa Vargas and Moon-Kie Jung contend, anti-Blackness is not a type of racism or logic of "domination and subjection"; instead, it is "an antisocial logic that not only dehumanizes Black people but also renders abject all that is associated with Blackness" (8). Although Barbara Harris Combs conceptualizes racism in *Bodies out of Place: Theorizing Anti-Blackness in U.S. Society* (2022) as a form of anti-Blackness (28), she also identifies George Yancy's discussion of the Black body in North American Whiteness as an example of a type of anti-Blackness (11–12). Given Yancey's description of Whiteness's Black body as "the monstrous," "an anomaly of nature" that is the "essence of vulgarity and immorality" as well as "criminality itself" (qtd. in Combs 12), Combs seems aware that anti-Blackness is, as Vargas and Jung put it, "a logic of social and ontological abjection" (Vargas and Jung 8).[10] As I show throughout *Anti-Blackness and Human Monstrosity*, while the White rage, respectability, not-ness, and serial killing monsters are dangerous because they can terrorize Black people with virtual impunity, what makes them repulsive and threats to common knowledge is the anti-Black sadism that encourages their violent and ahistorical disavowal of America's Blackness.

Racial sadism, as defined herein, refers to the pleasure that one receives from inflicting pain on members of a particular racialized group or watching that group in pain; therefore, anti-Black sadism is defined as the enjoyment

10. Nevertheless, according to Vargas and Jung, when we treat racism as a type of anti-Blackness, we might overlook the fact that racism "tends to focus on analogous experiences of oppression," while anti-Blackness emphasizes the differences in experiences between Black and non-Black people, rather than between Black and White people, by stressing "the singularity of Black people's dehumanization, antihumanization" (7, 9).

one receives from producing and consuming Black people in pain. This definition draws upon Claire Raymond's use of the term *sadism* in her analysis of Carrie Mae Weems's installation *From Here I Saw What Happened and I Cried* (1995–96), which depicts "the sadism of American slavery and racism" through its rephotographed images of Black women degraded by White men of science (44). Unlike Sigmund Freud, who saw sadism as primarily a sexual perversion, Raymond defines sadism as "a 'delight in cruelty'" and "a delight in watching cruelty, which could also be a delight in creating humiliating images of other human beings" (28). Thus, reading the human monsters of Black American horror fiction as anti-Black sadists means reading them as embodiments of the enduring and almost invisible everyday routines of domination that characterize much of Black life in the contemporary world, what Christina Sharpe refers to as the "sadomasochism of everyday black life" (*Monstrous Intimacies* 118–19). This also means that the pleasure that these monsters of anti-Blackness receive from producing and consuming Black people in pain is not only sexual, social, and psychological, but also ideological.

Patrick Jordan argues in *Designing Pleasurable Products* (2000), which examines "pleasure-based approaches to human factors in product design" (9), that "pleasurability" is more than "a property of the product"—it is also "the interaction between a product and a person" (12). In this understanding of pleasurability, a person's ideological commitments play a major role in determining if that person's interaction with a product is pleasurable. The intersection of ideology and pleasure is what Lionel Tiger, whom Jordan draws from, calls "ideopleasure," the joy that "people receive from experiencing or creating theoretical entities such as movies, buildings, plays, music, art objects, books. Or when they do crossword puzzles, or create scientific problems and excitedly try to solve them." This means, according to Tiger, that ideopleasure is "mental, aesthetic, often intensely private"; therefore, "an observer might never know the person experiencing ideopleasure is experiencing anything at all" (59). Considering Tiger's definition, a product must be able to manifest the "mental, aesthetic, often intensely private" perspective or experience of a customer to make that customer feel good about consuming that product. As Jordan sees it, if a product does not represent a customer's ideological position, then that product lacks "ideopleasure," which refers to "people's values" and describes "the aesthetics of a product and the values that a product embodies" (14). Although Jordan theorizes ideo-pleasure through the person-product interaction and is not intended to be a theory of pleasure or explain why people experience pleasure (15), I believe that it is useful for understanding the pleasure that the human monster derives from its interaction with its victims. Although human beings are not products, they have been and continue to be treated as such, and the ideological pleasure that the human monster receives from its interaction with its victim is comparable to that produced by the person-product interaction, since the monsters of anti-Blackness produce and consume Black bodies in pain to defend or aspire to certain notions of Americanness. Indeed, the Black horror stories in which these human monsters are depicted ask us to interrogate the ideological pleasures that are produced by their denial of America's Blackness and, at the same time, why such pleasures make them repulsive and barely human.

In chapter 1, I examine the monsters of White rage in W. E. B. Du Bois's "Jesus Christ in Texas" (1920), John Henrik Clarke's "Santa Claus Is a White Man" (1939), Tananarive Due's *The Between* (1995), and Victor LaValle's *The Changeling* (2018). According to Carol Anderson, since White rage is not about the "visible violence" of White supremacy, it does not have to "wear sheets, burn crosses, or take to the streets" to make its presence felt. Indeed, White rage not only works through the halls of power (e.g., the courts, the legislatures, and other government bureaucracies) to achieve its anti-Black ends, but it is, more importantly, triggered by "black advancement" (3). Thus, the objective of White rage is to limit Black access to the American Dream through the production and/or reinforcement of anti-Black laws, policies, institutions, and social practices. While White rage is not about visible violence, the texts by Du Bois, Clarke, Due, and LaValle suggest that White rage is sustained by its human monsters. I argue that the monsters of White rage are horrifying for the Black protagonists in these texts because they are human manifestations of the Black gains–White loss assumption that is at the heart of White rage and its vision of the American Dream, the assumption that Black advancement automatically entails White descent.

In chapter 2, I direct my attention to the human monsters in Black American horror fiction who seek to harm or kill Black women and girls because of their hatred of and sexual longing for the Black female body. I argue that the human monsters in Alice Walker's "The Child Who Favored Daughter" (1973), Octavia E. Butler's *Kindred* (1979), and Nnedi Okorafor's *Who Fears Death* (2018) are respectability monsters, those humans who use the myth of Black female hypersexuality, which is at the center of respectability politics, to justify terrorizing Black women and girls. Respectability politics, according to Susana M. Morris, is a "strategy" that advocates the adoption of a "set of mainstream ideals regarding behavior" that will supposedly improve the life chances of Black people in an anti-Black world (5). However, because they exist in such a world, Black women could never be fully respectable because hypersexuality is attached to the Black female body, leading to what Morris calls a "paradox of respectability," the desire to be and the virtual impossibility to become "respectable according to the ideals of respectability politics" (3). As the texts by Walker, Butler, and Okorafor demonstrate, respectability monsters are dangerous and repulsive because they can represent their sexual abuse of Black women as virtuous and themselves as respectable precisely because desiring Black women and the desires of Black women are inherently immoral in an anti-Black world.

Similar to chapter 2, chapter 3 examines the myth of the hypersexual Black male in Richard Wright's "The Man Who Killed a Shadow" (1946/1949), Robert Fleming's "The Ultimate Bad Luck" (2004), Rickey Windell George's "Good 'Nough to Eat" (2006), and Lexi Davis's "Are You My Daddy?" (2007). I argue that these short stories offer us different versions of what I call the not-ness monster, those humans who employ the myth of the hypersexual Black male to put or keep Black males in a state of what Tommy J. Curry calls "Man-Not-ness."[11] According to Curry, Man-Not-ness describes "the vulnerability that Black men and boys have to having their selves substituted/determined by the fears and desires of other individuals. The Black male stands in relation to others as always vulnerable because his personhood, who he actually is to himself, is not only denied but also negated by society" (Man-Not 34). Thus, not-ness monsters, like their respectability siblings, are those individuals and groups whose hatred of and desire for Black males lead them to deny and negate Black male personhood, which includes terrorizing, harming, and/or killing Black men. As we will see, the horrors created by the respectability and not-ness monsters are fostered by the dangerous and disgusting belief that Black people cannot be raped.

I focus on the serial killers of Black American horror fiction in chapter 4. As I noted earlier, one of the "warring discourses" represented by popular culture's typical depiction of the serial killer, the discourse of insanity, is absent from the serial killing monsters of Black American horror fiction. By removing insanity as an explanation for the serial killer's actions, I argue that R. J. Meaddough III's "The Death of Tommy Grimes" (1962), Chesya

---

11. I use "not-ness" to show that the term derives from Curry's notion of Man-Not-ness and to distinguish it from "notness." Whereas notness describes the state of nonexistence or not being, not-ness describes the state of negative modifying, since "not" is a modifier of negation and the suffix "ness" emphasizes the state, quality, or condition of "not." Thus, not-ness monsters are those who derive pleasure from negatively modifying the Black male into a Man-Not to justify the pleasure they receive from watching or producing Black males in pain.

Burke's "Chocolate Park" (2004), Michael Boatman's "Our Kind of People" (2006), and Dia Reeves's *Slice of Cherry* (2011) propose not only that serial killing monsters are lethal and disgusting because they are sane but also that motive and victim selection are key factors in determining the humanity or monstrosity of a serial killer. Since the fictional serial killers in the works by Meaddough, Burke, Boatman, and Reeves are sane and not forced by others to murder people, their decision to kill is intentional as well as their choice of victims. Moreover, in their questioning of popular culture's untreatable serial killer, the sane serial killers depicted in the stories by Meaddough, Burke, Boatman, and Reeves suggest that a distinction between *good* and *bad* serial killers exist in Black American horror fiction and that distinction is defined by intentionality. By highlighting the importance of intentionality, their stories insist that what makes serial killers horrifyingly disturbing is not their methods of murder but the thinking and desires that motivate them to kill and to determine who should be killed.

Although I direct most of my attention to showing how the human monsters in Black American horror fiction are created by ideologies that de-Blacken Americanness and call for the production and consumption of Black bodies in pain, I am also interested in, as discussed in the conclusion, the strategies offered by these stories on how Black people should "go on" in their everyday lives, knowing that the human monsters depicted in its texts might be permanent fixtures in American society. As Nickel notes in his discussion of what is good about horror's ability to "threaten our background cognitive reliance on others and the world around us" is that it forces us to realize that we can "continue to act in the presence of fear," that we can "still go on, even in the absence of perfect certainty" (28–29). Like Nickel, Katerina Bantinaki argues,

> Through our encounter with horror fiction we are given a chance to confront or learn to cope with fear in a safe environment: we learn to control our fear feelings and display mastery over our reactions to frightening stimuli; to direct our thoughts—often aided by the narrative—to aspects of the situation that counter the fear (for instance, to the weak traits of the 'monster' or to the resources that a protagonist has to confront it); or when the challenge is overwhelming, to manage it by seeking comfort in peers. (390)

Indeed, one of the pleasures and benefits of Black American horror fiction is that it offers readers the opportunity to learn about the discourses that give birth to the human monsters of anti-Blackness and, more importantly, about the individual and communal resources that Black people have used and might use in the future to combat these monsters. As I discuss in the conclusion, the intellectual resources offered by the horror fiction covered in this book center on two approaches to dealing with anti-Blackness and its monsters, what Frank Wilderson III refers to as "Afropessimism" and what Kevin Quashie calls "black aliveness." I attempt to show that while those approaches disagree on how to think about Black hope and Black agency, both are concerned with how to make America and the modern world places where anti-Blackness is not the foundation of their sociality and notions of the human.

CHAPTER 1

The Monsters of White Rage

In *Facing Up to the American Dream: Race, Class, and the Soul of the Nation* (1995), Jennifer Hochschild dates the concept of the American Dream to John Locke's *Second Treatise of Government* (1690), where he claims that the whole world was "America" in the beginning. According to Hochschild, Locke's conception of America as a primitive society that lacks "a cash nexus . . . evokes the unsullied newness, infinite possibility, limitless resources that are commonly understood to be the essence of the 'American dream'" (15). However, James Truslow Adams, who coined the term *American Dream* in his *The Epic of America* (1931), believes that the concept is older than Locke's text. As Carlton Floyd and Thomas Reifer point out in *The American Dream and Dreams Deferred: A Dialectical Fairy Tale* (2023), Adams begins the American Dream with Columbus's voyage to the Americas (35), and in his retelling of Columbus's arrival to the Americas, which is a typical but disturbingly inaccurate trope of settler colonialism, "Columbus, an agent of the Catholic Spanish empire, conjures the Garden of Eden (Paradise), the Fall, and the restoration of paradise" (36). While Locke and Adams are writing in different eras, both demonstrate that the concept of the American Dream requires an "un-telling" of the Americas and America, a story that, in this instance, omits the indigenous people inhabiting the Americas and the violence that they suffered at the hands of European colonizers that led to the creation of America.[1] Since its inception, in other words, the American Dream has been imagined as a White achievement that always comes at the expense of non-White people. Given that context, White rage can be seen as a response to moments in US history when Black people challenged the idea that the American Dream is just a White dream.

I noted in the introduction that Carol Anderson's conception of "white rage" can be defined as the laws, policies, institutions, and social practices that seek to limit Black people's access to the American Dream. Thus, as Anderson writes, the mere presence of Black people is not the problem for White rage; rather, "it is blackness with ambition, with drive, with purpose, with aspirations, and with demands for full and equal citizenship. It is blackness that refuses to accept subjugation, to give up" (3–4). For example, although Black progress occurred during Reconstruction, White rage ensured that "real change was infinitesimal at best" (38). The emergence of the Black Codes—a series of state laws designed to undercut the Black people's pursuit of economic independence and educational, political, and legal equality—helped to transform Reconstruction into "nothing less than an age of violence and terror" (31). Unfortunately, the post-Reconstruction era, defined mostly by Jim Crow and Black people's fight against that system of degradation and terror, was not much better. For instance, during the Great Migration (1910–40), what Ira Berlin calls the beginning of the "third passage" of Black people's journey to make America their home that occurred between World War I and 1970 (154; 272n2),[2] many of the anti-Black Whites who attempted to prevent Black Southerners from seeking a better life in the North were political elites and members of the South's upper classes: "mayors, governors, legislators, business leaders, and police chiefs . . . devised an array of obstacles and laws to stop African Americans, as US citizens, from exercising the right to find better jobs, to search for good schools, indeed simply to escape the ever-present terror of lynch mobs" (C.

---

1. An "un-telling," according to Katie Sciurba and myself, describes "the process of (willfully or unintentionally) neglecting, omitting, revising, or recasting key elements of historical events" (4). While we acknowledge that "some form of un-telling always takes place when recounting a historical event or cultural moment because a single narrative cannot possibly address all elements or individuals who brought that event or moment into being" (4), we also insist that "despite an author's or illustrator's intentions, an un-telling not only conceals certain aspects of a historical moment or event but also articulates an ideological stance related to what occurred" (5).

2. "The entire African American experience," according to Berlin, "can be best read as a series of great migrations or *passages,* during which immigrants—at first forced and then free—transformed an alien place into a home, becoming deeply rooted in a land that once was foreign, unwanted, and even despised" (9).

Anderson 41–42). As the examples above suggest, while White rage does not need "visible violence" to make its presence felt in American society (3), its presence always leads to visible anti-Black violence.

I argue that W. E. B. Du Bois's "Jesus Christ in Texas" (1920), John Henrik Clarke's "Santa Claus Is a White Man" (1939), Tananarive Due's *The Between* (1995), and Victor LaValle's *The Changeling* (2018) propose that one of the underlining reasons for anti-Black violence in the US is the depiction of Black advancement as immoral and a threat to White life by the monsters of White rage. The White rage monsters depicted in the horror fiction by Du Bois, Clarke, Due, and LaValle are human manifestations of the Black gains–White loss assumption that is at the heart of White rage and its conception of the American Dream. Their stories suggest that these monsters view the ideo-pleasure they derive from producing and consuming Black people in pain as morally valid. Susan Searles Giroux would refer to such thinking as an example of "moral sadism." According to Giroux, who draws upon the work of Judith Butler and, by proxy, Melanie Klein, moral sadism refers to a "destructive discourse" that "transforms horrific violence into a 'justified,' 'legitimate' and even 'virtuous' act" (22). In the stories by Du Bois, Clarke, Due, and LaValle, the moral sadism of White rage's monsters is physically and cognitively threatening because it insists that Black people *should* always have less than White people. Consequently, according to that anti-Black logic, since Black progress is inherently immoral and threatening to White life, the monsters of White rage can guiltlessly terrorize Black people who are ambitious, since these monsters, ironically, imagine themselves as ridding the nation of "evil doers" (see Giroux 22). As Anderson notes, "White rage manages to maintain not only the upper hand but also, apparently, the moral high ground" in its attack on Black progress (4). What I hope to make clear in this chapter is that Black American horror fiction that features White rage's monsters are asking us to consider the future of Black progress in a nation where it is demonized. They ask us, in other words, if the American Dream can be saved from its White-only origins, or do we need a new dream altogether?

Jim Crow's Monsters of White Rage

Even though there is a publication gap of nearly twenty years between Du Bois's "Jesus Christ in Texas" and Clarke's "Santa Claus Is a White Man," both demonstrate the ways in which the horrors of lynching impacted everyday Black life during the Jim Crow era. Set in Waco, Texas, and published four years after Du Bois's "The Waco Horror" (1916), an article that describes the events that led to the lynching of Jesse Washington and where Du Bois "officially launches the NAACP's Anti-Lynching Campaign" (Bernstein 159–61), "Jesus Christ in Texas" tells the story of a man referred to as "the stranger," who appears to be Jesus Christ, attempting to rid Waco's White elite—which includes a colonel, a business promoter, and a farmer and his wife—of their anti-Blackness. The stranger, who is described as a "mulatto" by White folks (97) and as a "n———" by the Black convict whom the visitor is trying to save from being lynched (100), has supernatural powers, but his powers are unable to change the hearts and minds of the White elite. Thus, the Black convict, whose mouth embodied "revolt" (96), is lynched due to the false accusation that he attempted to assault the farmer's wife. Clarke's "Santa Claus Is a White Man" takes place in Jim Crow Louisiana and tells the story of Randolph Johnson's horrific adventure to a downtown department store during a mid-December day. Randolph is a "little colored boy" who receives some money, twenty-five cents to be exact, from his mother to go Christmas shopping. However, instead of buying Christmas presents for his family, he is robbed and almost lynched by a group of poor White kids and a White man in a Santa Claus suit. Although the White Santa saves Randolph from being lynched, declaring that he is "too lil'l to lynch" and it is "Christmas time" (185), he takes Randolph's quarter because he believes that it is immoral for Black people, especially a Black kid, to have more money than any White person.

Du Bois's and Clarke's horror stories represent what Maisha Wester calls a "new era of black Gothic," which also includes works such as Pauline E. Hopkins's *Of One Blood: Or, The Hidden Self* (1902–3), Jean Toomer's *Cane* (1923), Zora Neale Hurston's "Spunk" (1925), Richard Wright's *Native Son* (1940), and Ralph Ellison's *Invisible Man* (1952). Shaped by the drive to assimilate into American society and by the failures, strife, and disappointments of Reconstruction, post-Reconstruction, and the Great Migration, the writers of Black gothic during Jim Crow "sought to negotiate the drive to re-member their Southern origins and pressures to progress beyond the violent racialisms inherent in that heritage to become something 'new'" (Wester 102). However, as Wester argues in her examination of the works of Toomer and Ellison, early twentieth-century Black gothic critiqued not only the notion that the South or the North was a definitive site of Black progress but also New Negro and Talented Tenth movements and leaders. In addition to being absent as protagonists in Toomer's and Ellison's texts, the New Negro and Talented Tenth leaders, along with the Black masses, are depicted as "horrible" and "barely human" due to their corruption and lack of criticality

(105). Wester concludes that the texts by Toomer and Ellison refuse to identify "an ideal space for black freedom and racial advancement"; instead,
"the terrains of the psyche," or "the underground," become the location of
Black progress and its future (146). While Du Bois's "Jesus Christ in Texas"
and Clarke's "Santa Claus Is a White Man," like the Black gothic-horror of
the Jim Crow era, grapple with questions regarding the time and place of
Black progress, I focus on how they link the American Dream to the moral
sadism of anti-Black violence. I submit that the monsters of White rage in
the stories by Du Bois and Clarke represent how the American Dream can
function as a destructive discourse that justifies anti-Black violence.

As proposed by both stories, since all White people are not monsters,
readers need to know how to distinguish White people who are monsters
from those who are fully human. One distinction between the two, according to these stories, is that the monsters of White rage believe that White
people's exploitation of Black people is good for Black people as well as for
themselves. In "Jesus Christ in Texas," every White character in the story,
save for the colonel's daughter, is a White rage monster. The story begins
with the colonel, a business promoter, and a convict guard discussing how
to exploit the labor of Black convicts to build a railroad line that will make
the colonel a millionaire. When the stranger, who suddenly appears in the
room containing these White men, asks if this deal will be "a good thing"
for the Black convicts, the promoter says it will be good for the White men
in the room if these convicts are "driven" to work hard and are underpaid
(95–96). While the colonel agrees with the promoter, he tries to justify the
promoter's response after looking into the stranger's eyes: "Yes, it will do
them good; or at any rate it won't make them any worse than they are" (96).
Like the colonel and promoter, the farmer forces the Black convict, who will
be lynched for a crime that he did not commit, into an exploitative labor
contract by threatening to call the convict guard (101), implying that if he
wants to stay out of jail, he must agree to be oppressed in his freedom.
Sharing her husband's sentiments, the farmer's wife believes that free Black
folks are the main reason why she and her husband are having difficulty
acquiring a new farm: "She said it was hard to get n—— to work. She said
they ought all to be in the chain-gang and made to work" (102). According to these human monsters, Black oppression is crucial to achieving the
American Dream and is morally valid, since such oppression is imagined as
a "good thing" for them and their Black victims.

Like "Jesus Christ in Texas," virtually all the White characters in "Santa
Claus Is a White Man" can be described as White rage monsters. Indeed,
the narrator notes that it was not only the White Santa and the gang of kids

who surround and terrorize Randolph, but also "ill-nourished children," "men in dirty overalls, showing their tobacco-stained teeth," "women whose rutted faces had never known cosmetics" (185), "older persons," and even a "passerby" (182). Yet, since Randolph was searching for a "sympathetic adult face" (183), he also believes that not all White people are monsters, that there are White people who would find his situation horrifying and would be willing to help free him from these monsters. But, unlike the White human, the monster of White rage views terrorizing Black people as a form of entertainment as well as a form of punishment. For example, when the White Santa, who is homeless and walks like someone with a "subnormal mentality" (183),[3] demands to know Randolph's name, the monster tells the crowd that Randolph is "no name fer er n——! No n——'s got no business wit er nice name like dat!" As such, the monster declares that his new name is "Jem" (184). Moreover, when the White Santa discovers that Randolph received the quarter from his mother, the monster states, while the crowd demands that Randolph be lynched, that "N—— ain't got no business wit' money whilst white folks is starving" (185). While terrorizing Randolph is punishment for having more than poor White folks, since the monsters of White rage believe that Black people "got no business" with having a better name, better job, or more money than White people, the threat of lynching Randolph is entertaining for the White Santa and the monstrous crowd because lynching was also spectacle. Anderson notes that one of lynching's "most macabre formats" was the "spectacle lynching." A spectacle lynching, as Anderson explains, "advertised the killing of a black person and provided special promotional trains to bring the audience, including women and children, to the slaughter. These gruesome events were standard family entertainment; severed body parts became souvenirs and decorations hung proudly in homes" (43). If terrorizing Randolph with the threat of being lynched is "good" for the monsters of White rage, why do these monsters believe that it is good for Randolph? They seem to believe that they taught Randolph a very valuable lesson about Black survival during Jim Crow—he will survive if he lacks aspiration.

Another distinction between the fully human White and the monster of White rage is the monster's fear of racial sameness, that is, the fear that

---

3. While Clarke's use of "subnormal mentality" to describe the White Santa's gait would be considered ableist by some, who might not be convinced by the story's link between the term and racism, it would have been considered the normal way of describing someone with a mental disability at the time that the story was published. For example, John E. V. Pieski has noted that the term, up until the 1960s, was associated with crime and was "utilized by the courts as synonymous with 'feebleminded,' 'weakminded,' 'subnormal mental age,' 'stupid,' and 'mentally deficient'" (772).

Black and White people belong to the same race. In "The Anatomy of Lynching," Robyn Wiegman argues that the Black male's threat to White masculine power is due to the fear of gender and racial "sameness," a sameness that could extend the privileges of Whiteness and patriarchy to Black men (352–53). In the stories by Du Bois and Clarke, it is the fear of racial sameness that inspires the monsters of White rage to produce and consume Black people in pain, since racial sameness means that "we are nothing more than gradations of blackness" (Jenkins, *Paradox* 180). For example, when the stranger in Du Bois's "Jesus Christ in Texas" asks the farmer's wife if she loves her neighbors as she loves herself, she initially says yes after gossiping about them. However, after looking at a "little, half-ruined cabin," the farmer's wife says that she tries to love her neighbors in that way, "but they are n——s!" (102). After realizing what she has said, the farmer's wife grabs a lamp to see what the stranger looks like and shrieks in "angry terror" after seeing his "dark face and curly hair" (103). What seems to terrify and anger the farmer's wife is that the stranger is forcing her to acknowledge what she does not want to believe—that she must love Black people as she loves herself to be Christian and fully human. That point seems to derive from the concluding paragraph of "The Waco Horror," where Du Bois explains what is at stake regarding America's lynching record: "What are we going to do about this record? The civilization of America is at stake. The sincerity of Christianity is challenged" (qtd. in Bernstein 161).

White rage's fear of racial sameness and its monsters' responses to it are also represented in "Santa Claus Is a White Man," especially through Clarke's depiction of the monsters mocking Randolph's fear and helplessness. As the crowd of human monsters surround Randolph, "a little colored boy who had done nothing wrong, and harmed no one," he notices that the crowd is "laughing at him because he [i]s frightened" (183). The pleasure these monsters receive from terrorizing Randolph causes him to start crying. In response to Randolph's crying, the White Santa, speaking with "anger and disgust," threatens to kill him: "If you don't stop dat damn cryin,' we'll send you t'see Saint Peter" (184). One can read that threat of anger and disgust as acknowledgement of Randolph's humanity,[4] which is interfering with the ideo-pleasure that the White Santa is receiving from terrorizing Randolph.

---

4. Kwame Anthony Appiah notes in his discussion of the "modes of response underlying our moral sentiments" that the ingroup/outgroup distinction is a mode that can "license extraordinary acts of cruelty" (143). However, Appiah continues, the reason for these acts is not simply due to the dehumanization of the outgroup: "The persecutors may liken the objects of their enmity to cockroaches and germs, but they acknowledge their victims' humanity in the very act of humiliating, stigmatizing, reviling, and torturing them" (144). The White Santa's treatment of Randolph, I argue, is an example of Jim Crow's ingroup/outgroup mode of response that underlines its moral sadism.

To stop that interference, the White Santa threatens Randolph with physical violence, or else he will have to acknowledge the truth—that he and the White folks in the crowd, not Randolph, are the real monsters in this scenario. Such thinking also helps to explain why he saves Randolph from being lynched. Indeed, to assert that Randolph is "one lil'l n—— who ain't ripe enough to be lynched" (186), the White Santa acknowledges that he is a little boy and, therefore, deserves the same chance as the White boy to get to adulthood. At the same time, to reassure himself and the crowd that terrorizing Randolph is morally valid, he gives Randolph's quarter to the White boy who got the rope to lynch Randolph, an act that serves as a reminder that Black and White people are not the same in Jim Crow America and as an explanation for why Black people should have less than White people.

Finally, both stories argue that the White rage monster's belief in Jesus Christ and celebration of Santa Claus only exits because these figures, like the American Dream, are racialized as White.[5] For instance, the monsters of White rage in Du Bois's story are depicted as White Christians who would renounce their faith in Jesus Christ if he appeared to them in any other body besides a White male body. Indeed, while all the Black people in the story who encounter the stranger immediately identify him as the Christ figure, none of the White characters identify him as such, save for the colonel's young daughter, who talks with the stranger about the "'Kingdom of Heaven'" for a few moments (98). Moreover, the "amazement," "anger," and "terror" expressed by the colonel, his wife, and the farmer's wife after they discover that the stranger is a dark-skinned mulatto with curly hair indicate that they would treat a non-White Christ the same as they treat Black people. Although the farmer's wife comes to see the stranger as Christ, she only comes to that realization after the Black convict is lynched in her name (103). Thus, "Jesus Christ in Texas" proposes not only that the racialization of Christ as White

---

5. The racialization of Jesus Christ and Santa Claus as White is still relevant for some contemporary White Americans. The most infamous example of this racialization was expressed by Megyn Kelly on her former Fox News television show, *The Kelly File*. In a December 2013 episode of her show, Kelly insisted that Jesus Christ and Santa Claus were White. Kelly was responding to Aisha Harris's claim that it is time to develop an image of Santa Claus that all American children can identify with. Thus, Harris proposes that "America abandon Santa-as-fat-old-white-man and create a new symbol of Christmas cheer. From here on out, Santa Claus should be a penguin" (par. 7). However, in order to push the argument that Santa and Jesus were White men, Kelly intentionally misreads Harris's argument as calling for Santa to be represented as Black: "By the way, for all you kids watching at home, Santa just is white. But this person is just arguing that maybe we should also have a black Santa" (*The Kelly File*). In this light, Du Bois's and Clarke's stories point to some of the historical reasons why most parts of White America continue to be invested in racializing these figures as White.

serves to justify anti-Black exploitation and violence[6] but also that a key distinction between fully human White Christians and the Christian monsters of White rage is that the fully human ones, represented by the colonel's young daughter, would remain Christian after learning that their savior is Black.

Like its belief in Jesus Christ, the White rage monster's celebration of Santa Claus in Clarke's story is shaped by the idea that this mythical figure only rewards White people. For example, the narrator not telling us the race of the "real" Santa Claus whom Randolph saw at a downtown department store is noteworthy because it suggests that Randolph believed that the "real" Santa, even if he is White, is raceless and not racist (182). Moreover, Randolph seemed to believe that the real Santa would give him everything that he wanted for Christmas, which assumes that Santa wants all kids, regardless of race, to be happy. Indeed, before "he reached the outskirts of the business district, where the bulk of the city's poor whites lived," Randolph was "the happiest little colored boy in all Louisiana" due to his visit with the real Santa weeks prior (181). Thus, after the White Santa steals Randolph's quarter and gives it the White boy who wanted to lynch him, who declares, "Sure there's a Santa Claus," Randolph is left "crestfallen," "whimpering," and "bewildered beyond words" because he no longer knows "what to think about Santa Claus" (186). Randolph's fear and confusion about Santa Claus represents Black people's fear and confusion about the American Dream, "a dream that was not originally theirs" (Hochschild 15). As Floyd and Reifer point out, that exclusion is reflected by Adams's own vision of the American Dream, a dream in which "each is afforded equal opportunity, unhindered by social, cultural, and economic conditions that impinged on the full development of their abilities, and their humanity, yet which simultaneously could not imagine African Americans as part of the American people" (*American* 118). In this light, what seems to confuse and scare Randolph is that Santa Claus, like the American Dream, is imagined as available to all, but in the real world, Santa Claus and the Dream are only for White Americans. Thus, as Randolph learns from the White Santa who "had taken [Randolph's] fortune

---

6. The practice of racializing God as White is an example of what I refer to as the "God-as-human" concept. One of the problems with that concept is that believers are required to give God a racial and gender identity: "Since race and gender in a racialized heteropatriarchal society, such as the United States, mythically naturalizes what the races and the genders enjoy, think, or do, identifying God as human assumes that God identifies itself as belonging to a race and a gender and, therefore, acts accordingly. In this context, God is ultimately on the side of those it looks like, and those who do not look like God exist as props to teach its lookalikes how to live a godly life" ("Is Religiosity" 13–14). Similarly, Du Bois's story proposes that the God-as-human concept is a crucial reason why the monster of White rage exists, since these monsters believe that their savior can only be White and male.

from him," knowing that "there was nothing he could do about it" (186), the monsters of White rage believe that the American Dream is a dream that comes to fruition through White theft of Black wealth.

The monsters of White rage in Du Bois's and Clarke's text represent how anti-Black Whites use the American Dream to justify anti-Black violence. As their stories show, since White rage and its monsters direct their violence primarily at Black people who have, as Anderson puts it, "drive, initiative, and resolve" (4), such as the Black convict whose closed mouth represents revolt and the Black boy who dared to be happy in an anti-Black world, the Black nightmare of the American Dream is the treatment of Black advancement as evil and anti-Black violence as a virtuous act. Given this context, Du Bois's "Jesus Christ in Texas" and Clarke's "Santa Claus Is a White Man" can be read as fictional documentation of what Floyd and Reifer refer to as the "epochal reshuffling" of the American Dream that occurred in the 1930s ("What Happens" 65). What makes this reshuffling noteworthy for the purposes of this chapter is that it occurred when Adolph Hitler and the Nazis became invested in the American Dream and when Du Bois began to see the dangers of the Dream for Black people and human progress. For instance, Timothy Snyder argues that since "the exemplary land of empire" for Hitler and the German imperialists before him was the US, we should not be surprised that "globalization led Hitler to the American dream" (qtd. in Floyd and Reifer, "What Happens" 64). While Hitler and the Nazis did not need, as Isabel Wilkerson puts it, "outsiders to plant the seeds of hatred within them" (79),[7] they were "impressed by the American custom of lynching its subordinate caste of African-Americans, having become aware of the ritual torture and mutilations that typically accompanied them. Hitler especially marveled at the American 'knack for maintaining an air of robust innocence in the wake of mass death'" (81). Grappling with the fact that White people at home and abroad imagine the American Dream as a White dream, Du Bois began to lose hope that the American Dream could be a dream for Black people. As Floyd and Reifer write, "At one time assuming the inherently humanizing effects of culture, religion and literature, as part and parcel of the progress of the world, the German and American experience revealed to Du Bois something much more ominous and disturbing, the power of the irrational, evident in both world events and the American Dreams shaping them and the related logic of total destruction" ("What Happens" 64–65).

---

7. For example, Angela Saini notes that Germany built its first concentration camp in Namibia and committed "the first genocide of the twentieth century" when it killed tens of thousands of Namibians for rebelling against colonial rule. Moreover, Saini continues, some estimates assert that "up to three thousand skulls belonging to members of the Herero ethnic group were sent back to Berlin to be studied by race scientists" (47).

The monsters of White rage depicted in "Jesus Christ in Texas" and "Santa Claus Is a White Man" embody the ominous and disturbing power of the irrational that accompanied the reshuffling of the American Dream. As these stories demonstrate, one of the horrors produced by the irrational was the practice of lynching and its link to achieving the American Dream. The ominous and disturbing power of the irrational is also captured in their depictions of America's icons of universal humanity, Jesus Christ and Santa Claus. Not only are these icons revered by the monsters of White rage because they appear in White male bodies, but they are also represented in these stories as useless in preventing the monsters of White rage from terrorizing Black people, since these monsters believe that Christ and Claus are on their side. Moreover, the ideological pleasure that the monsters of White rage receive from producing and consuming Black people in pain also represents the ominous and disturbing power of the irrational operating in the German and American versions of the American Dream. Since both versions of the Dream view lynching as a practice that will help White people achieve the Dream, anti-Black violence becomes ideologically pleasurable because the victims of that violence are viewed as threats to White wealth, and the monsters of White rage who perpetuate that violence are viewed as protectors of that wealth. Thus, the underlining horror in these stories is that the monsters of White rage are driven by the belief that Black advancement is always a threat to White people; therefore, it must be stopped at all costs. Sadly, as suggested by Tananarive Due's *The Between*, White rage's monsters will continue to wreak havoc on Black life in the final third of the twentieth century, and they will be largely inspired by what has been called the Southern strategy.

The Southern Strategy's Monsters of White Rage

Including "traces" of Due's life in Miami during her formative years,[8] *The Between* is not only a "combination of horror novel, detective story, and suspense/thriller" (Nevins 189), but it is also a fictional study of Black America's economically privileged at the end of the twentieth century, particularly their fight against the monsters of White rage. The novel takes us

---

8. In the 2002 interview that I referenced in the introduction, Due states the following: "Hilton's wife is a judge (my parents had supported a black Miami woman who ran for judge), Hilton is a social worker and activist (both of my parents have experience there), the family had a hostile neighbor (as my family did when we moved into all-white neighborhoods in my youth), Hilton's psychologist is Puerto Rican (as was my first boyfriend in Miami, an Afro-Hispanic who gave me entrée into that world), and the list goes on" (Glave 698).

back to 1963, the year of the famous March on Washington and the infamous response to the March—the bombing of the 16th Street Baptist Church
in Birmingham, Alabama, by White supremacists in which four Black girls
were killed. Organized as a peaceful, multiracial demonstration during
the centennial of the Emancipation Proclamation, the March on Washington is the result of Black Americans discovering that "demonstrations had
accomplished what other measures had not" up to that point—to make
emancipation a reality and not just a proclamation (Franklin and Moss 502).
However, the bombing of the church nearly three weeks after the March
was a reminder that White supremacists will do everything in their power
to prevent Black advancement. These events provide the background for
understanding Eunice Kelly's first and second deaths as well as those of
Hilton James, her grandson and the novel's protagonist.

Although Hilton spent a short time of his formative years with Eunice,
whom he calls Nana, she is the reason why he was able to achieve upward
mobility during the 1980s and early 1990s. Although Nana's second and
final death was in 1963, when she saved the seven-year-old Hilton from
drowning in the ocean, her first death happened close to a year before, when
Hilton discovered her on the floor of their two-room home with skin that
felt "as cold as just-drawn well water" (Due 2). When Hilton returns with a
neighbor to see if Nana is dead, she is up cooking and asking where Hilton
had gone. Once the neighbor leaves, Nana tells Hilton, as his eyes fill with
tears, that she is not going to leave him (3). The reason why Nana is not
going to leave Hilton is that she believes that "there were bigger things in
store for him" than what was offered to poor and working-class Black folks,
such as herself, who harvested sugarcane or picked string beans in Florida
(1–2). Indeed, Hilton's aunt and uncle, Auntie and CJ James, who adopted
Hilton after Nana's second death, believe that Nana's decision to drown
so that Hilton could live was more than an example of a grandmother's
love for her grandson. According to CJ, as Nana was drowning, her mouth
expressed "contentment" and accomplishment, "like she was saying, 'There.
That's done'" (252). Moreover, since Hilton had also died that day, but was
resuscitated by a family member, Auntie tells Hilton, "We knew there was
a plan for you" (253). It appears that Nana's sacrifice was not in vain, given
that Hilton obtains a master's degree in public administration, becomes the
director of a semiprivate facility that treats drug addiction, marries Dede
who becomes an elected circuit court judge in Florida, and fathers two lov-
able children. What makes Hilton's accomplishments noteworthy is that
they happened when "[President] Reagan's job cuts, retooling of student
financial aid to eliminate those most in need, and decimation of antipoverty
and social welfare programs [had] 'virtually ensured that the goal of the

African American community for economic stability and progress would crumble and fade'" (C. Anderson 123).

Reagan's policies are an example of the White rage that defined what has been called the "Southern strategy." Originally called "Operation Dixie," the Southern strategy was launched by Barry Goldwater's 1964 presidential campaign, which "directly and aggressively champion[ed] his vote against the 1964 Civil Rights Act" (Maxwell par. 5). Learning from Goldwater's loss to Lyndon B. Johnson, George Wallace and Richard Nixon made the Southern strategy more palatable to White voters during their presidential bids in 1968 (see Smith 130–37). After receiving congratulatory responses from Northern Whites for trying to prevent Black students from enrolling at the University of Alabama at Tuscaloosa in 1963, Wallace, who was Alabama's governor at the time, came to believe that all White people hate Black people and that all White people are Southerners at heart (C. Anderson 101). With that revelation in mind, Wallace used "race-neutral language to explain what was at stake for disgruntled working-class whites, particularly those whose neighborhoods butted right up against black enclaves." What is perhaps most important and disturbing about Wallace's approach to the Southern strategy is that it reiterated the dangerous all-or-nothing understanding of race in America—the assumption that "Black gains . . . could come only at the expense of whites" (102). While adopting Wallace's approach to the Southern strategy, Nixon's campaign team seemed to understand the risks of Goldwater's and Wallace's overt attacks against civil rights; thus, Nixon used "dog-whistle appeals" (e.g., crime, welfare, and neighborhood schools) to "trigger Pavlovian anti-black responses" without appearing to do so (104). However, according to Strom Thurmond, the senator from South Carolina whose filibuster against the 1957 Civil Rights Act is the record for the Senate's longest individual speech ("Strom"), Nixon's presidential campaign did not do a good job at hiding its anti-Black goals: "If Nixon becomes president, he has promised that he won't enforce either the Civil Rights or the Voting Rights Acts. Stick with him" (qtd. in Maxwell par. 6).[9]

---

9. Nixon's approach to the Civil Rights movement lived up to Thurmond's claim about him. Carol Anderson notes that one of the tasks that the Nixon administration executed to "crush the promise" represented by the Civil Rights Act of 1964 and the Voting Rights Act of 1965 was reducing the Civil Rights movement to "the harmless symbolism of a bus seat and a water fountain," which would allow him to declare in 1965, as paraphrased by Anderson, that nearly all roadblocks to equal opportunity for Black people disappeared "when the COLORED ONLY signs went down" (99). According to the logic of this disingenuous declaration, which history has shown to be extremely naïve or insidious, there is no need for the Civil Rights or the Voting Rights Acts because the majority of anti-Black Whites stop being anti-Black once anti-Black discrimination became illegal.

Although the Southern strategy was *refined* by Wallace and Nixon, Anderson argues that Reagan was a "more effective southern strategist" than Nixon or Wallace because "Reagan's aura of sincerity and 'aw shucks' geniality lent a welcoming, friendly façade to any harshness of the Southern Strategy—something that Nixon's brooding nor Wallace's angry countenance had ever been able to convey" (118). Indeed, during his first presidential campaign appearance, Reagan invoked the discourse of states' rights, which was code in the South for the "right of whites to oppress blacks," and he made subtler appeals to racist Whites in California during his first campaign for governor (Smith 2). Reagan is also responsible for the popularity of the mythical "welfare queen," a fictious Black woman who is "irresponsible," "sexually promiscuous," and living "comfortably, even extravagantly, on the taxpayers' dime" (White et al. 577–78). Once he became president, Reagan focused on coding the Great Society as a "giveaway program for blacks," developing budget proposals that "targeted very specifically those programs in which blacks were overrepresented" (C. Anderson 119), and his fight against affirmative action, like that of his Southern strategy predecessors, was grounded in the discourse of reverse discrimination that was powered by the very dangerous myth that Black gains can only be achieved at the expense of White people (102). Thus, Reagan's appointment of Ralph Scott to the chair of the Iowa Advisory Commission on Civil Rights in 1985 was "suspect" and "alarming" precisely because Scott, a professor of education psychology, was "a man known to be actively involved in blocking policies aimed at achieving desegregation," believing that racially integrated schools were harming White students and not helping Black students because of the so-called genetic differences between the two groups (Saini 75–76).

While Hilton succeeds despite Reagan's anti-Black policies and appointments, his battle with Charles Ray Goode indicates that he is unable to escape the White rage embodied in those policies. I argue that Goode is a monster of White rage born from the Southern strategy's myth that the racial climate in late twentieth-century America favored Black folks over White folks. What makes that myth dangerous and disturbing, as Due points out in *The Between*, is that it creates human monsters like Goode who believe that Black success is a threat to White survival in America. Thus, Due's novel interrogates a popular image of the American Dream that developed after Adams's 1931 introduction of the concept and was popular at the time of the novel's publication—that the Dream is or has become a raceless dream. That understanding of the American Dream is captured by President Clinton during his speech to the Democratic Leadership Council in 1993: "The American dream that we were all raised on is a simple but powerful one—if you work hard and play by the rules you should be given a chance to go as far as your God-given ability will take you" (qtd. in Hochschild 18).

While there is a lot to unpack in Clinton's definition, including the assumption about what "we were all raised on," I want to focus on who "should be given a chance" to achieve the American Dream because it dismisses the Dream's White-only origins and how White rage seeks to keep the Dream a White-only dream. Indeed, the fight to keep the American Dream for White dreamers only was expressed by the notorious Republican consultant Lee Atwater in a 1981 interview where he discusses the evolution of the Southern strategy:

> You start out in 1954 by saying, 'N——, n——, n——.' By 1968, you can't say 'n——'—that hurts you. Backfires. So you say stuff like forced busing, states' rights and all that stuff. You're getting so abstract now you're talking about cutting taxes, and all these things you're talking about are totally economic things and a byproduct of them is [that] blacks get hurt worse than whites.
>
> And subconsciously maybe that is part of it. I'm not saying that. But I'm saying that if it is getting that abstract, and that coded, that we are doing away with the racial problem one way or the other. (qtd. in Herbert par. 5–6)

Considering Atwater's admission, Due's depiction of Goode as a monster of White rage born out of Reagan's Southern strategy proposes that many White Americans at the end of the twentieth century believed that it is morally right that "blacks get hurt worse than whites" precisely because the American Dream, as they imagined it, is not for Black dreamers.

Goode is a former Green Beret officer who was recruited from an Ivy League university in 1977 and discharged in 1985 for being a munitions advisor for a neo-Nazi terrorist group who killed a Jewish radio talk-show host the year prior.[10] However, since the FBI was unable to prove that Goode was tied to the murder, the agency decided to sweep "the whole thing . . . under the rug" (Due 151). After his history with the FBI is concealed, Goode

---

10. The talk show host referenced here is Alan Berg, who was killed in his Denver, Colorado, neighborhood in 1984 by a White supremacist group called The Order, which began in 1983. According to Stephen Singular, who wrote the book *Talked to Death: The Life and Murder of Alan Berg* (1987), The Order formed when a "group of 11 men got together in the woods and basically said: 'It's time for a revolution in America [and] we're going to get rid of minorities, feminists, gays, [and] whoever we decide are our enemies.'" Moreover, as Singular continues, "They said: 'Our first assassination target will be Alan Berg'" (qtd. in Dukakis par. 8).

is convicted of aggravated battery for beating his girlfriend, "whose skull he had gashed with a crowbar" (152), but Hilton learns that "the judge practically let him off" (121). Hilton also learns that Dede was the prosecutor in Goode's aggravated battery case, which explains why Goode sends anonymous letters threatening to kill Dede and her children. While the dead Hiltons of the underworld have recruited Goode to carry out their plan to kill Hilton because Hilton has made them "an abomination," they note that Goode was "so willing" to do their bidding that "he'd have almost thought of [their plan] himself" (127). As implied by the underworld Hiltons, Goode's hatred of Hilton and the Black advancement he represents is not their doing. Indeed, as represented by the two face-to-face meetings between Hilton and Goode, that hatred is born out of the belief that the American Dream is a White-only dream.

The first meeting between Hilton and Goode is organized by law enforcement, and it takes place at Goode's trailer park home, where he is handcuffed and questioned about the racist letters sent to Dede in which the writer threatens to kill her and her children. As the handcuffed Goode is taken to meet Hilton, he makes a comment to his neighbor that gets to the heart of White rage at the end of the twentieth century: "It's official now. It's finally a crime to be a white man in the United States of America" (Due 154). Goode's comments evoke Stephan and Abigail Thernstrom's problematic claim that the racial climate in America by the 1990s was one of "black anger and white surrender" in which "the balance of power in racial confrontations has shifted" between Blacks and Whites to such a degree that "when blacks raise their voice, whites most often retreat" (494–95). Like the Thernstroms, Goode believes that being handcuffed and questioned by law enforcement on the behalf of a Black person is evidence that Black people have more social, economic, and political power than White people. In other words, Goode's statement engages in a rhetorical practice common among defenders of White privilege then and today—"relegat[ing] black grievances against whites to the past while situating white complaints about blacks in the present" (Lipsitz 222). Thus, it appears that Due's goal in having Goode articulate the myth that America is a White man's country is to show not only that White rage is the child of White privilege but also that the anger that fueled White rage in the late twentieth century was largely shaped by the belief that the state prevented White people from harming, killing, and/or discriminating against Black people with impunity. While the defenders of White rage claim publicly that the state has helped create an America of Black anger and White surrender, Due's depiction of Hilton and Goode's second face-to-face encounter implies that the defenders of White rage know that Black people are lone wolves in their fight against them.

The second meeting between Hilton and Goode, which is absent of law enforcement, takes place at a convenience store, where Goode tells Hilton that he learned a great deal about Black people from his friends who fought in the US war in Vietnam: "You know, it was mostly n——s they sent over there. And my buddies had to live with them, fight with them. They said you never scrap with a n——. You know why? They don't have anything to lose. They can beat your ass. I never underestimate a n——. Never" (Due 221). While Goode gives the impression that he is afraid of Black rage because Black people have nothing to lose, he also lets Hilton know that he is not worried because Black folks are on their own in the struggle against White rage and the monsters it engenders: "You're a lone wolf now. You're sick of the system's way, and so you've come up with your own way" (221). For example, even though an FBI agent informed Hilton at the first meeting that "Goode has a history with the FBI," the agent cannot take him into custody because the FBI only has enough information about Goode to keep him under surveillance (156). However, given what the FBI knows about Goode, it is shocking and terrifying that Goode is not in prison. Moreover, although Goode is under FBI surveillance for the letters sent to Dede, the surveillance is so bad that Goode describes the agents watching him as "useless" and has named one of them "Goober." According to Goode, "Sometimes I wake him up to let him know when I'm going to work. I think he'd sleep all day, otherwise. He and a second man switch off. You're a better tail than both of them put together" (220). Finally, when Goode decides to leave the Miami area for another job in Florida, Curt, the Black police officer working on the Goode case, tells Hilton that the FBI is "so glad to get rid of him, they're helping pay his expenses, if you can believe that" (239).

In light of Goode's history of criminality and the state's response to it, Hilton comes to the realization that his "way," which is to shoot Goode with the gun that he is carrying in his pocket, will not work because the "system" would punish him for defending himself.[11] Indeed, after Goode tells Hilton that "fate" is the reason why he cannot kill him, Hilton grabs the gun in his jacket at the same time Goober walks into the store. While Hilton can still shoot Goode, he does not because, as Goode puts it, Hilton would also be "shooting it out with the FBI" (222). What Hilton learns here is that the dead Hiltons of the underworld are not Goode's only protection against Black

---

11. Hilton's fear that he would be punished for defending himself evokes the Georgia Supreme Court's ruling in *John v. State* (1854). In that case, the court ruled that "any slave accused of killing a white person had to be charged with murder, even if he or she had acted in self-defense" (White et al. 193). According to that ruling, White people could legally harm Black people, and Black people had no right to defend themselves against White assault.

self-defense; it is also the state. Thus, what makes Goode's monstrosity lethal is not his anti-Black beliefs, which has been a constant in America since its beginnings, but the freedom to act on his beliefs. As bell hooks observed in 1995, White on Black violence in the US is "condoned by the state":

> We live in a society where we hear about white folks killing black people to express their rage. We can identify specific incidents throughout our history in this country whether it be Emmett Till, Bensonhurst, Howard Beach, etc. We can identify rare incidents where black folks have randomly responded to their fear of white assault by killing. White rage is acceptable, can be both expressed and condoned, but black rage has no place and everyone knows it. (15)

Considering hooks's comments, Due's depiction of Goode can be read as an indictment of US laws and institutions for their role in the creation and cultivation of White rage and its monsters. Indeed, even if Goode did not have supernatural assistance, Hilton would still be powerless to stop Goode from killing him because the state excuses and protects anti-Blackness. While the state's inability and/or unwillingness to punish Goode for his White-rage crimes is what makes Goode's monstrosity lethal, the reason for his rage is what makes his monstrosity disgusting.

For Goode to be a horror monster, he must not only be deadly, as I discussed above, but also embody "the disgust elicited by impurity" (Brooks 5). As Carroll explains, "The character's affective reaction to the monstrous in horror stories is not merely a matter of fear, i.e., of being frightened by something that threatens danger. Rather threat is compounded with revulsion, nausea, and disgust" (22). For example, when Hilton initially learns of Goode's background and his ability to escape imprisonment for his crimes, "he fe[els] a leap in his stomach, nausea tickling his throat" (Due 151). While Hilton's reaction to Goode is evidence that Goode is a disgusting monster as well as a lethal one, Goode's repulsiveness is also rooted in a disturbing view of the racial climate in late twentieth-century America, a view captured by Goode's first letter to Dede:

> Am I to believe it is mere coincidence they sent an African-coon-tarbaby-n——-American bitch to persecute me? And you, the child of Ham's clans, marked by Satan himself, beholding me with contempt and irreverence, your insides raging with unborn seeds of your insidious kind, of monkey-men?

> Do you believe I'm only a monkey, too, adept at the art of mimicry? You
> are wrong, sadly wrong. You and your herd won't live to mock me further,
> nor will your offspring ever grow up to taint and murder mine. (Due 60)

What makes Goode disgusting is that his view of the racial climate in late
twentieth-century America is an intentionally inaccurate depiction of that
climate. While Goode's light sentence for his aggravated battery conviction as well as his education, military career, and history with the legal system indicate that his White rage has state support, he somehow believes,
as expressed by his letter to Dede, that Black people have more institutional power than White people. Indeed, the intellectual impossible-ness of
Goode's claim, which functions in the same way as the physical impossible-
ness of the horror monster in that both can make those who encounter them
mentally ill, is partly responsible for Hilton's mental crisis.

The impossible-ness of Goode's view of the racial climate is nurtured by
the discourse of reverse discrimination, which perpetuates the fear of racial
sameness that we see in Du Bois's and Clarke's stories as well as the myths
that anti-Black racism was no longer a threat to Black life at the dawn of
the twenty-first century and that Black advancement always entails White
poverty. While Goode's description of Dede as a "monkey" and "the child of
Ham's clans, marked by Satan himself" invokes the discourse of Black dehumanization in which Black inferiority is viewed as the product of nature or
divine decree, it also evokes the fear that White people are nothing more
than just a shade of Blackness. As Goode sees it, Whiteness, Americanness,
and manhood are being "mock[ed]" when the state places Black people,
especially Black women, in positions where they have the power to judge
the thoughts and actions of White men. Indeed, Goode's letter to Dede can
be read as a modern take on Chief Justice Taney's view of Black people
in his deliverance of the Court's majority opinion in *Dred Scott v. Sandford*
(1856). Taney claimed not only that people of African descent could not be
US citizens because they are commodities but also that Black people are so
inferior that "they had no rights which the white man was bound to respect"
(www.loc.gov/item/usrep060393a/). In 1990s America, Goode is confronted
by one of the fears expressed in Taney's opinion—being "bound to respect"
the rights of Black people. Goode seems to read Dede's judgeship as the
state telling him that he and Dede are both "monkey-men," which Goode
believes is "sadly wrong." Thus, while Goode threatens to kill Dede and
her kids because he wants to protect his future offspring from living in an
America where his kids must respect the rights of Dede's kids, he is also

scared that his kids may be "tainted" by the belief that Black and White people are racially the same, since his kids must acknowledge that both groups have the same rights in that America, including equal access to the American Dream.

Due's depiction of Goode highlights the ideological forces that gave birth to the monsters of White rage during the late twentieth century. Indeed, Southern strategists from Goldwater to Reagan claimed, as Anderson notes, that slavery was an American institution in which "few if any whites had ever benefitted because their 'families never owned slaves,'" that affirmative action and President Lyndon B. Johnson's Great Society were forms of "reverse discrimination" against hardworking Whites and handouts for lazy Black people, and that the Ku Klux Klan is *the* symbol of racism in America, therefore, reducing White racism to "its most virulent and visible form" and simultaneously designating it as "an individual aberration rather than something systemic, institutional, and pervasive" (100). With these forces in play, it is not surprising that Goode becomes a White rage monster whose rage is directed at an economically privileged Black family. Indeed, Goode's letters to Dede and his face-to-face encounters with Hilton indicate that he believes not only that his anti-Black violence is morally reasonable but also that Dede's and Hilton's socioeconomic success explains his socioeconomic failure. In the eyes of Goode, the production and consumption of Black people in pain is crucial to both White acquisition of the American Dream and the ideological pleasure of White rage, since anti-Black violence in this context disavows Black-White racial sameness while posing as a morally righteous response to the Black gains–White loss myth exploited by Southern strategists. Like *The Between* but with less focus on the Southern strategy, Victor LaValle's *The Changeling* proposes that the disavowal of racial sameness and the belief in the Black gains–White loss myth engender White rage monsters who believe that the destruction of the Black middle-class family is crucial to White achievement of the American Dream.

The Monsters of White Rage and the Black Dream Family

Hortense J. Spillers reminds us that Africans held and practiced concepts of family that were as complex as those of the "mythically revered" nuclear family in the West, and *"the revised 'Black Family' of enslavement"* is "one of the supreme social achievements of African-Americans under conditions of enslavement" (218–19). Yet, as E. Frances White notes, "black family life has consistently served as a model of abnormality [in White bourgeois nationalism]. Black families were matriarchal both when the ideal white family was considered to be male dominated and now, when the ideal white family has become a family headed by an equal heterosexual pair" (122). The belief that all Black families, regardless of type, are abnormalities largely explains why stereotypes about the Black family's "brokenness or pathology," despite the scholarship that refutes those stereotypes, continue in the twenty-first century (C. Jenkins 85). For instance, Clare Huntington notes that even though some First Families, including the first First Family, were "far from nuclear" (351), Donald Trump is the only American president in the twentieth or twenty-first century who has had children with three different women (352n4). Yet, as Huntington continues, "President Obama had to replace the 'tangle of pathology' image of Black families . . . with a Norman Rockwell painting. President and Mrs. Obama worked hard to preserve this image, and when they strayed even slightly, the criticism was rife" (351). Implicit in Huntington's observations is that White families who abandon the "mythically revered" nuclear family but are successful can be transformed into models of respectability,[12] whereas successful Black families must maintain strict adherence to that mythical family structure to be considered respectable. That racialized double standard, as proposed by LaValle's *The Changeling*, is the product of White rage, whose goal is to transform successful Black families into Black families in pain. Although *The Changeling* focuses on the terrifying way that Apollo Kagwa, a biracial Black father and husband who works as a self-employed book trader, learns how to bury the "monster" of fatherlessness (427), it is also a tale of how the monsters of White rage work to prevent the Black family from acquiring or maintaining the American Dream.

While the majority of LaValle's novel is set in the second decade of the twenty-first century, the narrator begins the novel by identifying Apollo's story as a "fairy tale" that began in 1968, when his mother and father came to New York City (3). Nearly ten years later, Lillian Kagwa and Brian West, from Uganda and Syracuse, New York, respectively, created Apollo and began their "shared dream" of parenthood, "a story two people start telling

12. For example, Adam Withnall reported in 2016 that while the sixteen-year-old Ivanka was hosting the 1997 Miss Teen USA pageant, Trump asked the then-Miss Universe the following: "Don't you think my daughter's hot? She's hot, right?" Moreover, Withnall continues, "In the almost 20 years since, Mr. Trump has called his eldest daughter 'voluptuous.' He's said it's OK to describe her as 'a piece of ass,' though she is a senior executive in his business empire. And he's said that, if she wasn't his daughter, 'perhaps [he'd] be dating her.'"

together" (7). Apollo's story shifts from fairy tale to nightmare when Brian unexpectedly vanishes from his life. Although Brian did not leave his family for another person or move back to Syracuse, Apollo discovers as an adult that Brian had planned to kill the entire family, including himself, after discovering that Lillian had filed for divorce. Before this horrifying discovery, Apollo marries Emma Valentine, who also learns the tragic story of her parents' deaths as an adult—the house fire that killed Emma's parents and almost killed her and her sister was started by her mother. Apollo and Emma learn about their parental histories after they become the parents of Brian Kagwa. While Apollo and Emma are determined to realize the "shared dream" of parenthood that was unable to last with their parents, William Wheeler, who identifies himself as Kinder Garten, steals baby Brian to feed him to a monstrous troll hiding in the Little Norway section of Queens.

Known as the "trolde" or "jotunn," the troll, whom Wheeler serves, came from Norway on a sloop with Nils Knudsen, Wheeler's great-great-great-great grandfather, in 1825. According to Jorgen Knudsen, Wheeler's father, Nils was planning to leave Norway for the US, but he was not sure if he and his wife Anna Sofie would survive the fourteen-week journey, since the sloop that they would be sailing in was dangerously too small for all its passengers. Thus, Nils made a deal with a troll in which the troll would ensure that Nils, Anna Sofie, and the other passengers arrive safely in New York, and he would be the troll's "caretaker" in their new home, supplying it with a child to raise. Nils thinks he has fulfilled his end of the bargain when he gives Agnes, whom Anna Sofie bore on the sloop, to the troll, but the troll's attempt at fatherhood failed, a pattern that will continue into the twenty-first century, so he ate Agnes and demanded another child. When Nils refused to give the troll a child from his union with Petra, his second wife and one of the passengers on the sloop, the troll began to destroy what the passengers developed in their new homeland. To keep the troll pleased, Nils began to kidnap immigrant children and sacrifice them to the troll, which also ensured that his kids would have the opportunity to pursue and achieve the American Dream. While Wheeler, the last male of the Knudsen line, seeks to continue the tradition started by Nils, he also attempts to destroy a middle-class Black family in the process by creating a situation in which Apollo and Emma are pitted against each other—Emma is led to believe that Apollo is somehow responsible for baby Brian's disappearance, which leads to her hitting him in the head with a claw hammer, and Apollo is coaxed into believing that Emma killed baby Brian.

Even though Apollo and Emma will save baby Brian and their marriage as well as kill Wheeler, Jorgen, and the troll, their story does not end like the typical fairytale in which their family lives "happily ever after." As Emma puts it, they will live "happily today" (431). I plan to show in the following pages that Emma's desire to end Apollo's story and their shared dream of parenthood with "today" instead of "ever after" highlights the "gap between our imagined American Dream and equally stark historical realities" (Floyd and Reifer, *American* 1). To understand how the dream-reality gap negatively affects Apollo and Emma's family, I draw upon Hochschild's critique of the American Dream's four tenets of success: "that everyone can participate equally and can always start over" (26), "the reasonable anticipation of success" (27), "that success results from actions and traits under one's own control" (30), and "the association of success with virtue" (30). As Hochschild argues, "most Americans must have faith in each component of the dream for the whole dream to bear the vast emotional and political weight that it now carries" (257). Indeed, if people reject or discredit one or more of the tenets, the Dream loses its ability to portray America and Americans as exceptional, since it is no longer viewed as a rational, original, or virtuous path to success. I argue that LaValle's depictions of the differences between the New Dads and Old Dads as well as Wheeler's transformation into Kinder Garten highlight the ways in which the American Dream has been and continues to be used by White rage's monsters to imagine themselves as those whom nature or a supernatural being has designed to succeed and dominate.

In his discussion of how the notion of the "free" American was impacted by the shift from work and production to leisure and consumption, Eric Foner notes the following: "By the twentieth century, as the promise of economic abundance blunted hostility to the wage system, 'slave wages' replaced 'wage slavery' as a mark of servitude, and a family's level of consumption—the so-called American standard to living—came to define the essence of the American dream" (qtd. in Floyd and Reifer, *American* 8). Thus, the American Dream family is a family who owns the commodities that have been deemed symbols of success. That consumption-based conception of the American Dream, according to Floyd and Reifer, encouraged Americans to "look away from freedom and autonomy in their working lives, and to seek these attributes in their ability to consume the increasing amount of goods the new industrial society produced" (*American* 8). Implicit in that understanding of the Dream family is the second tenet, "the reasonable anticipation of success." As Hochschild argues, while the second tenet, which is the "emotional heart" of the American Dream (30), does not claim that people are guaranteed to achieve the Dream, it does promise something that has been and continues to be impossible to do in America—providing "enough resources and opportunities that everyone has a reasonable chance of having some expectations met" (27). This means that our consumption-based American Dream, despite its promises of economic abundance, will always be unavailable to many of the families who work hard, make smart decisions, and are morally upright. The danger of believing in the second tenet, as suggested by *The Changeling*, is that it can turn its believers, such as Wheeler and the Old Dads, into monsters.

Wheeler and the Old Dads, which includes Nils, Jorgen, and Apollo's dad, see the nuclear family and its heteropatriarchal structure as key to achieving the American Dream or as evidence one has achieved the Dream. For example, Wheeler's decision to kill Agnes, his daughter, by feeding her to the troll is driven by the idea that the father-husband owns the members of the family. As Greta, Wheeler's ex-wife, tells Apollo, Wheeler thinks that she, Agnes, and Grace, their remaining daughter, are "his" (269). Thus, when Wheeler kills Greta via a drone attack, it functions as punishment for defying her role as a commodity in the nuclear family, since he sees such defiance as part of the reason why the family did not achieve the American Dream. Indeed, while Greta saw Agnes's death as filicide, Wheeler continues to see it as an act of love. As Jorgen explains, "He loved them so much, he would sacrifice his own child—and Greta abandoned him! That broke him. . . . My son lost his mind" (370). According to Jorgen's and Wheeler's view of Agnes's murder, since killing Agnes was done to allow the remaining members of the family to attain the Dream, Wheeler should have received praise from Greta rather than her scorn and abandonment. Like the bourgeois husband in Karl Marx and Friedrich Engels's *Manifesto of the Communist Party* (1848), who "sees in his wife a mere instrument of production" and "hears that the instruments of production are to be exploited" (101), Wheeler and the Old Dads believe that husbands own their wives and children, whose role in the Dream family is virtually the same as that of the nice house, school, and car—to function as commodities that validate "his" success.

Unlike the Old Dads, the "New Dads," whom Apollo mocked before Brian's birth, are those dads who "blithely assumed their online friends were gluttons for punishment. *Here's my baby lying on his back! And here's my baby also lying on his back! And how about this one: blurry baby on his back!* Good God, the vanity of it all, the epic self-centeredness" (82). Indeed, none of the New Dads whom Apollo befriended, including himself, "talked about their jobs, or their hopes and dreams, not when there were children to discuss" (90). Despite their unaware self-centeredness, the New Dads are "so much better than the Old Dads of the past," fixing the "mistakes" made in earlier conceptions of the American family, especially the mistakes concerning childcare, domestic chores, and emotional availability (89). Moreover, Apollo and the New Dads expect that their wives want to and/or must share bread-winning duties with them, implying that the nuclear family's heteropatriar-chal structure does not guarantee or even offer a reasonable expectation that such a family will achieve or maintain the American Dream. For instance, Apollo did not expect Emma to be a stay-at-home mother, since she enjoyed her work as a librarian and, more importantly, "retained her health insur-ance" when she returned to work. Although Apollo made more money when Emma's work hours were cut from full-time to part-time, "her health insur-ance made a big difference" (91). In Apollo's New Dadism, Emma is not like Greta, an accessory of family success; rather, she is, like Apollo, a creator of that success. This means that the New Dad does not see his wife and kids as "his"; rather, he is "theirs." As the narrator points out, New Dads do not remember each other's names because they are identified by "the names of each other's children, and that mattered more" (89). Similarly, when Apollo meets Greta, he introduces himself as "I'm Emma's" (268); however, such identification is not about ownership but about unity, since it "allied" Apollo to Emma (269).

Thus, New Dads acknowledge not only that family success is a com-munal accomplishment, instead of an individual one as presumed by the Old Dads, but also that family structure does not guarantee success or fail-ure, since "some people fail in the best of circumstances and others suc-ceed in the worst" (Hochschild 181). This also means that the third tenet, "the belief that success results from actions and traits under one's own control," offers a very problematic understanding of those families who do not achieve the American Dream—it is their fault. The problem with such thinking, as Hochschild points out, is that it is illogical—it assumes that "if success results from individual volition, then failure results from lack of volition" (30). Indeed, if there are not enough resources and opportunities to go around, then a family's success or failure is not solely determined by its choices but by forces external to the family such as laws, luck, discrimi-nation, and the economy. Since family structure does not guarantee success or failure, then the fourth tenet of the American Dream, "the association of success with virtue," is disturbing and dangerous because it demonizes and justifies failure (Hochschild 30). According to Hochschild, the "psycho-logic" (30) of that tenet insists that nature or supernatural being(s) made some people destined to succeed and fail as well as to dominate and be dominated: "For some Americans always, and for many Americans in some periods of our history, virtuous success has been defined as the dominance of some groups over others" (34). Indeed, LaValle's depictions of Wheeler's transformation into Kinder Garten highlights a major problem with the fourth tenet—it can be used to justify White rage's anti-Blackness and its monsters' anti-Black violence.

Cal, the leader of the community of women and children in which Emma has become a member, tells Apollo that though she and the women on the island are witches, known as the Wise Ones, Wheeler "consorts with monsters" (260).[13] The monsters that Wheeler associates with are human and nonhuman. The nonhuman monster, as noted earlier, is the troll, and Wheeler inherited his association with the troll from Nils. Given this fact, one might be tempted to argue that Wheeler's monstrosity is not his own because his practice of kidnapping and killing children was forced upon him. However, when Wheeler reveals his "real name" to Apollo, he not only reveals the human monsters that he consorts with but also the desires that make him a monster: "I didn't know my real name either. Didn't know who I really was. Then I found the place where I belonged. Found people who understood me. . . . When I was there, I took off William Wheeler's face and found my true face underneath" (277). Wheeler's "real name" is Kinder Garten, and it does not refer to him only but to "ten thousand men" (277). As he sees it, he is the product of Jorgen's past mistake, and correcting it requires monetizing his service to the troll:

My father did his service for free, but that was never how it was supposed to work. The pact was that we, the Knudsen men, would make the ultimate sacrifice. But in return, we would prosper. My father failed to make the proper sacrifice and received no blessing. He kept the troll from rampaging, but that didn't pay my goddamn mortgage. (405)

To profit from his service, Kinder Garten developed a website where his ten thousand men, for a monthly fee, can watch the troll eat children, and baby Brian is his "beta test," his trial run in the everyday world (405–6).

On the one hand, Kinder Garten's monstrosity is the product of his pursuit of the American Dream. As he sees it, killing children, including one of his own, is justified if he becomes economically successful or able to pay the "goddamn mortgage." Given the fourth tenet of the Dream, Kinder Garten must believe that his means to achieving success is virtuous because

---

13. LaValle's depiction of the Wise Ones can be read as a critique of the witch that one encounters in most horror films, which tend to focus on the myths of post-fourteenth-century Europe, when witches were viewed by the church as evil penis stealers. Indeed, the Wise Ones are like the pre-fourteenth-century witches, who were considered in some cultures as healers, midwives, and practitioners of medicine (see Renegade Cut).

to think otherwise is to admit that one has failed to achieve the Dream. As Hochschild notes, the fourth tenet requires that Americans believe that "success without virtue is not really success—otherwise the restraints required by virtue will seem worthwhile only to suckers and saints" (257). To circumvent virtue's restraints, Kinder Garten draws upon a popular belief in American culture that was mentioned earlier in this chapter—the idea that dominance of a group is virtuous success. That idea explains not only why Kinder Garten, as well as Jorgen, thinks of his murder of Agnes as the "ultimate sacrifice" for his family rather than a horrific murder by a human monster but also why Jorgen insists that Nils was not "evil," regardless of what Apollo and others might think of him, since his seven children with Petra told "stories of his kindness" (365). Thus, the problem that LaValle exposes in his depictions of Kinder Garten and the Knudsen men is the fourth tenet's assumption about virtue. Indeed, if virtue is associated with success, then either the means of success, regardless of who or what is harmed, are also associated with virtue, or the moral status of the means does not matter because the virtuousness of success is defined by the ends, not by the means. In either case, as symbolized by Jorgen's and Kinder Garten's justifications for killing children, the fourth tenet does not encourage people to be virtuous in their pursuit of the American Dream; rather, it encourages people to define their pursuits as virtuous.

On the other hand, Kinder Garten's monstrosity is also the product of White rage. For example, Jorgen claims that the move toward "fairness" and "balance" in the workplace is one of the reasons why his son never achieved the American Dream:

> My son . . . had a wife and two daughters. A good job, working with computers, but it hardly made him enough. There was a time in this country when a man like him could be sure his children would do better than he had done. Once that was the birthright of every white man in America. But not anymore. Suddenly men like my son were being passed over in the name of things like "fairness" and "balance." Where's the justice in that? (369–70)

Like Charles Ray Goode, the monster of White rage in Due's *The Between*, Jorgen believes that his son has not achieved the American Dream because his "birthright" has been stolen by people who are not White and male. However, given Jorgen's view of White and non-White people's relationship to the American Dream, how do we explain the presence of White kids among the Knudsen men's victims, whose pictures and other renderings are hanging on Jorgen's living room walls? Indeed, these victims imply that race was irrelevant in whom Jorgen decided to kidnap and feed to the troll, as Apollo notices that all the victims were under the age of one and formed "a roster as varied as the general assembly of the United Nations," which included boys and girls who were "black and brown, yellow, white, and red" (365). Moreover, Jorgen's explanation of how he spotted his victims seems to support the idea that race was not a determining factor in which babies he would steal: "In the eighties I drove everywhere in my white van. . . . But eventually I would find a candidate. A boy or girl without protection. A baby that no one was watching. The castoffs. They have a look to them. I learned to recognize it instantly" (366).

While Jorgen's description of his victims as "castoffs," as children without "protection," appears to be raceless, his view of the White man's birthright suggests that race was a determining factor in whom the Knudsen men decided to feed to the troll. Jorgen seems to believe that the White kids whom he and the Knudsen men kidnapped were not "real" White people, implying that "there is more to being white than having a white body" (Jenkins, *Paradox* 179n3). Pamela Perry has noted that the "class, gender, and sexual hierarchies within whiteness" have objectified and sanctioned poor White Americans, typically referred to as "white trash," for not performing "the proper class decorums of whiteness" (245). Regarding the Knudsen men's victims, the one trait that they all lacked was the protection of Whiteness. Without that protection, people cannot access the American Dream, nor can they be protected from the horrors that come with not having access to the Dream.[14] In other words, Jorgen's belief that the American Dream is a White man's dream and his method for determining which kids to kill not only rejects the premise of the second tenet but also the first one, "that everyone can participate equally and can always start over." According to Hochschild, the first tenet is the least believed precisely because racism, sexism, heterosexism, and class discrimination and exploitation, to name a few, limit who can start anew and achieve the American Dream (26). Thus, by defining Black success as the theft of White opportunity, Jorgen's demonization of "fairness" and "balance" as anti-White is an example of how White rage uses the fourth tenet to vilify racial diversity and Black success. It also

---

14. The protection of Whiteness for many Trump supporters, including non-White ones, is real, as indicated by the people who have used the novelty White Privilege Card: Trump's Everything after getting caught breaking the law. For example, a Filipina who traveled to Anchorage for a July 2022 Trump rally claimed that her "White Privilege Card" helped her avoid getting a ticket for swerving on the road. She even took a smiling selfie with an Anchorage Police Department officer while holding the novelty card (Thiessen).

provides, as LaValle's depiction of Kinder Garten points out, the moral justification for anti-Black violence.

Kinder Garten begins his service to the troll by killing his daughter, but he begins his monetization of his service by attempting to kill baby Brian. While both horrific events are about achieving the American Dream, they are also about limiting the Dream to White dreamers. For example, because Kinder Garten believed that the troll was a "blessing" and not a "burden," his murder of Agnes was, according to Jorgen, his attempt to return to the "old ways," to the days when the Knudsen men were "great" (370). As Kinder Garten sees it, once Nils failed to sacrifice one of Petra's children, he also limited the Knudsen men's access to the American Dream. To make the Knudsen men "great" again, when the Dream was their perceived birthright, Kinder Garten concludes that he and his father, with their "whole hearts," had to revive the tradition that gave them their Whiteness (370). Kinder Garten's return to the "old ways," like Trump's "Make America Great Again" campaign, calls for reviving past traditions of oppression, such as anti-Black and antiwoman oppression, to produce White male success in the present. Indeed, his attempts to destroy a middle-class Black family and profit from killing its Black child indicate that he believes, like the White Santa in Clarke's story, that it is an injustice that Black families can enjoy the American Dream while his White family is unable to do so. For Kinder Garten to hold such thoughts, he must believe, like Goode and Jorgen, that the American Dream is the birthright of White men and, therefore, Black success is the theft of that birthright. Thus, killing baby Brian, in the mind of Kinder Garten, is both just compensation for Black success and a form of White self-defense that seeks to stop the reproduction of Black success. In this instance, Kinder Garten represents the undead life of slavery in twenty-first-century America, since he believes that Black families in pain are crucial to White survival and success. As Spillers reminds us, Black kinship was always in danger in US slavery, since it could be *"invaded at any given and arbitrary moment by the property relations"* (218). Like the system of US slavery, Kinder Garten's attempt to monetize his work for the troll entails destroying Black kinship ties, since he is attempting to transform baby Brian from Black child into White property.

Fear, Pleasure, and the Monsters of White Rage

I have noted elsewhere that "the increase in the number of white supremacist groups since the beginning of President Obama's presidency, recent claims by white nationalist groups that diversity and multiculturalism are attempts at white genocide, and the election of Donald Trump as president indicate that a significant number of white Americans still believe that race is real and that America is a *white* nation" (*Paradox* 177). For example, on June 17, 2015, Dylann Roof, a monster of White rage, killed nine Black people who were worshipping in a Charleston, South Carolina, church. One of the main sources of Roof's rage, as Anderson reminds us, was the "hatred and lies" posted on the website of the Council of Conservative Citizens (CCC), the offspring of the 1950s White Citizens' Council that terrorized Black people and worked with state governments to defy federal civil rights laws (159). Roof cited web posts by Earl Holt III, a known White nationalist from St. Louis and president of the CCC at the time, to explain why he killed the Black church worshippers, who were "the very model of respectability"—he believed that Black people were "taking over" America, which he considered a White country (160).[15] Disturbingly, the month after Roof's anti-Black violence, Trump makes a "macabre promise" to an audience of thousands that invokes Roof's White rage: "Don't worry, we'll take our country back" (qtd. in C. Anderson 161). Less than a decade after Roof's anti-Black violence, Payton Gendron murdered ten Black people, wounded one more, and killed two White people at a Buffalo, New York, grocery store on May 14, 2022. According to a federal complaint, Gendron, a self-avowed White supremacist and anti-Semite, "wrote an apology note to his family and said he carried out the attack 'for the future of the White race'" (M. Burke par. 1). Moreover, as the complaint asserts, "Gendron's motive for the mass shooting was to prevent black people from replacing white people and eliminating the white race, and to inspire others to commit similar attacks" (par. 8). Gendron's horrific acts have been linked to Tucker Carlson, a former Fox News television host and Trump supporter who has promoted what has been called "replacement theory" in over 400 episodes of one of his shows (Ali par. 6).[16]

---

15. Since the mid-1990s, the CCC has, despite being an avowed White supremacist organization, "enjoyed precisely the cachet of respectability that racism requires to achieve its own goals within American society" (C. Anderson 160). For example, the Southern Poverty Law Center has noted that in 2001 the CCC website included statements such as "God is the author of racism," "God is the One who divided mankind into different types," and "Mixing the races is rebelliousness against God" ("Council"). Moreover, Holt stated in 2019 that the CCC's mission is "nothing less than the preservation of the white race, Western Civilization and even Christianity itself from the fools, trash, traitors and barbarians inside and outside the gates" (qtd. in Keith par. 4).

16. According to Nina Gonzalez, Replacement theory, also known as the "Great Replacement," is a far-right, White supremacist conspiracy theory that claims that non-White people, immigrants, and Jewish people are replacing the White race (ii). However, as Gonzalez argues, the theory does not originate with the rise of the internet age and White-supremacist online communities, as some have suggested; rather, it has a history in the US that dates to at least the late nineteenth century (9).

The fear that Black people are taking over America is a fear shared by the real and fictional monsters of White rage. For these monsters, who are human manifestations of the Black gains–White loss assumption, Black progress is a direct threat to White life in America; therefore, their production and consumption of Black people in pain is viewed as a matter of racial and national survival. Indeed, "if the American Dream has been and continues to be 'on the backs of blacks,' then it is also the case that audiences of black bodies in pain do not learn anything about the people experiencing the pain; rather, they learn, among other lessons, how [those bodies] can be exploited to achieve the American Dream" (Jenkins, *Paradox* 41). As highlighted in Du Bois's "Jesus Christ in Texas," Clarke's "Santa Claus Is a White Man," Due's *The Between*, and LaValle's *The Changeling*, the monsters of White rage imagine themselves as defenders of the American Dream, as those who protect American success from non-Americans and non-White Americans. By framing their anti-Black violence in that way, White rage's monsters can view their terrorization of Black life as morally righteous and Black socioeconomic success as immoral and anti-White. Such thinking allows these monsters to enjoy, free of guilt, their anti-Black violence, since they imagine themselves as ridding the nation of "evil doers," who are, in this context, Black people with ambition. The ideo-pleasure that these monsters receive from inflicting pain on Black people or watching them suffer is akin to that produced by the person-product interaction. Given that ideo-pleasure is partly about how the products we acquire represent how we wish to be perceived by others (Jordan 18), White rage's monsters produce and consume Black bodies in pain to be perceived as defenders of the nation, the American Dream, and the White race. As the horror stories by Du Bois, Clarke, Due, and LaValle point out, while the monsters of White rage are dangerous because they are able terrorize Black people with virtual impunity, what makes them repulsive and threats to common knowledge is not only their violent and ahistorical disavowal of America's Blackness but also their anti-Black sadism. That anti-Black sadism, as I attempt to demonstrate in chapter 2, is also rooted in the American tradition of harming, killing, or exploiting Black women to advance racialized conceptions of womanhood, a tradition embodied by what I call the respectability monster.

The Monsters of Respectability

The hypersexualization of Black women in the US has produced a history of decriminalizing sexual violence against Black women. According to E. Frances White, "White bourgeois nationalism has repeatedly portrayed African Americans as a threat to respectability. Specifically, white nationalists have described both black men and women as hypersexual" (122). For instance, historians have noted that slavery's White Southerners attempted to justify their sexual abuse of Black women by claiming that "black women were naturally promiscuous and seduced white men" or that "the sexual exploitation of black women by white men reduced prostitution and promoted purity among white women" (Hine et al. 153). Moreover, laws were enacted as an attempt to ensure that the myth of the hypersexual Black woman was true and that Black women had no legal recourse against their rapists. As Saidiya Hartman puts it, given that "the enslaved is legally unable to give consent or offer resistance, she is presumed to be always willing" (81). Moreover, the status of free Black women in postbellum America did not drastically differ from their enslaved foremothers, as Ida B. Wells highlighted in 1892: "The miscegenation laws of the South only operate against the legitimate union of the races; they leave the white man free to seduce all the colored girls he can" (*Southern Horrors* 53). Indeed, those laws not only banned consensual unions between Black men and White women but also legalized sexual abuse of Black women. In 1913, for example, Governor Coleman Blease of South Carolina justified his decision to pardon Black and White men who raped Black women because he always held "very serious doubts as to whether the crime of rape can be committed upon a negro" (qtd. in Hine et al. 353). In addition to implying that Black women are not *real* women, Blease's anti-Blackness is also disturbing because it criminalizes Black women who fight against being raped, since he believes that they are always willing. In fact, as Daina Ramey Berry and Kali Nicole Gross note, "a number of Black female lynching victims met their end resisting white rapists" (107).

In response to White America's hypersexualization of Black women, elite Black women in the late nineteenth and early twentieth centuries developed what has been referred to as Black respectability politics. According to Susana M. Morris, respectability politics, first theorized by Evelyn Brooks Higginbotham, "is a strategy for navigating a hostile society that characterizes Blackness as the definition of deviance—animalistic, hypersexual, ignorant, uncivilized; it makes bettering one's life chances depend on adhering to a set of mainstream ideals regarding behavior, and it takes place where the public sphere meets the private" (5). The link between bettering one's life chances and adhering to racialized notions of respectable behavior creates what Morris calls a "paradox of respectability," which means "simultaneously desiring to be respectable according to the ideals of respectability politics and finding this difficult, if not impossible" (3). Because of this paradox, Brittney C. Cooper discusses the politics of respectability in conjunction with "the culture of dissemblance," as theorized by Darlene Clark Hine and colleagues, to highlight that both strategies were concerned with "minimiz[ing] the threat of sexual assault and other forms of bodily harm routinely inflicted upon Black women" and, therefore, "attempted to make Black women's bodies as inconspicuous and as sexually innocuous as possible." However, as Cooper points out, the Black women who deployed dissemblance and respectability strategies were "acutely aware of the limitations of making themselves invisible in a world predicated on the surveillance of Black bodies" (3). That awareness alludes to what E. Frances White refers to as the "double-edged" nature of respectability politics. While it is an ideological tactic developed by Black Americans to "create unity," the politics of respectability often does not consider that "African Americans are structured in dominance by class, gender, sexuality, and more," which, thus, hinders its goal to produce an effective and sustainable Black unity (14–15).

The myth of the hypersexual Black woman and the respectability response to it are shaped by an overall discourse of Black female immorality. For example, by the early nineteenth century, according to Sabrina Strings, "fatness became stigmatized [in the US] as both black and sinful. And by the early twentieth century, slenderness was increasingly promoted in the popular media as the correct embodiment for white Anglo-Saxon Protestant women" (6). Since Black women's bodies represented fatness and sin in the White American psyche, it is not surprising that Black women's sexualities have historically been tied to crime. For instance, in her discussion of the "U.S. punishment industry" at the end of the twentieth century, Angela Davis reveals the ways in which Black women are hypersexualized and criminalized to support that industry:

> Th[e] female criminalization process has more to do with the marking of certain groups of women as undomesticated and hypersexual, as women who refuse to embrace the nuclear family as paradigm. The current liberal-conservative discourse around welfare criminalizes black single mothers, who are represented as deficient, manless, drug-using breeders of children, and as reproducers of an attendant culture of poverty. (275)

While the discourse of Black female immorality within America's punishment industry focuses on the hypersexualization and subsequent criminalization of working-class Black women, we should not assume that that discourse did not and does not affect their middle- and upper-class counterparts.

Patricia Hill Collins argues that at the dawn of the twenty-first century "the mass media has generated class-specific images of Black women that help justify and shape the new racism of desegregated, colorblind America" (147). In contrast to the "bitch" and "Bad Black Mothers," mass media's generated images of poor and working-class Black women, "Black ladies, modern mammies, and educated Black bitches" are mass media's representations of Black women who are not that different from their middle- and upper-class White counterparts and are, therefore, "ready for racial integration" (122–23). While the images of the b— and the Bad Black Mother became the "texts of what *not* to be" for middle- and upper-class Black women (138–39), the images of Black ladies, modern mammies, and educated Black b—s are no less damaging because they help justify workplace discrimination against middle- and upper-class Black women by depicting them as either lacking "loyalty," "not ladylike enough," or so "cutthroat and ruthless that they cannot be trusted." Moreover, as Collins continues, these images are also invoked to explain why many straight Black women are romantically alone—"they allegedly work too hard, do not know how to support black men, and/or have character traits that make them unappealing to middle-class Black men" (146).

In this chapter, I examine the ways in which the human monsters in Alice Walker's "The Child Who Favored Daughter" (1973), Octavia Butler's *Kindred* (1979), and Nnedi Okorafor's *Who Fears Death* (2018) interrogate the myth of Black female immorality. I argue that the human monsters that populate the horror fiction by Walker, Butler, and Okorafor are respectability monsters, humans who use the myth of Black female immorality to justify harming and terrorizing Black women and girls. Like the monsters of White rage, the monsters of respectability are frightening because their violence against Black women and girls is done without fear of punishment. Unlike White rage's monsters, the monsters of respectability are repulsive and threats to common knowledge because their violence against Black women is born out of their desire for Black women. In other words, the monsters of respectability are dangerous and repulsive because they believe that desiring a Black woman and the desires of Black women are inherently immoral. Such thinking is horrifying, according to the texts by Walker, Butler, and Okorafor, because it implies that violence against Black women and girls is socially and morally necessary to maintaining or even challenging current racial hegemonies.

Black Progress and the Respectability Monster

Set in the South during the Jim Crow era and published during horror literature's paperback wave, Walker's "The Child Who Favored Daughter" tells the horrific story of "a black man's incestuous feelings toward his sister and later toward the daughter who resembles his sister" (T. Harris 497). The story begins after the unnamed father reads a letter detailing his daughter's love for and sex with a White man. The father decides to sit on the porch of their house, with an empty shotgun nearby, to confront his daughter about the veracity of the letter. As the father sees it, "if he cannot frighten her into chastity with his voice he will threaten her with the gun" (Walker 37). Before he confronts his daughter, the father reminiscences about his late sister, who was called Daughter, his incestuous love for her, and how her love for a White man broke his heart. Those feelings shape how the father engaged his relationship with his late wife and how he deals with his own daughter, who refuses to deny the contents of the letter. Disturbingly, the father's memories about Daughter and his un-Christian or too-Christian desires will lead him to cut off the breasts of his daughter. According to Wester, Walker's story is a "post-Civil Rights African American Gothic text" in which "stable identity" is articulated as an "imprisoning locale of terror and torment" (155). Indeed, the respectability monster in "The Child Who Favored Daughter" is a Black man who embraces a transhistorical understanding of Blackness at the detriment of Black women, indicating that the monsters of White rage are not the only ones who impede Black progress. I argue that the father is a Black respectability monster who embodies the horrors of using race realism and Christian doctrine to define Black progress. Such an understanding of Black progress, according to Walker's story, is rooted in the myth of Black female hypersexuality, a myth used to justify the social and physical deaths of Black women.

In *Slavery and Social Death* (1982), Orlando Patterson demonstrates that in virtually all slaveholding societies, the slave was defined as a "socially dead person" because this person did not have a social existence outside of the master (38). According to Patterson, there are two ways in which the social death of the slave is represented: "intrusive" and "extrusive." The intrusive approach to representing social death depicted the slave as "someone who did not belong because he was an outsider," whereas the extrusive approach represented the slave as "an outsider because he did not (or no longer) belonged" (44). The link between Black women's social death and racial belonging in "The Child Who Favored Daughter" takes place in the home, which is identified as one of the social spaces where Black respectability monsters are made. Indeed, if we read Walker's story as a "kind of inverted slave narrative," as Neal Lester does, we find that the story is "an account of black female enslavement by black men who position themselves as 'masters'" (290). One of the horrifying outcomes of this paradoxical understanding of home, a place of safety and danger, is the production and consumption of Black women in pain, such as the father's sister, wife, and daughter who are "mutilated, tortured, and destroyed" (Wester 163–64). For example, the father not only beats his wife into "a cripple to prevent her from returning the imaginary overtures of the white landlord" (Walker 40) but also brutalizes his daughter for falling in love with a married White man by cutting "two bleeding craters the size of grapefruits on her bare bronze chest and fling[ing] what he finds in his hands to the yelping dogs" (45).

According to Margaret Bauer, since Daughter killed herself before he could punish her for her so-called transgression, "he brutally takes revenge on the other women in his life" (145). Indeed, the father's hatred of Black women who love White men or willingly sleep with them was born out of his intense desire for his sister and his intense hatred for her after discovering that "she had chosen to give her love to the very man in whose cruel, hot, and lonely fields he, her brother, worked" (Walker 38). Thus, when Daughter impales herself on a fence post near the family home to escape her family's dehumanizing "ostracism," the father believes that Daughter's fate was deserved even though he insists that his sister's White lover had "shamed them all" (39). Implicit in the father's reaction to Daughter's fate is that incestuous love and sex is less shameful and better for Black progress than interracial love and sex. In the father's mind, Daughter and his daughter are race traitors because they stepped out of their "expected roles" as Southern Black women by choosing to fall in love with White men (see Bauer 146). According to the father's politics of respectability, these roles require Black women to suppress their desires in the name of Black progress, a discourse that was hotly contested during the Black Power movement, when Walker's story was published. In other words, Walker's story represents a critique of the notion that Black progress is Black male progress, what Jewelle Gomez refers to as the "single-issue" view of Black freedom—the idea that the only -ism that negatively affects the Black community is racism and that straight Black men are racism's primary victims ("Speculative" 951). According to the story, the ideological tradition of equating Blackness with manhood is one of the reasons why some Black men become respectability monsters, since that tradition insists that Black progress also requires Black women's social death. Indeed, if the father and his father are the "masters" of their homes, then Daughter and the father's wife and daughter were born socially dead. This means that Daughter and the father's daughter were punished for not only having sex with White men but also for acting as if they were socially alive, for acting like they had a social existence outside the wills of their fathers.

What stands out in the father's respectability politics is that Daughter, his daughter, and his wife, not the White men whom they willingly or imaginarily loved, are the ones accused of stepping out of their expected roles. This suggests, on the one hand, that the father's decision to not confront the real or imagined White men who are shaming the family and the race is due to the lack of power that Black people have in defending themselves and their families against anti-Black Whites during Jim Crow, given that "the white 'boys' the daughters date are imagined as authorities over the father in racist articulation" (Wester 165). On the other hand, the father's respectability politics reveals his unspoken desire to have the privileges of White heteropatriarchy extended to him. Indeed, one of the reasons why the Black home is problematic for the women in the father's family is that it seeks to emulate the "mythically revered" nuclear family and its patriarchal structure. That family, as I discussed in chapter 1, is partly shaped by a consumption-based conception of the American Dream in which a successful family is defined as one who owns the commodities that have been deemed symbols of success, which include wives and children. Thus, if the father and his father are the "masters" of their families, then wife, sister, and daughter are "theirs," which means that they can hurt or discard Black women in the same ways as the White slaveowner did in antebellum America. As Wester argues, while the father and his father "horrifically understand their place in the field as beasts," they also "violently reproduce white assaults upon the bodies of their daughters," rendering these women as "less-than-beasts at home" (169).

Walker demonstrates in "The Child Who Favored Daughter" that one of the main problems with respectability ideology, as Morris argues in her analysis of the ways in which Louis Farrakhan's Black nationalism is critiqued in Sapphire's *Push* (1996), is that the horrors engendered by respectability ideology are blamed solely on the "destructiveness of white supremacy." By marginalizing the effects of anti-Black sexism against Black women and making White people the "proverbial bogeymen," respectability ideology "fails to underscore that whites are not the only ones who mobilize domination and hegemony," a failure that highlights the "limited usefulness of respectability politics in truly improving circumstances for African Americans in wide-reaching ways" (117). Indeed, the story suggests that the failure to acknowledge that Black men can become just as dangerous and repulsive as the proverbial White bogeyman reinforces the insidious idea that the race of the person producing and consuming Black women in pain determines whether such anti-Black female violence is justified or can be overlooked. In this light, the problem with race realism, as expressed by Walker's story, is that it impedes Black progress, since those who believe that race is real also believe that Black progress requires the social deaths of Black women who embrace Black nationalist thinking and the physical deaths of Black women who do not.

While "The Child Who Favored Daughter" examines the problems that emerge when Black progress is tied to the oppression of Black women, it also identifies Christianity as providing the rationale for validating the respectability monster's violence against Black women. For instance, the Bible scriptures that call for, as Lester puts it, "a quiet submission of Christian women to men whether Christian or not" (e.g., Ephesians 5: 22–24; 1 Peter: 1–2, 5–6; 1 Timothy 2: 11–12; and 1 Corinthians 14: 34–35) are treated in "The Child Who Favored Daughter" as attempts to transform women into obedient slaves (291–92n3). Indeed, due to Christianity, which functions as the ideological foundation of the father's monstrous respectability and, therefore, Black women's pain, is one of the reasons why the Black home in Walker's story is a paradoxical space of horror and safety. For example, the story begins with a reference to the Christian family structure, a structure that is shaped by the belief that the Christian god has made men, not women, in its image: "*Father, judge, giver of life*" (35). In this version of the "God-as-human" concept, God is the god of men with women functioning as "props" to teach men how to live a godly life (see chapter 1). Indeed, in addition to the biblical passages mentioned earlier, 1 Corinthians states that "a man ought not to have his head covered, since he is the image and glory of God; but the woman is the glory of man" (11:7). Thus, when the daughter, like Daughter, decides to claim her body and desires as her own by having sex and falling in love with, as the father calls him, the "white devil who has disowned her to marry one of his kind" (Walker 42), the father believes he has the divine right to scar her body and even kill her, since she has dishonored the "glory of man" who is the "image and glory of God." Given this context, when the father calls his daughter a "White man's slut" (41), he is implying not only that the myth of Black female immorality is real but also that the Christian god does not support interracial relationships or daughters resisting familial enslavement. While such thinking excuses the father's desires for his daughter, allowing him to destroy "the source of the temptation" rather than his "temptation to sin" (T. Harris 502–3), it also reveals that the ideological parents of the respectability monster are anti-Black racism and Christianity.

Given the father's ideological parents, his monstrosity is not the product of insanity, which would imply that the father is not truly responsible for his actions. According to Trudier Harris, attributing the father's desires and violence to insanity would be the "simple interpretation" of the father, an interpretation that avoids discussing incest, which is the "real theme of the story" (504). As Harris explains, because the father knows that he desired and desires Daughter and his daughter, he becomes "moody" and "fanatically obsessed with the actions of his wife," evidence that "the insanity possibility seems more tenuous than the incest." Moreover, as Harris continues, "even if we add racism to his problem—the specific fact that he is acutely oppressed by the idea that his sister would run away with the man who has treated him like a beast—the origins of his problems in incest are no less diminished" (504). Considering Harris's critique of reading the father as one suffering from mental illness, Walker's depiction of the father as a respectability monster can be read as her attempt to force the reader to think about the ideologies that justify the father's violence toward the women in his family. According to the story, in addition to anti-Black racism, the "hard Southern rudeness" of Christianity, which agonizes over women's "selfishness" or freedom (Walker 43), is the theology of the father's monstrosity.

Through its depiction of the father's faith, "The Child Who Favored Daughter" functions as a warning about the dangers of Christianity for Black women, since it promotes what I call the salvation-through-oppression discourse. Candace Gorham's explanation of why some Black Americans believe that slavery was good for Black people captures the essence of that discourse: "Some black people have gone so far as to profess their gratitude for slavery because it introduced their ancestors to Jesus and paved the way for their salvation. Without slavery, the thinking goes, they would have been born into a pagan tribe and doomed to spend all eternity in hell" (27). As implied by Gorham, one of the many problems with the salvation-through-oppression discourse is that it requires one to view Christian salvation as the *most* important achievement in a Black person's life. To make such a claim, one must believe that being Christian has benefited Black America. However, "The Child Who Favored Daughter" asks us to consider the veracity of that claim. For example, Christian doctrine in Walker's story demands that the Black family become an institution of Black male ownership to receive God's blessings while simultaneously implying that a Black family defined by ally-ship, such as that of Apollo and Emma's in LaValle's *The Changeling*,[1] is detrimental to Black progress. Besides his ability to harm Black women with virtual impunity, what makes the father repulsive as a respectability monster is his justification of the violence he inflicts on the women in his family—he believes that they are "his," but he could never be "theirs." Indeed, the father's Christian-based conception of the family insists that wives and daughters are born socially dead; therefore, their safety is determined by their ability to follow their "master's" rules. In such a conception of the family, Black women are only guaranteed justice in the afterlife, not in the every-day world, which helps to explain the wife's and Daughter's suicides. For these women, Christianity is not only ineffective and oppressive but also the religion of the respectability monster precisely because it provides divine support for that monster's violence against Black women by claiming that men, not women, are created in the image and glory of the Christian god.[2]

While Walker's story examines how Christianity and anti-Black racism produced Black respectability monsters during the Jim Crow era, which was "neoslavery, pure and simple" (Patterson xix), Octavia Butler's *Kindred* is

---

1. I noted in chapter 1 that Apollo is a husband-father of a Black heteronuclear family who believes that he belongs to his wife and kids, that he is "theirs." Such thinking, as I argued, is not thought of in terms of ownership (i.e., as someone's property or commodity) but in terms of allyship, terms that are aligned with partner, supporter, reciprocity, mutuality, and mutual benefit.

2. I have noted elsewhere that "in a patriarchal society grounded in Abrahamic theology (e.g., Judaism, Christianity, and Islam), it is believed that men are closer to God than women because God is assumed to be a man"; therefore, "it is assumed that men can be good without being religious, while the only way for women to be good is to be religious" ("Is Religiosity" 9–10). Such thinking helps to explain the sense of righteousness that the father feels as he mutilates his daughter and reminisces about his sister's death.

a neo-slave horror narrative that interrogates slavery's White respectability monsters and the social death of enslaved Black women. Butler's novel examines the horrors that occurred because of the White slaveholder's simultaneous hatred of and desire for Black women. Indeed, unlike Walker's respectability monster, whose production and consumption of Black women in pain relies on hierarchical conceptions of Black progress, the respectability monsters in *Kindred* are legally allowed to hurt Black women because such violence is crucial to sustaining slavery. Yet, like all respectability monsters, the oppression of Black women and girls is viewed as a racially virtuous act.

Anti-Black Necrophilia and the Respectability Monsters of Slavery

Although the term "neo-slave narratives" was coined in 1987 by Bernard Bell, who famously described them as "residually oral, modern narratives of escape from bondage to freedom," Ashraf Rushdy dates the origin of the genre to Margaret Walker's *Jubilee* (1966). Citing the works of Bell, Rushdy, James Olney, and Guy Mark Foster, Alison Francis suggests that we can think of "neo-slave narratives" as modern tales about bondage and liberation that involve the interplay of past and present while assuming and adopting the slave narrative's form, conventions, and first-person voice (15–16). This understanding of the neo-slave narrative, I believe, accounts for Sherryl Vint's concern about scholars neglecting "the importance of the fantastic" in works like Butler's *Kindred* and Toni Morrison's *Beloved* (241). As Joan Anim-Addo and Maria Helena Lima assert in "The Power of the Neo-Slave Narrative Genre" (2017), the "main reasons" for the rise of the neo-slave narrative, which involves rewriting a genre that "officially lost its usefulness" with the end of racialized slavery, "are the will to re-affirm the historical value of the original slave narrative and to reclaim the humanity of the enslaved by (re)imagining their subjectivity" (3).[3] The "(re)imag-

3. In addition to the neo-slave texts produced by Black British writers (see Anim-Addo and Lima 4), the neo-slave narrative has attracted authors who are neither Black nor American. For example, Oluyomi Oduwobi argues that Manu Herbstein's *Ama, a Story of the Atlantic Slave Trade* (2000) is a postcolonial neo-slave narrative that "highlights how the trans-Atlantic slave trade damaged the humanity of the slave masters (victimisers) as it damaged the humanity of the slaves (victims)" (103–4). Although Herbstein is a White South African of Jewish European descent, Oduwobi contends that *Ama* represents Herbstein's attempt to "conjure up the spirits of the enslaved Africans who perished during the trans-Atlantic slave trade" by creating Ama as "a fictional character whose life is sketched as a result of questions interrogating how she would have reacted to the real circumstances of slavery" (102).

ining" that takes place in neo-slave narratives involves the fantastic, since these texts "rely on speculative memories despite the narrative truths used to render them" (Francis 15). The narrative truths that the neo-slave narrative's "speculative memories" rely on tell "a vexed history of trauma and violence" (Anim-Addo and Lima 5), a history that demonstrates that, as Wester argues in her examination of Victor Séjour's use of the gothic in "The Mulatto" (1837), "the entire system of slavery and its oppressions of the black body are predicated upon the subjugation of the black woman's body" (74). Wester's reading of Séjour's story is a starting point for understanding the horrors embodied by the respectability monsters in *Kindred*, given that Butler's Black female protagonist is, as Lisa Long puts it, "penetrated by the past" and, therefore, endures "the rape of history" (464).

Told in the first person and set in 1976 California and early nineteenth-century Maryland, *Kindred* is a story about the terrifying experiences of a young Black woman who becomes an involuntary time traveler. Our time traveler's name is Dana, a shortened version of Edana, and she has just moved into a home in a Los Angeles suburb with her husband Kevin, a White man who, like her, writes fiction. Dana's time travels, which begin the month before America's bicentennial celebration, take her to the past of her enslaved and slave-owning ancestors. As Long puts it in her discussion of *Kindred* and Phyllis Alesia Perry's *Stigmata* (1998), the goal of these texts "is not so much to set the record straight, as historical fiction such as Margaret Walker's *Jubilee* does, nor even to 'raise the dead,' as Morrison's *Beloved* does so compellingly, but to become the dead, to embody and enact the protagonists' families' personal histories and our national past" (460). According to Christine Montgomery and Ellen C. Caldwell, the "socially dead" are privileged in *Kindred*, "as Dana is literally transported back to her ancestors" (152). Indeed, Dana's survival depends on whether she will save the life of Rufus Weylin, her slave-owning ancestor whose raping of Alice Greenwood, her enslaved foremother, will lead to the birth of a child who will allow Dana to exist in 1976. Since Rufus's near-death experiences bring Dana to Maryland and her near-death experiences bring her back to California, Dana appears to be given a choice by the supernatural force(s) responsible for her time travel: die by killing Rufus before he rapes Alice or live by saving Rufus's life until he rapes Alice. Thus, as Gregory Hampton notes, Dana does not really have a choice: "It is this utter dependency on the actions of her ancestors that eliminates Dana's options from doing anything but ensuring the birth of Hagar by any means necessary" (8). This lack of power is what makes *Kindred* a horrifying novel—the Black people in the novel, especially the Black women, are unable to harm or kill the monsters who enjoy producing, consuming, and profiting from their pain.

The circumstances that put Dana in a situation in which she must ensure the life of a monster who will repeatedly hurt her foremother is one of the reasons why *Kindred* is a neo-slave horror novel, a tale in which the conventions of the horror story—for example, the "appearance of the evil supernatural or of the monstrous" and "the intentional elicitation of dread, visceral disgust, fear, or startlement in the spectator or reader" (Nickel 15)— account for most or all of the "fantastic" or "(re)imagining" that occurs in neo-slave narratives. As Heather Duerre Humann argues, while Butler is thought of as a science fiction writer, and rightly so, "she ultimately both builds upon and subverts the genre by borrowing from other literary traditions as part of her storytelling" (91). With respect to *Kindred*, Humann contends that Butler's "blending" or "hybridization" of the neo-slave narrative and science fiction's time travel narrative "opens up narrative and symbolic possibilities each genre alone does not" (95–96). Citing Christina Sharpe, Christopher Lewis points out that Butler's *Kindred*, along with Morrison's *Beloved* and Gomez's *The Gilda Stories*, critiques dominant historical narratives of slavery by engaging "the antebellum system of enslavement and its legacies as horror in order to emphasize slavery's 'mundane horrors that aren't acknowledged to be horrors'" with the intent to show "how white slaveholding society's unwillingness to see enslaved black people as human beings and fellow citizens positioned them as social monsters" (447). In this light, *Kindred* is an example of what Kinitra Brooks refers to as "fluid fiction," defined as "a racially gendered framework that revises genre fiction in that it purposefully obfuscates the boundaries of science fiction/ fantasy/horror writing" (71–72). In my examination of *Kindred* as a horror novel, I will expand upon Lewis's claim about the social monsters of *Kindred* by directing my attention to how the novel distinguishes unlikable humans from human monsters.

Though the monsters of respectability that populate Butler's novel are White men, being White and male is not the reason why they are threatening and repulsive. The monstrosity of these White men, I argue, derives from their anti-Black necrophilia, their erotic interest in or sexual intercourse with socially dead Black people. The enslaved Black woman is the ideal woman for the anti-Black necrophiliacs in Butler's novel partly because her social death, which is intrusive in nature, means she lacks respectability. Indeed, because the slave owners in the novel view their wives and themselves as respectable, they cannot rape their wives as they do their slaves because respectability implies social aliveness and, therefore, legal protection. As Hartman notes, while "the sexual exploitation of slave women [was] cloaked as the legitimate use of property" in antebellum law, that law also defined slave women as persons, making them both "will-less and always willing" (80–81). Thus, the law legalized anti-Black misogyny, which can be read as an example of what Moya Bailey calls "misogynoir" (6), since its caricatured and mendacious representation of the enslaved Black woman as a will-less and always willing property-person sanctions and encourages violence against Black women. In addition to embodying the horrors of legalized anti-Black violence, the respectability monsters in *Kindred* are repulsive because they believe that their sexual violence against Black women is economically and socially justified. The economic justification, which is based on the myth of the slave woman's will-less-ness, views raping Black women as an attempt to increase the slave owner's capital through the reproduction of free labor, whereas the social justification, which derives from the slave woman's mythical always willingness, claims that raping Black women is sometimes an expression of the slaveowner's love since a White man publicly loving a Black woman is one way to lose his respectability among White folks. As the following pages will show, the anti-Black necrophilia in *Kindred* is an example of what Achille Mbembe refers to as "necropolitics," which are "forms of subjugating life to the power of death" that produce "*death-worlds*," such as the plantation and the colony, where "vast populations [e.g., Black women] are subjected to living conditions that confer upon them the status of the *living dead*" (92).

Rufus tells Dana during her fourth trip to antebellum Maryland that his father, Tom Weylin, is "not likable," but he is a "fair man" (Butler 134). According to Rufus, what makes Tom a fair man is that he "cares as much about giving his word to a black as to a white" (181). Indeed, Tom has made the same promise to the young Rufus and to his slaves about what will happen if they challenge his authority on the plantation—he will beat them. For example, Tom used a whip, like the one he uses on his slaves and horses, to beat Rufus to the point of death for stealing a dollar (25–26), and he forced his slaves, including Dana, to watch him whip a naked field hand for "answering back" (91–92). Like the young Rufus and the Black field hand, Dana is also savagely whipped by Tom for "reading," especially in front of Black people, since he was treating her "good" by letting her read to Rufus (106–7). Although Tom beats Rufus for the same reasons that he beats Dana and his slaves, his beating of Rufus functions as a teaching moment about being a White male slaveowner—do not allow your wife, kids, or slaves to challenge your authority—while his beating of Black folks was done to enforce Black submission, given that anti-Black violence in nineteenth-century court rulings was "sanctioned if not deemed essential to proper relations of free white persons and black captives and the maintenance of black submission" (Hartman 83). Thus, the promises made by Tom to White people, including Rufus, are qualitatively different from those made to Black people precisely because Tom's promises to Black people are promises of pain, physical or otherwise, if they act like they are White and, therefore, not his property. For instance, Rufus tells Dana that the reason why his father sold Luke—the adoptive father of Nigel, Tom's enslaved son who resembles Tom more than Rufus—was not due to him being inept or unable to do the work; rather, it was because Tom "got tired" of Luke acting and thinking that he is "white," so Tom thought "it would be better to sale Luke than to whip him until he ran away" (Butler 138). In short, Tom uses all forms of pain, such as whippings and selling slaves away from friends and family, to remind them that they are nothing more than "his" commodities.

Because slaves are commodities, Tom treats slave reproduction as the reproduction of wealth. According to Katherine McKittrick, owning Black women during slavery was "a spatialized, gendered, often public, violence: the black female body was viewed as naturally submissive, sexually available, public, reproductive technology" (44). Indeed, like "Bloodchild" (1984), Butler's award-winning short story that considers "forms of oppression that exist in the social valuing of reproduction outside the context of slavery," *Kindred* depicts the horrors that Black women suffered due to slaveowners using "reproduction as a bargaining chip in social relations" (see Jenkins and Sciurba 131–32). For example, Alice's mother told Dana that Tom demanded her husband, one of Tom's slaves who refused to get a pass to see his wife, to "choose a new wife there on the plantation. That way, Mister Tom'll own all his children" (Butler 40). In another instance, Sarah—the attractive, light-skinned, middle-aged cook for the Weylin plantation—had three of her children sold away by Tom because Miss Margaret, his second wife and Rufus's mother, "wanted new furniture, new china dishes, fancy things" that "she didn't even need" (95). Tom also views his enslaved children and grandchildren as property rather than descendants, as indicated by Nigel's comments to Dana after Tom gives him new clothes for having a baby with Chloe, the mute child of Sarah: "'Cause of Carrie and me, he's one n—— richer" (161). In fact, unlike other slaveowners who beat their pregnant slaves until the baby dropped to the ground, Dana believes that Weylin might not do such a thing because his "business sense" would view such violence as "dead mother, dead baby—dead loss" (191). Dana is reminded of Tom's business sense as she recalls the slave woman who lost three of her fingers because her former master "caught her writing," an act that should have made Tom suspicious of buying her, since he beat Dana for reading.

However, as Dana notes, this woman "had a baby nearly every year. . . . Nine so far, seven surviving. Weylin called her a good breeder, and he never whipped her. He was selling off her children, though, one by one" (191–92).

As Tom sees it, the familial bonds of slaves, whether among slaves or between slaves and masters, never outweigh their economic value in his decision to beat, rape, sell, or reward them. Thus, "good" business sense for Tom and his slave-owning peers necessitates treating slave women's reproduction as an economic tool to increase their master's capital and, at the same time, to reinforce their will-less-ness by forcing them to give life to the system that produces their social death. Because she is will-less property, the enslaved Black woman does not, should not, and cannot be treated as respectable, since granting her respectability would mean that she is socially alive; therefore, raping her would be a crime given that nineteenth-century common law, as Hartman reminds us, defined rape as "the forcible carnal knowledge of a female against her will and without her consent" (79). The enslaved woman's lack of respectability not only allows Tom to rape the Black women on his plantation with impunity and a guilt-free conscience, but it also conceals his anti-Black necrophilia by defining such desire in economic terms. While Tom does not find any woman who is more educated than him as attractive, which explains his decision to marry Miss Margaret, whom Sarah calls "white-trash Margaret" and Dana describes as "a poor, uneducated, nervous, startlingly pretty young woman" (Butler 94–95), he seems to prefer raping socially dead Black women over sexual intercourse with his White wives. As Kari Winter notes in her discussion of the "angel-whore dichotomy" in the slave household, where White women were idealized as "the angel in the house" and Black women were "demonized as subhuman chattel and whores," the angels were "expected to be asexual and to be content while their husbands vented their 'animal lusts' on black women" (57). The horror embodied by Tom's anti-Black necrophilia can be described as what McKittrick refers to as the "territorialization" of the Black female body, a body that becomes "publicly and financially claimed, owned, and controlled by an outsider." What makes territorialization horrifying is that it turns "ideas that justify bondage into corporeal evidence of racial difference" in which the Black female body is "marked as decipherable and knowable—as subordinate, inhuman, rape-able, deviant, procreative, placeless" (44–45). Thus, implicit in Tom's anti-Black necrophilia is that the ideo- and physio-pleasures he receives from territorializing his Black female slaves, pleasures he is unable to receive from the angel of his house or from free Black women, is due to his conception of enslaved Black female bodies as "seeable sites of wealth, sexuality, and punishment" (McKittrick 44).

Despite the pain and suffering that Tom has inflicted on Dana and enslaved Black folks, she believes that he is just extremely unlikable, that he has not crossed the line that separates the unlikable human from the human monster: "[Tom] wasn't the monster he could have been with the power he held over his slaves. He wasn't a monster at all. Just an ordinary man who sometimes did the monstrous things his society said were legal and proper" (Butler 134). For Dana, law and custom are responsible for Tom's treatment of Black people, implying that the horrific things that Tom has done are inhumanely human. Although Kevin, who accompanies Dana on her third trip to Maryland and poses as her owner from New York, could not find any "humanity" in Tom because he was not disgusted by anything that Kevin said he would do to her, Dana tells him that Tom is "human enough" (80–81). According to Dana, what makes Tom "human" is his inhumanity, since he thinks of slaves in the same ways as slave owners have done throughout history. As Patterson notes, "The slave was the ultimate human tool, as imprintable and as disposable as the master wished. And this is true, at least in theory, of all slaves, no matter how elevated. Paul Rycaut's description of the Janissaries as men whom their master, the sultan, 'can raise without Envy and destroy without Danger' holds true for all slaves in all times" (7–8). Considering Patterson's argument, Dana's view of Tom as an ordinary person following the laws and customs of his day suggests that he is not a monster because he has not done all the things that he could do as a slave owner in antebellum Maryland.

Although Dana argues that Tom is just an unlikable human, her fear that Rufus could turn out to be like his father suggests otherwise. Indeed, a few sentences after she contends that Tom is "human enough," Dana tells Kevin that their goal while in Maryland is to "keep [Rufus] from growing up into a red-haired version of his father" (81). After stating that Tom is an "ordinary man who sometimes did the monstrous things," Dana discovers, in "disbelief," that Tom lets Black people die if they become sick or injured because, as Rufus puts it, "Daddy won't pay for a doctor to fix n——" (147). Moreover, when Kevin asks Dana what Rufus, who has become master of the Weylin plantation after Tom's death, did to make her cut her wrists so she could return to California, she tells him that Rufus did nothing to her (i.e., he did not rape her) or anything "important": "He sold a man away from his family when there was no need for him to. He hit me when I objected. Maybe he'll never be as hard as his father was, but he's a man of his time" (242). In each of these instances, Dana emphasizes that Tom is more monstrous than Rufus; thus, how should we read her contradictory assessment of Tom's monstrosity? One way to read her assessment is to see it as exposing the main problem with the law and custom argument about the slaveowners' inhumanity—it excuses the slaveowners' acts of depravity against Black people by claiming that they were being inhumanely human or living in an era when their depravity was encouraged by custom and protected by law. As Dana acknowledges in her use of New York as her state of origin and her reference to Harriet Tubman, the law and custom argument ignores the fact that free states and a vibrant abolitionist movement existed in early nineteenth-century America, indicating that all White people did not believe that slavery should be law and that slaveowners had a choice in how they treated their slaves or in divesting from slavery altogether. Thus, Dana's contradictory assessment of Tom's monstrosity suggests that Tom, as well as Rufus, can be both: a human monster and a product of what society considers "legal and proper."

While the violence from Tom's anti-Black necrophilia is economically justified by law and custom, Rufus believes that raping Alice is justified because it is done out of his "love" for her. The first time Rufus rapes Alice, she is a free woman and married to Isaac, a field slave, who is beating Rufus close to death for harming Alice, which transports Dana to Maryland. Although Rufus and Alice were childhood friends, Rufus believes that she should be his concubine now that they are adults simply because he desires her to be so. Disturbingly, Rufus cannot understand why Alice would choose to marry a slave rather than be his sex slave: "I would have taken better care of her than any field hand could. I wouldn't have hurt her if she hadn't just kept saying no." When Dana tells him that Alice has the right to say no and to choose her husband, Rufus declares that Alice's "rights" as a free woman do not outweigh his desire for her; therefore, her future enslavement is her "own fault" because "she'd rather have a buck n—— than me!" (123). According to Rufus, since he "begged" Alice to be with him and she rejected his plea, she deserves the physical and emotional pain that will come to her when she and Isaac are caught, and he deserves to be "rewarded" for his rape of Alice since he lives in a society in which there was, as Dana puts it, "no shame in raping a black woman, but there could be shame in loving one" (124).

Rufus's explanation for his acts of depravity against Alice is based on what Hartman refers to as the "discourse of seduction" in which "seduction denotes a theory of power that demands the absolute and 'perfect' submission of the enslaved as the guiding principle of slave relations and yet seeks to mitigate the avowedly necessary brutality of slave relations through the shared affections of owner and captive" (88). Thus, when Rufus said Alice's future enslavement is her own fault, he is also saying that his brutality is the result of her not willingly submitting to his brutality. The insidiousness of such logic is the power that Rufus assigns to Alice—it makes her, not him, "the master of her subjection" (see Hartman 89). Indeed, if Alice is the master of her subjection, then she should also be the master of her freedom since masters have the power to choose their fates. However, as Rufus reminds Dana in his demand for her to help him rape Alice, if a White man desires a Black woman in the antebellum South, the only power she has is choosing whether she will submit willingly or unwillingly to his desires. Indeed, when Dana refuses to help Rufus in his rape plan, he tells her that her refusal means more pain for Alice: "Go to her. Send her to me. I'll have her whether you help or not. All I want you to do is fix it so I don't have to beat her. You're no friend of hers if you won't do that much!" (Butler 164). Since Rufus is not married, raping Alice is not done to protect the "angel in the house" from his animal lust; instead, it is done in the name of being a "respectable" White man. In other words, if loving a Black woman is one way a White man could lose his respectability status, then raping Alice functions as Rufus's way of maintaining or achieving that status, since the White people who know him, save for his mother, are not sure if he is a respectable White man.

If being a respectable White male slaveowner meant being a monster, then how did enslaved women benefit from the love of their owners, as the law and Rufus claim? They did not benefit, as indicated by the circumstances surrounding Alice's physical death. In fact, Rufus's love is what makes him a monster precisely because it is "destructive" (147), evokes feelings of "revulsion" (164), and engenders Alice's "misfortune" (124). For example, during her last trip to Maryland, Dana discovers that Alice has hanged herself because Rufus not only beat her for running away, but he also pretended to sell their children, Joseph and Hagar, "to punish her, scare her. To make her see what could happen if she didn't . . . if she tried to leave me" (251). Like Daughter from Walker's story, Alice was so repulsed by being in the presence of her monster that she killed herself. Alice's suicide represents one form of resistance that Black women deployed when separated from family or in the aftermath of a sale during slavery, as in the nonfictional case of an enslaved woman from Maryland. The unnamed Black woman, whose story is told in a deposition given by Francis Scott Key, cut her throat after being separated from her husband (Berry and Gross 80–81). The horror of these women's suicides is not that they broke some moral or divine code, but that physical death was the only option they had available to them to escape their social death. Thus, Rufus's love is responsible for Alice's social and physical death, since his love demands Alice to not hate him for repeatedly hurting her. Rufus's love for Dana, which has become sexual after Alice's death, is just as disturbing because he wants Dana to "take the place of the dead" (Butler 259). Although Rufus told Dana prior to Alice's death that he would kill himself if he ever loved Dana the way he loves Alice, he has always believed, as he reminds Dana before he attempts to rape her, that she and Alice were "one woman," "two halves of a whole" (257). That view of Alice and Dana not only suggests that Rufus believes all Black women, whether free or enslaved, are not fully human, an allusion to the US Constitution's infamous three-fifths clause, but it also captures his anti-Black necrophilia since he is erotically obsessed with Black women who are socially dead as well as with causing the social death of socially alive Black women.

Reading *Kindred* as a neo-slave horror novel allows us to examine Butler's conception of human monstrosity, especially the monster of respectability during slavery. As pointed out in the novel, one feature that distinguishes the unlikable human from the human monster is the monster's necrophilia. Indeed, Butler's depictions of Tom and Rufus suggests that slavery's respectability monsters are anti-Black necrophiliacs whose ultimate fantasy is to live in an America where all Black women are socially dead, where free and/or educated Black women do not exist. Because of such desire, these monsters could never really love Black women, as Rufus claims, since he and his father uphold the laws, customs, and economics of slavery, which dictate that White men, particularly slaveowners, who love Black women are shameful and lack good business sense. Moreover, in contrast to the "symbiotic love" proposed in Butler's "Bloodchild," the idea that "our relationships must be driven not only by our need for others, but also by a desire to ensure the wellbeing of others" (Jenkins and Sciurba 133–34), Rufus's love is one-sided, repulsive, and destructive as it acknowledges his need for Alice but is not concerned with ensuring her wellbeing. Thus, Butler's depictions of Tom and Rufus as respectability monsters make the same point as actual slave narratives: "slavery did not produce good masters" (Winter 69).

Even though Tom and Rufus are men of their time, their monstrosity cannot be solely attributed to the laws, customs, or economics of racialized slavery, since White men in that socioeconomic system had the power to choose if they will or will not treat Black people inhumanely. Indeed, their decision to rape Black women was not due to a mental illness or a biological imperative (i.e., their race or sex) but due to their desire to be viewed as "respectable" White men. In this context, raping Black women serves as a way for "respectable" White men to defend themselves against the Black woman's so-called seductive powers, since Black women's sexuality was viewed as having the power to lead White men to their downfall (see Hartman 87). Such thinking is why Rufus's demand that Alice enjoy his production and consumption of her pain is repulsive and terrifying—although he knows that he does not need such consent and will never get it, he demands it anyway, as if to prove to himself and others (e.g., his father and the slaves who are suspicious of Dana and Alice because of their closeness to Rufus) that Alice wants him to rape her, that Alice has willingly consented to her oppression. Thus, Butler submits in *Kindred* that the plantation did not produce the monsters of slavery; rather, the monsters of slavery produced the horrors that made the plantation a "death-world."

I noted earlier in this discussion of *Kindred* that a death-world, drawing on the work of Mbembe, is a place where its living conditions transform vast populations of people into the "living dead." According to Mbembe, the plantation is not a "community," where everyone has the right to the "power of speech and thought," but a "space where the slave belongs to the master" and is "kept alive, but in a *state of injury*, in a phantom-like world of horrors and intense cruelty and profanity" (75). Indeed, *Kindred* is, as McKittrick asserts, "a spatial story that is unresolved and caught up in the uncertain, sometimes disturbing, demands of geography" (35), a story that shows that enslaved Black women's will-less-ness and always willingness were partly determined by the spaces on the plantation that their bodies occupied (e.g., the slaveowner's fields, kitchen, or bedroom), spaces where "the relations between life and death, the politics of cruelty and the symbolism of profanity, get blurred" (Mbembe 76). As I show in my examination of Nnedi Okorafor's *Who Fears Death*, the monsters of respectability are not isolated to America's cultural and geographical landscapes. Indeed, the novel suggest that these monsters might exist in the African continent's future for the same reasons that they exist in America's past and present—the simultaneous hatred of and desire for the Black female body, a key ideological feature of death-worlds shaped by African enslavement.

The Respectability Monster in Africanjujuist Horror Fiction

Set in a far-future, postapocalyptic kingdom that used to be part of the Sudan, *Who Fears Death* is one of Okorafor's "thought-experiments regarding young women who challenge the hierarchical power structures and cultural traditions that hinder their moral development" (Lindow 46). In the novel's acknowledgments, Okorafor reveals that Emily Wax's 2004 news article about "weaponized rape in the Sudan" was the inspiration that "created the passageway through which Onyesonwu slipped into [her] world." *Who Fears Death* is Onyesonwu's first-person account of how she discovered, found, and punished the human monster who raped her mother and is seeking to murder her. Onyesonwu, whose name means "who fears death," which is "both question and renunciation" (Byrd 59), is not only Eshu (i.e., a shape-shifting human) but also Ewu, whose biraciality reveals the origin of her conception—a Nuru man raping an Okeke woman. According to Najeeba, Onye's mother, Nuru people have "yellow-brown skin, narrow noses, and brown or black hair that was like a well-groomed horse's mane," whereas the Okeke have "dark brown skin, wide nostrils, thick lips, and thick black hair like the hide of a sheep" (Okorafor, *WFD* 25). However, Najeeba continues, Ewu children "look neither Okeke nor Nuru, more like desert spirits," and no one can explain why that is so (25). Onye discovers that her Nuru father and mother's rapist is Daib, a military general whom Mwita, Onye's Ewu-born lover, describes as a "powerful, *powerful* sorcerer" who not only has "a heart full of the most evil stuff" but can also "bend time," "make things appear that should never be there," and "make people think wrong things" (185). While Daib's powers make him an embodiment of fear, the pleasure that he receives from inflicting pain on the Okeke, Ewu, and Nuru who treat Okeke and Ewu as fully human makes him the embodiment of disgust.

While scholars have examined Nnedi Okorafor's *Who Fears Death* as a fantasy, science fiction, young adult, postcolonial/anticolonial, Afrofuturist/Africanfuturist, dystopian, and/or bildungsroman novel,[4] there was difficulty finding scholarship that examines the novel as horror fiction. I not only read *Who Fears Death* as a horror novel but also as an Africanjujuist horror novel that focuses on theorizing human monstrosity. According to Okorafor, her work is not an example of Afrofuturism but what she has coined "Africanfuturism" and "Africanjujuism." As a "sub-category of science fiction," Africanfuturism is like Afrofuturism but rooted more deeply in "African culture, history, mythology and point-of-view as it then branches into the Black diaspora, and it does not privilege or center the West." Similarly, Africanjujuism is "a subcategory of fantasy that respectfully acknowledges the seamless blend of true existing African spiritualties and cosmologies with the imaginative" (qtd. in Wabuke par. 5). As Okorafor sees it, "Afrofuturism: Wakanda builds its first outpost in Oakland, CA, USA. Africanfuturism: Wakanda builds its first outpost in a neighboring African country" (qtd. in Wabuke par. 6). I think Okorafor raises a valid point about the centrality of

---

4. See, for example, cited texts by Burnett, Samatar, Pahl, Bryce, Kotecki, and Byrd.

America or the West as the locus of action and critique in Afrofuturism, but I also think that her framing of that critique can lead one to think that African-futurism and Africanjujuism are *Blacker* than Afrofuturism, as Hope Wabuke does: "By not centering themselves around the concept of 'American' in their definitions, Africanfuturism and Africanjujuism are freed from the white Western gaze. Indeed, this becomes the main defining difference between Afrofuturism and Africanfuturism. And while some texts can hold aspects of both Afrofuturism and Africanfuturism—an Afrofuturist text and an Afri-canfuturist text are quite different indeed" (par. 7).[5] Though Wabuke's cri-tique of the absence of Africa from Mark Dery's conception of Afrofuturism is valid, her critique of *Kindred* relies on a racially essentialist understanding of American Blackness. Indeed, because Afrofuturism was initially identi-fied as a Black American cultural phenomenon and was coined by a White American critic, Wabuke claims that *Kindred*, unlike Butler's other works, which are "so thoroughly sunken in the Black American diasporic gaze," is a novel that "provides the reader's white gaze with Black forgiveness *and* the absolution of white guilt without holding whiteness culpable for its legacy of violence or demanding accountability and reparations" (par. 12).

While there are many problems with Wabuke's assessment of Butler's novel, too many to address here, one problem that stands out is the assump-tion that the novel is not "thoroughly sunken" in the Black American literary gaze. Not only does that assumption imply that there is only one literary gaze that Black Americans use to read texts, but it also seems to ignore Okorafor's assertion that Africanfuturism is "similar" to Afrofuturism (qtd. in Wabuke par. 5). In so doing, Wabuke appears to discount the role that Okorafor's Americanness plays in her work (see Kotecki 168). Indeed, Okorafor's use of "similar" is important because it suggests that *Who Fears Death*, "The Child Who Favored Daughter," and *Kindred* are addressing the same horrors associated with the monsters of respectability, but they are using different Black cultures, histories, and mythologies to address those

---

5. However, given that Black people in Africa and America have been partly shaped by the Western colonial project (e.g., Okorafor writing her novels in English), Afrofutur-ism, Africanfuturism, and Africanjujuism may never be free from the White Western gaze. This revelation helps to explain Okorafor's description of the imagined worlds she has created as a reflection of "a series of cultural mixes and clashes between being American and being Nigerian" (qtd. in Kotecki 168). In this light, Okorafor's distinction between Afrofuturism and Africanfuturism and Africanjujuism, despite its framing or tone, is not about determining which genres of Black speculative fiction are the most racially authentic; rather, that distinction is making the point that there is more than one way to be Black; therefore, privileging Afrofuturism as the Black literary philosophy that encapsulates all Black speculative fiction is racially essentializing.

horrors. Indeed, if we consider Alondra Nelson's amendment in "Introduction: Future Texts" (2002) to Dery's definition of Afrofuturism, then it is possible to see Afrofuturism as a movement, philosophy, and practice that, according to Sofia Samatar, "explores a Pan-African psychogeography, resists the framing of Africa as a latecomer to science fiction, and attests to the continued relevance of Afrofuturism for both Africa and the diaspora" (176). As I will show in the following pages, the human monsters in *Who Fears Death* are comparable to those in "The Child Who Favored Daughter" and *Kindred,* since they all receive ideo- and physio-pleasure from the production and consumption of Black girls and women in pain. I argue that Daib can be read as a monster of respectability whose violence against Okeke women is justified by the racist and religious ideologies upheld by the Okeke and the Nuru. Like Walker's "The Child Who Favored Daughter" and Butler's *Kindred,* Okorafor's *Who Fears Death* proposes that if humans, Black or non-Black, continue to believe that nature or a deity has created the human races, then Black women will continue to exist in a world that breeds monsters who believe it is respectable and possibly necessary to terrorize Black girls and women.

The mythology explaining why the Okeke and the Nuru look the way they do is grounded in the idea of race, the myth that nature or a deity has created and stratified the human races; in this instance, the goddess Ani created the Okeke, the Nuru, and the inequality that exist between them. "The Okeke people," as Nejeeba tells eleven-year-old Onye, "have skin the color of night because they were created before the day. They were first. Later, after much had happened, the Nuru arrived. They came from the stars and that's why their skin is the color of the sun" (Okorafor, *WFD* 16). While the Okeke, which means "the created ones," are the first humans, Najeeba notes that the Great Book, the sacred text of the Okeke and Nuru, says that the Okeke did something so terrible during the "Old Africa Era" that it warranted Ani making them the generational slaves of the Nuru (16). However, a few decades before Najeeba's birth, a group of Okeke men and women rejected their enslavement and demonstrated "ambition" (17), and the Nuru punished that ambition with a genocidal campaign that not only moved the Okeke to the wastelands of the East, but it also included raping Okeke girls and women with the intent of impregnating them so that the Nuru could "destroy Okeke families at the very root," since custom dictates that children are the children of their fathers and, therefore, an Okeke woman who has given birth to an Ewu child is "bound to the Nuru through her child" (20–21).

While not framed within a Black-White binary supported by an Abrahamic theology, *Who Fears Death* is nevertheless a discussion about the ways in which religion fosters racism. As Patrick Manning points out, the people of the twelfth and thirteenth centuries were unfamiliar with our current usage of "race," but they believed that "religion was as important as phenotype in determining race" (39). George Fredrickson defines racism as a set of beliefs and practices that "directly sustains or proposes to establish *a racial order*, a permanent group hierarchy that is believed to reflect the laws of nature or the decrees of God." Furthermore, racism is primarily, if not exclusively, a Western product that originated, at least in prototypical form, in the fourteenth and fifteenth centuries and "was originally articulated in the idioms of religion more than those in natural science" (6). For instance, the growth of "religious racism or racialized religiosity" in Europe during the sixteenth and seventeenth centuries can be seen in the application of the Curse of Ham, the myth that may have provided the rationale for enslaving Africans regardless of their faith. According to this legend, Ham and his descendants, Canaan and the Canaanites, were punished by God to be servants of his brothers and their descendants because Ham saw Noah, his father, naked and mocked him. While the ancient Hebrews used that curse to justify their conquest and subjugation of the Canaanites, medieval Arabs who were importing slaves to the Middle East from East Africa shifted the curse's emphasis from Canaan to Ham, who was "widely believed to be the physical ancestor of all Africans, and the physical result of the curse became a blackening of the skin" (43). In medieval Europe, the curse was applied to various Asian and European groups, but it was not thought of as a serious explanation for Black servitude until the middle of the fifteenth century, when the Portuguese reached West Africa (43). Similarly, America's racial categories, as Janet Jakobsen notes, "grew out of what was originally a religious distinction between Christians and 'strangers,' a categorization that differentiated between Christian indentured servants and African slaves" (202).

Like the anti-Black racism fueled by the Abrahamic religions, the anti-Okeke beliefs and practices of the Nuru are nurtured by the Great Book. Indeed, Daib was not always a monster according to Sola, his mentor. In fact, Bisi, Daib's single-parent mother, was a "free thinker" who rejected the Great Book and was "always shouting about how women were treated badly." She also helped some Okeke to safety during a wave of Okeke riots, and she had wished "with all of her heart" that Daib would bring good change to their kingdom (Okorafor, *WFD* 317). Although Sola does not explain why Daib went from "right" to "wrong," his actions indicate that his shift was partly due to his belief in the Great Book and a recognition that he enjoys producing and consuming bodies in pain. According to Joshua Yu Burnett, the Great Book has created "a colonialist dystopia for the Okeke" (143), a dystopia in which dominant groups maintain their power not only through force but also by "imprint[ing] ideologies onto themselves and the oppressed that remake the oppressors as extensions of the divine and the oppressed as something less than human" (144). Moreover, Miriam Pahl argues that this dystopia is presented as "an adversary even greater than the dictator reigning over the kingdom," given that "all social practices in the kingdom are based on the hierarchies dictated by the book" (215). Indeed, an examination of the Great Book's creation story reveals that Ani, not the Nuru, is the mother of Okeke subjugation and Nuru monstrosity.

According to an Okeke storyteller who survived a genocidal raid by the Nuru, Ani was "horrified" and "furious" because the Okeke, who sprang from the rivers she created before she took a multicentury nap, were "aggressive like the rushing rivers, forever wanting to move forward." Ani's anger was fueled by the Okeke's exploitation of her creations and desire to be like her: "They bent and twisted Ani's sand, water, sky, air, took her creatures and changed them" (92). In fact, Onye learns that the Lost Papers of the Great Book, which the Okeke are confusingly ashamed by, depicts Ani as displeased by the Okeke's "wild creativity," since they, without the assistance of Ani, invented methods and technologies that allowed them to "keep themselves young until they died," to make "food grow on dead land," and to cure "all diseases" (337). Due to the Okeke's actions, the story-teller continues, Ani grabbed a sun from the cosmos and pulled it to Earth, plucking the Nuru from it. Implying that the Nuru represent life and rebirth while the Okeke represent death and extinction, the Great Book states, as the storyteller puts it, that the same day the Nuru were plucked from the sun, "flowers realized they could bloom. Trees understood that they could grow. And Ani laid a curse on the Okeke" (93). Considering that the first time Ani speaks to the Okeke is when she cursed them to be slaves, her curse on the Okeke is unjust because she is punishing beings to whom she gave no clear or credible instruction on how she wished them to exist. Burnett contends that "Okorafor links her speculative future Africa to African American history as she signifies on the use of Christianity as a slaveholder's religion, creating a religious text, holy to both the Okeke and the Nuru but actively hostile to the Okeke" (142). Indeed, like the Curse of Ham, the curse of the Okeke not only demands that they be enslaved by their human siblings for perpetuity simply because they unknowingly committed acts that Ani was displeased with, but it also depicts Ani as the goddess and protector of the Nuru, not the Okeke, since she intentionally created the Nuru.

Given Ani's justification for enslaving the Okeke, Onye stopped believing in Ani and views the Great Book as dangerous because it legitimates Nuru monstrosity. For instance, Daib's speech to a middle-class Nuru community declares that their genocidal campaign against the Okeke is "doing what must be done," "following the Book" as Ani's "pious loyal people." By wiping out the Okeke, Daib continues, the Nuru can make Ani and the Great Book "proud" by building "an empire that is the most good of good!" (Okorafor, WFD 178). As represented by the eerie song sang by Nuru men and women as they watch or brutalize Okeke men, women, and children, Daib's success at getting most of the Nuru community onboard with his genocidal campaign represents the logical conclusion of the Great Book's creation story:

> The blood of the Okeke runs like water
> We take their goods and shame their forefathers.
> We beat them with a heavy hand
> Then take what they call their land.
> The power of Ani belongs to us
> And so we will slay you to dust
> Ugly filthy slaves, Ani has finally killed you! (18–19)

Thus, even without the Okeke's resistance to their divinely sanctioned enslavement, Nurus like Daib would still find it necessary to exterminate the Okeke precisely because their goddess has defined the dark-skinned people in the Great Book as slaves who are inherently immoral and, therefore, an existential threat to the Nuru people. According to Kristine Kotecki, because the Great Book "authorizes [Daib's] actions, he represents as righteous the violence of his rape of Onye's mother and of his campaign to dehumanize and destroy the Okeke" (170). Indeed, because racism and sexism reinforce each other, Ani is also the reason why the Okeke women are doubly oppressed and Ewu women are triply oppressed.

Given the Great Book's depiction of the Okeke, there is nothing that Okeke girls and women can do—including keeping the "old," "respected," and horrifying practice of the Eleventh Rite in which eleven-year-old girls suffer clitorectomies because it is believed that "to be uncircumcised past eleven brought bad luck and shame to your family" (Okorafor, WFD 33)—to be respectable in the eyes of Ani or the Nuru because they are permanent slaves and, therefore, will always be incomplete humans. In this instance, the Eleventh Rite is an example of how the Okeke of Jwahir, one of the first villages settled by the first Okeke to flee the West and where Onye lives, internalized what Burnett calls "their own Great Book–endorsed inadequacy" (144). This so-called inadequacy not only explains why Daib wants to kill Onye but also the pleasure he receives from torturing and murdering Okeke women. For example, on the day that Aro agrees to teach Onye the Great Mystic Points, which is based on Igbo cosmology (Okorafor, "Writing" 24), he tells her that Daib wants to kill her because she is a "failure," since she was "supposed to be a boy" (Okorafor, WFD 110). In fact, Daib tells Onye that although he prefers to "bash an Okeke woman's head in after [he has] had her," he let Najeeba live because he "enjoyed" her and wanted her to give him a "great, great son" (365). Daib wanted a son, as Aro explains, because "he would have an ally instead of an enemy" in fulfilling a Great Book prophecy (120). According to that prophecy, a Nuru sorcerer "will come and force the Great Book's rewriting" that will lead to "good change for Nuru *and* Okeke" (94). For Daib, the prophecy is referencing him, and his rewriting of the Great Book will exclude the Okeke as his vision of good change (364).

However, Onye and others discover that the prophecy is wrong or misinterpreted because Onye, an Ewu woman who embodies the horrors inspired by the Great Book, is revealed to be its rewriter (187). Aro suggests that Najeeba, an Okeke sorceress, might be the prophesized rewriter, since her "demands" to make Onye female overrode Daib's demand for a son (120). As Kotecki puts it, "Fate [in the novel] is a manifestation of Onye's mother's will subverting the territorial claims that rape as a tactic of ethnic cleansing entails, and it is the first chip in Daib's totalitarian armor" (170). Whether it is Najeeba or Onye, the sex of the rewriter is important for Daib because it indicates the rewriter's gender; that is, Daib's desire to have a son rather than a daughter assumes that a male Onye would be an oppressor instead of a liberator simply because he is born male (Burnett 144). The significance of Daib's desire for a son and his assumption about the sex-gender relationship is that it points to the intentionality of his cruelty. For example, Daib knows that his violence is inhumane, as suggested by his "moment of doubt and disgust with himself" as he raped Najeeba, but Onye tells us that his people's "rage," which originates from the Great Book, "took him again, filling his body with unnatural strength" (Okorafor WFD 151). The word "again" tells us that Daib has occasionally questioned his beliefs and actions, but he decides, by letting the rage take over, to be a monster because he is celebrated for his violence against the Okeke and, more importantly, he enjoys "the potential and taste for amazing cruelty" (151). Indeed, Daib has recorded himself on disks singing in almost every beating, rape, and murder he has committed, including his rape of Najeeba. Mwita tells Daib before he is killed that his "brain is diseased" for keeping and taking pride in owning a collection of horror in which he is recorded laughing and being aroused by violence (364). Mwita is not using mental illness as the reason for Daib's malevolence; rather, he is pointing out that the ideo- and physio-pleasure that Daib receives from inflicting pain on Okeke bodies is done by choice, done to prove that he is *not* a monster, but a respectable Nuru man who is loyal to his goddess and is admired so much by his people that parents "name their firstborn sons after him" (316). Thus, Onye concludes that Daib is beyond unlikable and, therefore, beyond ideological help, meaning that he must die and the Great Book must be revised in order to destroy the death-world that is designed to terrorize Okeke life.

As an Africanjujuist horror novel, *Who Fears Death* uses Igbo spiritualities and cosmologies to depict a human monster who is both lethal and sickening. Human monstrosity in the novel is not attributed to ill minds or abnormal bodies; instead, it is the product of ideology, the product of people's beliefs about themselves, others, and how the world works. The ideological source of human monstrosity in the novel is the theistic religion of the Great Book and its goddess Ani, which is not that different from the Abrahamic religions. Indeed, the ideo-pleasure Daib, the novel's human monster, receives from beating, raping, and killing Okeke women derives from his loyalty to Ani, who created and stratified the human races by designating the Okeke as the slaves of the Nuru. Moreover, since Daib's violence is sanctioned by Ani's anti-Okeke racism, he sees himself and is seen by most Nurus as a righteous and respectable man. However, to prevent readers from treating Daib's monstrosity as an eye-of-the-beholder issue, since he is admired by some and hated by others, Okorafor highlights the role that choice plays in Daib's monstrosity. For instance, since Daib is sometimes disgusted by his acts of brutality, he is not doomed to be a monster; rather, he chooses to be one because he is ideologically and physically aroused by inflicting violence on socially dead people. Thus, according to the novel's logic, Onye could not defeat the monster until she rejected Ani and rewrote the Great Book, the sources of the monster's ideological pleasure, which moralizes his physical pleasure. Indeed, Onye's defeat of Daib suggests that defeating the monsters of respectability requires more than becoming physically stronger than them—it also requires Black women to discredit or rewrite the religious beliefs these monsters follow, since these beliefs make it possible for the monsters to exist and to believe that terrorizing Black girls and women is evidence of their loyalty to their races and to their gods and/or goddesses.

The Horror of the Respectability Monster

What Walker, Butler, and Okorafor demonstrate in their texts is that the monsters of respectability, humans who deploy the myths of Black female hypersexuality and immorality to justify harming and terrorizing Black women and girls, embody the limitations and dangers of respectability politics. For example, Walker's "The Child Who Favored Daughter" suggests that Black female family members who refuse to adhere to the constraints of respectability ideology are viewed as deserving of the violence inflicted upon them by the monsters of respectability. However, given that the father's violence is driven by his desire for and hatred of his sister and daughter, Walker's story contends that "a family under the sway of respectability politics cannot be functional, even if its adherents gain or attempt to gain social privilege" (Morris 9). Moreover, since living up to the standards of respectability will not erase or alleviate the misogynoir that permeates American culture, Daughter, the father's daughter, Alice, Dana, and Onyesonwu represent Black women who, as Cooper might put it, have moved "beyond respectability." One could argue that these fictional Black women represent a rejection of the "continued use of the paradigms of respectability and dissemblance as the only ways to read the historic Black female body" (Cooper 144). Indeed, the horror fiction by Walker, Butler, and Okorafor is not just about condemning respectability politics as an ineffective strategy of Black progress—these texts are also about how human monsters seek respectability through the production and consumption of Black women in pain, as exemplified by Tom and Rufus Weylin's exploitation of enslaved Black women. In other words, the depictions of the father, the Weylin men, and Daib are manifestations of the paradox that informs the respectability monster's violence—the hatred of and attraction to Black women. Since the respectability monster desires a sexual relationship with his Black female victims that is prohibited by mainstream society (i.e., the father and his daughter and sister, Rufus and Alice, and Daib and Najeeba), the respectability monster, in contrast to the unlikable human, uses the discourse of Black female hypersexuality to force and validate that union. Tacitly claiming that the Black woman's race makes her sexuality inherently immoral, the monsters of respectability can present their sexual abuse of Black women as virtuous and themselves as respectable.

According to Morris, the structure of domination that shapes all others in respectability politics is what Elisabeth Schüssler Fiorenza calls "kyriarchy," which describes a "socio-cultural and religious system of domination constituted by intersecting multiplicative structures of oppression" (qtd. in Morris

9). Because it is rooted in kyriarchy, as Morris contends, respectability ideology is inherently repressive precisely because kyriarchy is "a system of social hierarchies connected to intersecting sets of oppression, whereby individuals with differing amounts of power and privilege—even those from traditionally marginalized groups—can dominate or attempt to dominate others as they navigate social institutions and interpersonal relationships" (110). Thinking of the respectability monster as a product of kyriarchy implies that race does not limit who can and cannot be a respectability monster since that monster, as represented by the father, the Weylin men, and Daib, is defined not by what it looks like but by what it does and why. This also means that sex or gender does not determine one's status as a respectability monster precisely because Black and non-Black women can also sexually abuse Black women and girls in the name of respectability. Thus, according to the texts by Walker, Butler, and Okorafor, what transforms people into respectability monsters are the beliefs that they *choose* to live by, since these beliefs encourage and validate their misogynoir-based violence. Consequently, this means that respectability monsters have no excuse for the pain and terror that they cause Black women and girls precisely because they are aware, on some level, that their actions are inhumane. As we shall see in the next chapter, Black men are also subjected to human monsters who terrorize them because of their race and sex. These human monsters, whom I call not-ness monsters, are also not defined by their race or sex, and they suggest that the paradigm of respectability is as dangerous for Black men as it is for Black women since it cannot protect them from those who act on their simultaneous hatred of and desire for the Black male body.

CHAPTER 3

The Monsters of Not-Ness

Like the myth of the hypersexual Black female discussed in chapter 2, the myth of the hypersexual Black male defines Black boys and men within a constant state of sexual willingness. While the myth of the hypersexual Black male was used to explain away White-on-Black sexual violence, given that Black men were "routinely raped and subject to sexual violence during slavery and Jim Crow" (Curry, "Foreword" xvii), it also criminalized Black men as a threat to both White womanhood and manhood. For example, Black men having consensual or nonconsensual sex with White women was, according to Brittany C. Slatton, "one of the greatest fears during both slavery and legal segregation." Slatton notes that Black men *accused* of raping a White woman were subjected to castration or the death penalty in antebellum America and condemned to the horrors of lynching during Jim Crow (36). As Ida B. Wells observed at the end of the nineteenth century, "It is certain that lynching mobs have not only refused to give the Negro a chance to defend himself, but have killed their victim with a full knowledge that the relationship of the alleged assailant with the [White] woman who accused him, was voluntary and clandestine" (*Red Record* 117–18). Implicit in Wells's observation is that lynching mobs were monstrous manifestations of the insidious belief that "being a black man was enough evidence to prove the intent of rape" (Slatton 36).

While the myth of the hypersexual Black male defined Black men as *the* threat to White women's sexual virtue, it also defined them as "well-endowed and able to please women sexually" (Slatton 36), making Black men's bodies "simultaneously appealing and appalling" (Kitossa xli). Ironically, by making the Black penis well-endowed and appealing, the White-generated myth of the hypersexual Black male identifies White men as lacking, forcing them to develop, acquire, reinforce, and/or redefine social and physical traits that are believed to trump the sexual power given to Black men by White people. Indeed, the work on the Black male in Black American feminist and gay criticism reveals, as Darieck Scott contends, that "the de rigueur application of the concept of double-consciousness to objects of knowledge assigned to the category of 'black,' 'male,' and 'African American' generally finds the 'black male' to be a self-contradicting and self-reinforcing position at once hypermasculine and feminine, exemplifying an erection/castration paradox" (19).[1] Thus, in addition to the use of bodily violence, such as the practice of lynching discussed in chapter 1, to physically castrate the mythical Black man's hypermasculine erection, that paradox also seeks to socially castrate Black men by representing them as abnormal, primitive, violent, and appalling. In fact, the reason why the erection/castration paradox exists is due to the ways in which "blackness is rendered by the various cultural, social, and economic processes of white supremacist domination as the exemplar of nonnormative genders and sexualities" (Scott 21). Consequently, combatting the appealing and appalling hypersexual Black male requires the processes of White supremacy that invented this mythical figure to make Black boys and men existential threats to Whiteness and White people.

What the myth of the hypersexual Black male tells us, drawing on the words of Ronald Hyam, is that "the peculiarly emotional hostility towards black men which [racism] has so often engendered requires a sexual explanation" (qtd. in Kitossa xlv). Tommy J. Curry makes a similar point in his discussion of Frantz Fanon's analysis of the Negrophobic man and woman: "While the nymphomania of the white woman is suggested as the basis of her heterosexual obsession with the Black phallus, the homoerotic manifestations of anti-Black racism—the disgust toward but lust for the Black male body—are rarely theorized as fundamentally linked to the violence Black men and boys suffer" (*Man-Not* 35). The Black American horror stories examined in this chapter take up Curry's challenge by highlighting the ways

---

1. Similarly, Curry notes that the contemporary understanding of *maleness* makes it synonymous with power, patriarchy, and Whiteness; thus, *maleness* has "no similar existential content for the Black male, who in an anti-Black world is denied maleness and is ascribed as feminine in relation to white masculinity." This means, according to Curry, that Black maleness is "a de-gendered negation of white maleness that is feminine because of its subordinate position to white masculinity, but *not female*, because Black maleness lacks a specific gender coordinate that corresponds to either white maleness or white femaleness" (*Man-Not* 6).

in which "the Negrophobia that drove white America to endorse lynching as a technology of murder is the same anxiety and fear that now allow the white public to endorse the murder of Black men and boys [by the police and others] as justifiable homicides" (7). I argue that Richard Wright's "The Man Who Killed a Shadow" (1946/1949),[2] Robert Fleming's "The Ultimate Bad Luck" (2004), Rickey Windell George's "Good 'Nough to Eat" (2006), and Lexi Davis's "Are You My Daddy?" (2007) offer different versions of what I call not-ness monsters, people whose desire and distaste for Black males leads them to terrorize, harm, and/or kill Black boys and men.

For Curry, as I noted in the introduction, Man-Not-ness names the "vulnerability" experienced by Black males due to their selves being denied, negated, and determined by the fears and desires of society. Those fears and desires, Curry adds, identify the Black male as a "brute and savage," an image of "horror" and "death" that needs to be exterminated (*Man-Not* 34). In this light, not-ness monsters are those humans who seek to transform Black men into Man-Nots or keep them in a state of Man-Not-ness. As we shall see, the stories by Wright, Fleming, George, and Davis reveal the ways in which the racial hatred of and sexual longing for Black men can result in Black and non-Black people believing that Black men are incapable of love or being loved. Such a view of Black men, as these stories suggest, informs the moral justification for the social and physical violence directed at Black boys and men in the US.

White Women as Not-Ness Monsters

As a response to the ways in which Blackness was rendered within White supremacist ideology, Scott notes that Black Power and Black Arts Movement intellectuals and writers such as Eldrige Cleaver and Amiri Baraka "identified sexuality as one of the primary means by which black subjugation was achieved and concomitantly as one of the primary arenas in which black liberation was to be won" (172). For writers like Baraka and Cleaver, situating Black subjugation and Black liberation within the context of sexuality meant treating homosexuality and rape as signifiers of White supremacy's essential nature, which was considered "perverse," "depraved," and "enforced through forms of sexual domination" (177). Thus, for Baraka and Cleaver, homosexuality and rape functioned as "oscillating metaphors" of a

---

2. Wright's story was published first in French in a "little" magazine, *Les Lettres Françaises*, on October 4, 1946. After its rejection by American editors, Wright's story "was next published, for the first time in English, in another 'little' magazine in France, *Zero*, in 1949" (Miller 210n1).

history defined by slavery and its legacies in the contemporary moment and as "opposing strategies for meeting the present emergency, either to be repudiated or embraced" (179). The present emergency in the 1960s was Black liberation, and since Black liberation was understood by Baraka and Cleaver as "the liberation of black male sexual prowess in the form of the rapist-warrior in at once cultural and biological combat," homosexuality functioned as the "sign of the patriarchal power denied to black men in the specific history of American slavery and segregation" (185). The themes of homosexuality, rape, Black liberation, and White domination that Scott finds in the works of Baraka and Cleaver are also found in Black American horror fiction where Black male sexuality is featured, as we see in Richard Wright's "The Man Who Killed a Shadow" and Robert Fleming's "The Ultimate Bad Luck."

While the subject of racism's sexualization is found in most, if not all, of Wright's works (e.g., *Native Son* [1940] and *Black Boy* [1945]), he gives the subject, as Earle V. Bryant argues, "its most concentrated and forceful treatment" in "The Man Who Killed a Shadow" (121). According to Paul Gilroy, Wright's story is "a discomforting tale that introduces the interrelation of racism and sexuality in a striking reversal of some stereotypical notions of predator and quarry" ("Introduction" xiii). Indeed, the story's critique of some of the "stereotypical notions of predator and quarry" can be read as Wright proposing that "white America has transmuted the black male-white female relationship into a terror-filled and murderous experience" (Bryant 119). Thus, in contrast to what some have speculated, Wright's story was not "dashed off for money" in an attempt to ride "the coattails of *Black Boy*" (Miller 210); rather, it offers, among other considerations, a conception of human monstrosity in an anti-Black world. Set in a Jim Crow southern town near Washington, DC, "The Man Who Killed a Shadow" is a story about how and why Saul Saunders, a Black man working as a janitor in a gothic-styled cathedral, kills Maybelle Eva Houseman, a forty-year-old White woman who died a virgin.[3] Ever since Saul was a "tiny boy," he lived in fear of the "shadows," the White people who embodied his fears as a Black

---

3. Eugene E. Miller notes that in addition to being shaped by Black American folklore, "The Man Who Killed a Shadow" is also shaped by a story relayed to Wright by the NAACP's legendary attorney Charles Houston in the mid-1940s. As described by Miller, "Houston told of a strange murder case that he was involved with, strange not because a black man had killed a white woman in broad daylight and in a church, but because of the black man's way of explaining what he had done" (217). Wright's explanation for this Black man's "cool, detached, off-handed" account of his actions that lacked "regret, remorse, guilt . . . or fear" is that he did not consider the White woman a real person: "The world little suspects how unreal the white race is to the majority of Negroes" (qtd. in Miller 217). That unreality, Miller argues, is "partially accounted for" in Wright's attempt to express Saul's mental/emotional frame of reference (217).

male born into a world that was "split in two, a white world and a black one" (R. Wright 185). As Saul aged, he grew more afraid of the "shadow-world," and his fear made him a "kind" and "attentive" young man until he found the pleasures of whisky, which gave him "a quick moment" to live, think, and do as if "the world of shadows was over" (189). However, when Maybelle decides to force Saul to have sex with her, he becomes appalled, not aroused as she seems to expect, and slaps her. After the slap, a violent form of rejection, Maybelle begins her screams of death, which lead to her accidental death and to Saul's institutional death. (Though his fate is uncertain, the voice of the court makes it clear that Saul will die at the hands of the legal system.)

Unlike Saul, Neptune Johnson, the protagonist of Fleming's "The Ultimate Bad Luck," escapes the shadow-world's death sentence; however, their experiences represent the horrific possibilities for Black men who are desired by White women during the era of legalized racial segregation and beyond. Fleming's story is a first-person narrative about how Neptune, with the assistance of some alligators, escaped being lynched in 1960s Louisiana. Neptune, who describes himself as "a big man, real big, dark buck, the kind pecker-woods get scared of in a hurry," has become a borderline alcoholic due to the deaths of his wife and two daughters in a home fire three years prior (Fleming, "Ultimate" 40). After a day of hard work at the cotton mill and a night of drinking at the local roadhouse, Neptune returns home to find Miz Gertrude, whom he refers to as "the white woman from over at the Source Planta-tion," in his shack with nothing on, save for bra and panties (41). Miz Gertrude uses the threat of lynching and her gun to force Neptune into sexual intercourse with her. Because Neptune is unable to satisfy her the way she imagines a "Mr. Big N—— Buck" should, Miz Gertrude begins to yell that Neptune raped her (45). As expected, Neptune finds himself being beaten by a group of peckerwoods, who decide during the beating that they would like to watch the alligators in a nearby swamp eat him. However, the lead alligator recognized Neptune as the person who saved it and its offspring from being killed by a group of peckerwoods several years ago, and it directed its crew to kill the peckerwoods and Miz Gertrude. After being escorted to a truck by the lead alligator, Neptune drives to Memphis, laughing about one of his Aunt Prince's favorite sayings: "No good deed goes unpunished" (49).

I argue that Wright's "The Man Who Killed a Shadow" and Fleming's "The Ultimate Bad Luck" offer us White women who are not-ness monsters and, therefore, believe in the horror-inducing myth that the authentic Black male is one who can never be raped. In the Man-Not-ness understanding of the Black male, a White woman raping a Black man is, as Curry puts it, "exceptionally confounding," since the Black male's supposed "hyper-masculinity, his savageness, is thought to make the rape of the Black male brute an impossibility" (*Man-Not* 151). Indeed, what makes the myth of the hypersexual Black male dangerous, as exhibited in Wright's and Fleming's stories, is its sanctioning of all sexual violence directed at Black men, and what makes that myth disgusting is its insistence that Black men enjoy or would enjoy being raped. Moreover, according to the Man-Not-ness image of the Black male, Black men who lack a desire for White women are inauthentic Black men, and White women who have sex with Black men do so not because they desire the Black male body, but because they are altruistic, curious, or being forced to do so. The danger that emerges from erasing White women's desire for the Black male body in their decisions to have sex with Black men, as Curry argues, is that it reinforces American culture's tacit assumption that rape can "never" be an act inspired by the desire for the Black male body (151), an assumption that, as suggested by Wright's and Fleming's stories, has been used to justify sexual violence against Black men.

Since Maybelle does not rape Saul, one might question identifying her as a not-ness monster. Indeed, one might view Maybelle as an unlikable White woman produced by America's racial patriarchy. As Bryant points out, "Both Saul and the shadow-woman are victims of racism's sexualization. . . . As the shadow-woman sees him, Saul is a typical 'n—— buck,' hot to trot, and accordingly she feels herself gravitating toward this supposed sexual dynamo. This is how she has been conditioned to view, and to respond to, 'his kind.' For his part, Saul has been conditioned to 'stay in his place' vis á vis the white female" (121). Although Maybelle and other shadow women are raised to believe in the myth of the hypersexual Black male, she also has the choice to not act on that belief. On the one hand, the narrator tell us that Maybelle's decision to demand Saul to "clean under her desk," as she sits with "her knees sprawled apart and her dress . . . drawn hallway up her legs," seems "as though she [i]s being impelled into an act which she d[oes] not want to perform but [i]s being driven to perform" (R. Wright 192–93). On the other hand, Maybelle's response to Saul's explanation for why he is frightened by her demands indicates that Maybelle's attempt to rape Saul was driven by her anti-Black necrophilia.

As I discussed in chapter 2, anti-Black necrophilia is the erotic interest in or sexual intercourse with socially dead Black people, which means that Maybelle's "tense but controlled voice" and her "stern[ ]" demand for cunnilingus from Saul is driven by something that goes beyond forbidden desire. Indeed, Maybelle's response to Saul telling her that she is making "trouble" for him reveals that her desire for Saul is ideological and physical:

"Why don't you do your work?" she blazed at him. "That's what your being paid to do, you black n——!" Her legs were still spread wide and she was sitting as though about to spring upon him and throw her naked thighs about his body. (193)

Like Tom and Rufus Weylin, the respectability monsters in Butler's *Kindred*, Maybelle imagines that the ideo- and physio-pleasures she will receive from raping Saul, whom she treats as socially dead, will not be available to her by having consensual sex with a White man or woman. In other words, Maybelle's anti-Black necrophilia allows her to be aroused only by socially dead Black men. Although Saul is not a slave, his social death is represented by his "many and simple" unskilled and underpaid jobs he has worked throughout his lifetime and by his desensitization to "hearing the siren of the police car screaming in the Black Belt [and] to seeing white cops dragging Negroes off to jail" (188–89). Since the Black Belt is represented as a kind of "death-world," a place filled with a vast population of people subjected to "living conditions that confer upon them the status of the *living dead*" (Mbembe 92), Maybelle is aware that Saul's social death ensures her master-like power of him, allowing her to treat him like an object because any Black man who occupies the same space as a White woman in Jim Crow America automatically loses his personhood. In other words, due to the myth of the hypersexual Black male and the lynchings that it produced, Saul became Maybelle's sexual property once she decided that she wanted to have sex with him, as indicated by her demand for him to do unpaid sex work. Saul's disturbing fate was secured long before Maybelle attempted to force him to have sex with her—it was secured the day he caught her, with other shadows in the room, staring at him in "a most peculiar way" (R. Wright 190).

One could argue, however, that Maybelle is the unlikable human and Saul is the human monster, given his brutal killing of her, which includes strangulation and cracking her skull (194–95). Although Saul's response to Maybelle's screaming is disturbingly monstrous, he is not the monster of the story. In fact, Saul's brutal murder of Maybelle, done out of fear and rage rather than pleasure and exploitation, not only represents his realization that Maybelle is using the social power of the White woman's scream to punish him for not consenting to his sexual exploitation, but it also suggests that he sees himself killing a human monster. Indeed, Maybelle is dangerous because she acts on the belief that her attraction to Saul automatically makes him her sexual property, giving her the power to determine if he will remain employed, free, or alive. She is disgusting because her actions insist that Saul, viewed through the lens of Man-Not-ness, cannot be raped because Black men never say no to the opportunity for sexual intercourse due to their mythical hypersexuality. Maybelle's not-ness monstrosity is the reason why, after Saul slapped her, she "sucked in her breath" to deliver a scream that was "like a lash cutting into his chest" (193)—Saul's death would be his punishment for refusing to do his "work," which is being a hypersexual Black man who is available to any White woman who desires him. Thus, while "The Man Who Killed a Shadow" posits that one of the most terrifying things that can happen to a Black man in Jim Crow America is a White woman being attracted to him, it is not a White woman's desire for a Black man that transforms her into a not-ness monster; rather, her not-ness monstrosity embodies the moment when her desire for Saul morphs into anti-Black necrophilia.

Like Maybelle, Miz Gertrude of Fleming's "The Ultimate Bad Luck" is a not-ness monster who derives ideo- and physio-pleasure from the production and consumption of Black men in pain. Unlike Maybelle, Miz Gertrude is a serial rapist who believes that her brand of sexual violence is altruistic. Indeed, the first words uttered to Neptune by Miz Gertrude, as she sits "pink naked in just her bra and panties" while holding a large gun, identify her as a sexual altruist: "Howdy, Mr. Neptune Johnson. Today's your lucky day" (Fleming, "Ultimate" 41). Since Miz Gertrude does not use the pronoun *our*, she is assuming that sexual intercourse with her is a gift that Neptune has always wanted precisely because he is a Black man. On the other hand, the absence of the pronoun *our* also suggests that today is not *her* lucky day, implying that having sex with Neptune is not something that she has always desired. Although Miz Gertrude contradicts herself immediately after her introductory words, her decision to frame her raping of Neptune as *his* lucky day serves as an attempt to position herself as performing an act of sexual altruism in which she allows Black men to fulfill what she considers their only sexual fantasy, a fantasy that Jim Crow and its anti-Black violence prevent from becoming a safe reality.

In addition to imagining herself as a sexual altruist, Miz Gertrude's moral sadism—her attempt to transform the horror of raping Neptune into a virtuous act—defines her desire for Neptune as a sexual curiosity, one akin to a scientific study:

I've been watching your big, black n—— ass walking around here like Mr. Big Coon Shit for over two years, six-eight, all muscles and dick," she said low and evil. "My brother, Halbert, say you got quite a reputation with the n—— wenches, say you hung like a stud stallion. I mean to get furrowed tonight. I want to see if you as good as they say at pleasuring. I want some of that dark snake between your legs, black boy. (41)

Defining her sexual altruism within the context of sexual curiosity, rather than erotic desire, Miz Gertrude's explanation for raping Neptune serves to produce an image of herself as a virtuous White woman. Ironically, Miz Gertrude's racist and dehumanizing description of Neptune reveals her desire for the Black male body, and her presentation of that desire as a curiosity about whether her brother's claim about Neptune's sexual prowess is true represents an attempt to deny that desire. According Miz Gertrude's illogic, since sexual curiosity is separate from sexual desire, her decision to rape Neptune is imagined as a sexual study inspired by the desire for knowledge about the Black male body, not by the desire for that body.

While Neptune acknowledges that part of the reason why Miz Gertrude thinks that sexual intercourse with her is a gift is due to some Black men's desire for White women, he also notes that White women's hyper-desire for Black men explains Miz Gertrude's desire to be, as she puts it, "furrowed" by Black men:

A lot of the white girls around here sneak off and meet some buck in the woods and get her first experience of real loving. The cracker gals were curious of colored mens, what they got down there, or had grown tired of pleasuring themselves with their fingers. But many of them got their minds wrecked by the colored mens they seduced, sexually put under a spell that few white mens could break. (42)

Neptune alludes to how separating sexual curiosity from sexual desire is used by Miz Gertrude to conceal her obsession with knowing what Black men "got down there." That obsession is so intense that local "cracker gals" like Miz Gertrude are willing to defy antimiscegenation laws to seduce Black men. However, once these women got some "real loving," they became addicted to the Black male body. Indeed, the "spell" that White women fell under after having sex with Black men "ruined" them because, as explained by one of the peckerwoods beating Neptune, "ain't no decent white man gon' want [them] now" (47). Such thinking is reminiscent of Fanon's recalling of a story by a White prostitute that echoes the peckerwood's beliefs about the consequences of Black male–White female sexual intercourse: "The prostitute whom I mentioned earlier told me that her hunt for Negroes dated from the time when she had been told this story: One night a woman who was in bed with a Negro went mad; she remained insane for two years, but then when she had been cured refused to go to bed with anyone else" (171). Like the prostitute, the peckerwood's discourse about the ruined White woman is really about the ruined White man, since he believes that White women who have gone to bed with Black men will no longer find White men sexually desirable. In this instance, Neptune and the peckerwood seem to agree that Black men have the upper hand in the arena of sexuality, since White men and women are unable to break the sexual spell conjured by the Black penis.

Neptune's narrative sounds like the discourse on Black sexuality and liberation articulated by Black Power/Black Arts writers in that the sexual "spell" Black men cast on White women is viewed by Neptune as something "to beat white men over the head with" and, at the same time, as something that must be kept under "strict control" (Scott 186). Given the way in which Blackness is constructed within White supremacist ideology, Black Power and Black Arts Movement intellectuals and writers "identified sexuality as one of the primary means by which black subjugation was achieved and concomitantly as one of the primary arenas in which black liberation was to be won" (172). However, while Neptune's description of Miz Gertrude counters the myths that all Black men are rapists and sexually excited by White women, his discussion of Miz Gertrude's monstrosity contradicts his claim about Black men's sexual prowess and serves as a critique of treating the sexual arena as a space of Black liberation. Indeed, what makes Miz Gertrude a "freak" and "real dangerous," according to Neptune, is not only her crazed obsession with the Black penis but also her ability to destroy the Black penis: "She ruined colored mens left and right, rode them until their nuts shriveled right up, hung like empty sacks of flour. Totally ruined their nature" (Fleming, "Ultimate" 42). Neptune's explanation of Miz Gertrude's monstrosity represents not only the potential dangers that Black men who sleep with White women might face, but also the realization that Black men in America do not have the upper hand in the bedroom with White women. Although Neptune has the kind of Black body that scares peckerwoods, he acknowledges, while being forced to strip down to his underwear by Miz Gertrude, that his "huge, powerful frame w[ill] do [him] no good here" (42).

What Neptune learns at that moment is that the myth of Black male hypersexuality is not something to beat White men or White women over the head with because, as Miz Gertrude demonstrates, not living up to the myth could be just as dangerous as living up to it. Indeed, after forcing Neptune to lick her vagina's "oily, bitter juices," which tasted like "quinine," Miz Gertrude kicks Neptune in the face and tells him that his life depends on if he can "give it to [her] good," that is, if he can please her in the same way as she imagines he would please a Black woman (44). When Neptune does not live up to her image of Black male sexual prowess, Miz Gertrude becomes so angry that her features change into that of "an evil white witch, all wrinkles and fangs." After her transformation, Miz Gertrude, like Maybelle, starts to scream that Neptune "took her," "hurt her," and "ruined [her] down there" (45), a scream that seeks to punish Neptune with death for not living up to her dehumanizing image of Black men.

Casting a sexual spell on White women, as Neptune discovers, does not lessen White women's power inside or outside the bedroom precisely because White women can rape and be raped in Black male–White female sexual encounters, but Black men can only rape. Fleming's story suggests, in other words, that the Man-Not-ness understanding of the Black male allows "white men and women to sexually assault and define Black masculinity in America" (Curry, *Man-Not* 152). Indeed, the myth of Black male sexual superiority makes the peckerwoods in "The Ultimate Bad Luck" sexually envious and racially hateful. For example, one of the peckerwoods beating Neptune wants to castrate Neptune and keep his castrated penis as a "souvenir" in a Mason jar at a local repair shop. Another peckerwood, who was urged to use his knife to gut Neptune, decides instead to make a small cut on Neptune's penis while "smiling with a mouthful of rotten, tobacco-stained teeth" (Fleming, "Ultimate" 46). Thus, Neptune's narrative does not celebrate the myth of Black male hypersexuality; rather, it treats that myth as a curse, since Black men can be harmed by White people for being better or worse than White men in the bedroom. That curse, which represents the horror that Miz Gertrude and the peckerwoods embody, also points to another fear that occupied Black Power/Black Arts writers during the 1960s—Black male homosexuality.

The link between homosexuality and rape in the works of Baraka and Cleaver, as observed by Scott, "renders axiomatic the idea that perverse sexuality governs black-white social and political relations" (179). Speaking about Baraka specifically, Scott notes that Black identity in Baraka's work is "born in a matrix of sadomasochistic relations between whites and blacks" (180). Similarly, in his explanation of the horror embodied in Miz Gertrude's ability to castrate Black men, Neptune implies that Black homosexuality is the product of White rape. Indeed, Miz Gertrude's monstrosity is not only defined by her ability to ruin the Black penis but also by her ability to somehow transform Black straight men into Black gay men: "After her, the mens could be nothing more than gal-boys, sissies, letting other mens ride them like wenches" (Fleming, "Ultimate" 42). Neptune's ahistorical and homophobic understanding of Black homosexuality defines "gal-boys" as "ruined" because they are not the men who are doing the riding but the men who are being ridden. Indeed, Neptune's ruined Black man is an example of what Scott calls the "figure of the bottom," who functions in the works of Cleaver and Baraka as "a handy reference both to historically produced political realities and to its sexual connotations as a powerful signification for the harm that has been done to black men" (164).[4] Considering Cleaver's and Baraka's use of the figure of the bottom, the problem with how Neptune uses that figure in his narrative is that Miz Gertrude's monstrosity is not tied to her being a rapist but to her ability to ride Black men in such a way that they become bottoms. Thus, while Neptune's narrative highlights the dangers of Black men engaging in sexual relationships with White women in the Jim Crow South, it also suggests that Black bottoms are inauthentic Black men, reaffirming the not-ness monster's conception of the "real" Black man as straight, hypersexual, obsessed with White women, and invulnerable to rape.

Like their respectability counterparts, Maybelle and Miz Gertrude are not-ness monsters who insist that they are not sexually assaulting their Black male victims because Black males are hypersexual. According to that logic, one cannot rape someone who is always willing to have sex; therefore, Maybelle and Miz Gertrude imagine themselves as sexual altruists who are helping Black men experience some happiness in the anti-Black world of Jim Crow by allowing them to engage in sexual intercourse with a White woman. While the moral sadism of Maybelle and Miz Gertrude reimagines the sexual abuse of Black men as a virtuous act, it also promotes what Jewelle Gomez refers to as the "single-issue" view of Black freedom, which claims that racism is the primary or only -ism that that negatively affects Black America and that straight Black men are racism's main target ("Speculative" 951). According to the single-issue view, as represented by Neptune's and Miz Gertrude's belief that the authentic Black man is straight and that Black bottoms are "ruined," Black gay men are not the target of Miz Gertrude's and the peckerwoods' violence because they are not viewed as pleasurable or as threats to Jim Crow. Fleming's depictions of Neptune and Miz Gertrude as voices of the single-issue view suggest that the victims of the

---

4. Scott notes that the two meanings of the bottom, "the nadir of a hierarchy" and a "sexual position," imply that the bottom figure can be used to represent power, pleasure, and resistance, as exhibited in his reading of Samuel R. Delany's *The Mad Man* (1994): "Delany's protagonist navigates the position of sexual/racial 'bottom' as a complex, empowered political persona and potentially demonstrates how a history of sexual domination endows the figure of blackness with nimble abilities, with a form of power" (206).

not-ness monster might hold ideas about Black masculinity that foster anti-Black male oppression. Indeed, given that the single-issue view normalizes the straight Black man as *the* image of Black freedom (Jenkins, *Paradox* 25), Neptune's and Miz Gertrude's views about the authentic Black man erase Black gay men from discussions of Black freedom because it is assumed that they are unable to generate the emotions that are needed to transform a person's desire for Black men into anti-Black necrophilia. However, as Maybelle and Miz Gertrude indicate in their decision to break antimiscegenation laws, any Black man whom they want to be "furrowed" by will pay the price of unemployment, imprisonment, or death if he is unable to pleasure them to their satisfaction. As highlighted by Rickey Windell George's "Good 'Nough to Eat," a Black male's self-defined sexuality does not matter to the not-ness monster precisely because that monster reduces the Black male to a penis, a thing that is defined by others because it lacks the ability to define itself.

Not-Ness Monstrosity in Extreme Horror

Set in a Black working-class neighborhood in urban America at the beginning of the twenty-first century, George's "Good 'Nough to Eat" documents the experiences that led Kelly, the story's protagonist, to be castrated at a ladies-only strip club. The story begins with Kelly, who is "one step from begging," desperately seeking employment because he and his girlfriend Sheila are on the verge of being evicted from their apartment, which he describes as a "god-damned, overpriced roach motel" (George 212). Although Sheila works as waitress to help pay rent, her wages cannot support the two of them, and Kelly does not want Sheila to ask her suburban middle-class father, who hates him, for money because Kelly sees himself as Shelia's "man," as her breadwinner. To make money in the absence of decent jobs, Kelly engages in what he considers indecent work, making money from his big penis, since "indecency promised to keep the lights on and the roof over his and Sheila's heads" (228). For example, Kelly will sometimes unzip his pants and charge a fee for those who want to see his unusually big penis in the flesh (209). According to the narrator, Kelly's penis is, when flaccid, "a half-foot strong all day every day, and thick too," but his penis grows "another half-foot" when erect (211). While everyone in Kelly's life, including Sheila, thinks his oversized penis is a gift, he sees it as his "very real nightmare" (209). However, to avoid eviction, Kelly accepts the offer from Big Mamma, the owner of the "ghetto whorehouse" that he often visits (222), to be become a male stripper at her friend's ladies-only club, "Savage

Thugs Male Review." The women at the club, like everyone Kelly has come across in his lifetime, become filled with "hunger" when they see his penis, a sexual hunger so intense that they pin him down and castrate him with their teeth.

In the introduction to *Voices from the Other Side: Dark Dreams II* (2006), the anthology of Black horror that contains "Good 'Nough to Eat," Brandon Massey describes George's story as "extreme horror" that "flips black-male sexual stereotypes upside down—and tears them inside out" (2). George's story evokes Fanon's and James Baldwin's discussions of how the Black male becomes a Black penis in the White imagination. In *Black Skin, White Masks*, Fanon argues that Michel Cournot's depiction of Black men and their penises captures European culture's "imago" of the Black man (169), an unconscious, idealized, mental image of Black men that shapes White behavior. For Cournot, the Black penis is a "sword" that can make White women "really fe[el] something" during sexual intercourse, and it is so enormous that four of them, when erect, "would fill a cathedral" (qtd. in Fanon 169). In addition to linking violence and abnormality to Black men's penises, Cournot's imagery makes the reader, as Fanon puts it, "no longer aware of the Negro but only of a penis; the Negro is eclipsed. He is turned into a penis. He *is* a penis" (170). Like Fanon, Baldwin's thoughts on Black maleness and American masculinity in his "love letter" discussing his admiration for Norman Mailer as a writer and friend alludes to the consequences of perceiving the Black male as a "walking phallic symbol": the Black male "pays, in one's own personality, for the sexual insecurity of others" (102). As Baldwin suggests, being perceived as just a big, powerful, and pleasurable penis by sexually insecure others, whom Fanon and Baldwin identify as White men,[5] does not benefit Black men because they are perceived as Man-Nots and, therefore, denied the social power to have the final say on how they define themselves.

Through its use of extreme horror, George's "Good 'Nough to Eat" builds upon Fanon's and Baldwin's critiques of what Tamari Kitossa calls the "Black Phallic Fantastic," a tripartite concept of the main ways in which Black men's and boy's bodies are imagined in America and elsewhere: "priapic, hypersexual, and prone to commit rape" (xli–xlii). I draw upon Aalya Ahmad's discussion of transgressive or extreme horror, which she uses interchangeably, to show how two formal elements of extreme horror,

---

5. As the critical essays in *Appealing Because He Is Appalling: Black Masculinities, Colonialism, and Erotic Racism* (2021) point out, White men are not the only sexually insecure others who have conceptualized Black males as walking phallic symbols, since this idea is prevalent in places affected by Western colonialism.

"body horror and its close relative the bad death" (372), are essential to the story's representations of the pain that the Black Phallic Fantastic inflicts on Black males. Broadly defined, extreme horror, like its etymological ancestor "splatterpunk,"[6] refers to horror fiction that presents "prolonged and graphic representations of body horror, torture, mutilation, abjection, and violence—subjects classified as deviant according to cultural norms—and the depiction of acts that shatter social and cultural taboos, causing reactions of shock and revulsion" (365). Despite the criticism directed toward it, Coco d'Hont argues that extreme horror fiction is "deeply intertwined with the politics and culture of its extra-textual content" (377), and it demonstrates that "horror is inherent to society itself and does not emerge from some unspecified 'outside'" (379). As a result, extreme horror can function as a "form of oppositional politics" that is capable of exposing "the cultural distinctions governing taste; what is acceptable to show and not show; what constitutes abnormality and Otherness and can powerfully expose and unsettle the normativity of dominant institutions and systems" (Ahmad 365). I argue that George's use of body horror and bad death in "Good 'Nough to Eat" suggests that every American is a potential not-ness monster because being American means, in part, believing that Black men are walking penises and, therefore, incapable of love or being loved. As we will see, the difference between the not-ness monsters and unlikable humans in George's story is that the not-ness monsters not only believe in the Black Phallic Fantastic, but they are also erotically aroused by treating Black men as unloved, unloving, and mindless.

Although Sheila and Josh, Kelly's longtime White friend, are not notness monsters or unlikable humans, they are Americans who are shaped by the Black Phallic Fantastic. For instance, Sheila declares "I love you" to Kelly after their lovemaking, an attempt to assure him that he is more than a penis to her. However, Sheila's explanation of why she continues to have sex with Kelly even though it hurts her reveals the power of the Black Phallic Fantastic: "I'd rather stop walking than stop fucking you" (George 227). Though hyperbolic, her behavior prior to their lovemaking indicates that

6. The term "splatterpunk" predates the categories that make up extreme horror fiction (e.g., "Phillip Brophy's 'horrality—horror, textuality, morality, hilarity,' Isabel Cristina Pinedo's 'carnography,' [and] John McCarty's 'splatstick,' 'gorno,' and 'zomedy'") and was coined by David Schow in 1986 at the World Fantasy Convention (Ahmad 365). According to S. T. Joshi, splatterpunk is horror fiction that "features frequent and graphic descriptions of grisly violence, bloody deaths, and extreme sex, built on the aesthetics of slasher movies, punk rock, and video pornography" that are linked with "urban horror, post-industrial decay, and a confrontational, 'in-your-face aesthetic'" (qtd. in Ahmad 366).

Sheila may not be exaggerating. According to the narrator, Sheila "could not take her eyes away from the magic of it," nor could she "help but smile at its beauty" (212). Indeed, Sheila insists on having sex with Kelly despite his worries about the eviction notice, the pain that is caused by his penis, and the fact that no one is "hiring." While Sheila acknowledges Kelly's initial disinterest, she is so enchanted by his penis that she disregards it and ties his penis into a knot, or what the narrator calls a "noose," to keep it "tight" (212). By keeping it "tight," Sheila can have sex with Kelly's penis without the need for Kelly's participation or consent, implying a disturbing link between pleasure and ownership that is captured by Sheila's response to Kelly's realization that he cannot free himself from the noose: "You're all mine 'til I say otherwise" (213). Although Kelly agrees to have sex with Sheila, despite his economic worries, he does it because he "love[s] her" and because he acknowledges that Sheila would "give any part of herself to what hung between his legs" (221). Indeed, Sheila's foreplay is disturbing because it indicates that she believes, on some level, that Kelly is an unconscious thing whose primary purpose in their relationship is to be always sexually available to her.

Like Sheila, Josh is so enchanted by his best friend's penis that he admits that he has always wanted to see it but was ashamed to ask. Josh's shame is tied to the fear that Kelly might see him as gay, even though Josh is envious of Kelly because he did not "get a dick like that" and reveals that he has been "forever" trying to "spy 'round urinal walls or peep [Kelly] out in locker rooms" (214). In the same way that Sheila is enchanted by the "magic" of Kelly's penis, Josh is "hypnotized by the cobra" with his eyes saying, as the narrator tells us, *I'm not gay, . . . but I'll suck your dick if you'll let me, just to see it full-grown, just to live through it for a few vicarious minutes*" (216). Josh's desire for Kelly's penis and his dismissal of that desire as "not gay" is an example of what Jane Ward calls straight White men's "not-gay homosexual activity." These men, as Ward argues, "painstakingly avoid being mistaken as sincere homosexuals by demonstrating that the sexual encounter is something other than sex, and in many cases, they do this by agreeing that the encounter was *compelled* by others (such as older fraternity brothers) or by circumstances that left them little choice (such as the apparently quite dire need to obtain access to a particular fraternity)" (27). Indeed, Josh not only defines his "forever" desire to see and suck Kelly's penis as "not gay," but he also implies that his goal to be an actor employed by his uncle, who has told Josh that he was not "hung enough" for his pornography films, is the reason for the "desperation" and "hunger" in his question regarding the size of Kelly's penis when erect (George 215).[7] Although Kelly grants the request posed by Josh's eyes, he is disheartened because it reveals that Josh has always been "the same" as everyone else he has encountered in his life—"hungry" for his penis (216).

While Sheila and Josh are aware that Kelly is not hypersexual or prone to commit rape, they do believe that his flaccid penis is always erect. This contradictory image of Kelly's penis represents sexual dehumanization as the cost that Black men pay for the sexual desires and insecurities of others, even those who are closest to them. Thus, by desexing, degendering, declassing, and deracializing those who believe in the Black Phallic Fantastic, George's story shows that treating Black men as walking penises is, like the myth of the hypersexual Black woman, an American fantasy, a fantasy so pervasive that it has "seeped into the consciousness of Americans of all races and . . . contributed to a racial folklore that is still in existence, still growing, and still remarkable in its reach" (Kennedy 14). In this light, Sheila and Josh are not not-ness monsters or unlikable humans; rather, they are Americans who are doing what is expected of them when encountering a Black man. Thus, what turns people into not-ness monsters in George's story is not just their belief in the Black Phallic Fantastic; rather, it is that belief coupled with treating Black men as unloving and unlovable.

The first not-ness monsters who terrorized Kelly due to his desirable and envy-inspiring penis were members of his high school's junior varsity football team. These monsters, who were "pink," "brown," and "dark chocolate," raped Kelly with their hands and bars of soap in the locker room shower because they assumed that he was a gay, interpreting his flaccid penis as an erection inspired by their nakedness. However, the way in which the boys looked at Kelly's penis made it "sadly obvious" that raping him was all about hiding their homoerotic desires: "They were the ones watching him, covetous and lusty, and covering up their own confusion with this nasty game of odd man out" (George 217). The body horror experienced by Kelly not only made him hateful of himself for enjoying sexual intercourse with men, as represented by his tearful declaration that "I'm not a faggot" while angrily thrusting his penis into Josh's mouth (219), but it also made him aware that he will always be vulnerable to bodily pain because the production and consumption of sexually abused Black males is, as I noted

---

7. According to Ward, straight White men like Josh can "circumvent homophobic stigma and assign heterosexual meaning to homosexual activity" by drawing on the resources and privileges of Whiteness in America, one of which is the ability to defuse "any imagined inconsistencies" in the sexual behavior of White men while heightening the "surveillance and misrepresentation" of the sexual fluidity of men of color (21).

at beginning of this chapter, an American pastime. Indeed, the monsters who raped Kelly only received two weeks of suspension, "a small price to pay for what they'd done," while Kelly had to wear "sanitary pads to school" to absorb the bleeding produced by their hands (218). Since any discussion of extreme horror "entails an examination of the social distinctions made between high and low cultures" (Ahmad 366), the "small price" levied against the monsters can be read as an insidious distinction between *tasteful* and *tasteless* ways of sexually abusing Black males. As Kelly suggests, the monsters who raped him were punished for *how* they raped him; that is, they are punished for using *tasteless* practices to satisfy their desire for and hatred of Kelly. The insidiousness of the school's punishment is the assumption that there are *tasteful* ways of raping Black males that incur no costs for the rapists.

Unlike their monstrous siblings, whose raping of Kelly was inspired by homoeroticism and homophobia, the women who chew off Kelly's penis, referred to as "cannibal females" (George 233), are inspired by American Dream consumerism. I noted in chapter 1 that the consumption-based conception of the American Dream that became dominant by the twentieth century encouraged folks to accumulate the commodities that are deemed symbols of success to signal that they are American dreamers. Since such commodities have historically included people (e.g., slaves, spouses, and children), the quest for ownership within the American Dream is terrifying for those who are owned precisely because being owned means one is socially dead and, therefore, always susceptible to body horror and bad death. The horror of being commodified is captured by the narrator's description of Kelly's castration. For example, the woman who "took the head off" of Kelly's penis was "chewing rather than spitting even as the carmine spray flashed her and a half dozen others in the face," and the last of the cannibal females left Kelly's scrotum in a "ragged tatter" as she was being pulled away from his body by a police officer (George 233). For the cannibal females, Kelly became, as his body "twitched" from the chewing, "a short-circuited sex toy vibrating underneath them as they ate down the pole of him, snapping and biting at each other in the awful process" (233). In other words, the cannibal females' inspiration for devouring Kelly's penis is their understanding of their consumer power in the consumption-based American Dream, the same power that Kelly feels when he goes to Big Mamma's brothel: "If he was paying, he didn't have to be gentle, and there he could order what he wanted" (222). Like Kelly the brothel customer, the cannibal females believed that they paid for the right to not be gentle to Kelly the penis. As the cannibal females see it, Kelly's penis has the same representational value as the expensive house, car, jewelry, and cuisine in the consumption-based American Dream—it is a scarce commodity, symbolized by the cannibal females' "snapping and biting at each other" for more of it, that identifies those who can buy it as successful.

One might argue that Big Mamma and Silvia are also not-ness monsters since they profit from representing Black men as priapic, hypersexual, and prone to rape. For example, Big Mamma encouraged Kelly to become a stripper, telling him that there "ain't no shame in usin' our God-given gifts to make a little money" (224). Similarly, Silvia's eyes became "full of hunger and dollar signs and hungry dollar signs" after seeing and touching Kelly's penis (228), introducing him to her patrons as the club's "new king of the jungle" (231), "a black Tarzan, wearing a leopard-skin thong specially cut for his dimensions" (229). Although Big Mamma and Silvia make a living from promoting the Black Phallic Fantastic, they are not not-ness monsters since they do not use body horror or bad death to satisfy their hunger for Kelly's penis. Thus, on the one hand, Big Mamma and Silvia are like Sheila and Josh in that they are doing what is expected of the upwardly mobile American who encounters a Black man in pain.[8] Unlike Shelia and Josh, on the other hand, Big Mamma and Silvia are unlikable humans whose monetization of Kelly's penis satisfies their hunger for it. In other words, Big Mamma and Silvia stand on the line that separates the unlikable human from the human monster, since their hunger for profits appears to be the only thing that prevents them crossing that line.

In contrast to the "splatterpunk" horror of the 1980s, which involved "mingling a subversive glee with its 'slapstick,'" Ahmad notes that "some extreme horror seems to evade such social confrontations for a more nihilistic outlook" (372). George's "Good 'Nough to Eat" represents that nihilistic form of extreme horror, encapsulated by Kelly's bad death. The terms that define the sexual nihilism of Black male life in George's story are those that constitute the Black Phallic Fantastic—priapic, hypersexual, and rapist. These terms, which depict Black boys and men as always hard, always willing, and always dangerous, reduced Kelly to a penis that is admired, desired, and feared but never loved. As the narrator puts it, "[Kelly's penis] was every man's dream, but all that adoration and worship had never felt like love—it was only appetite" (George 210). Indeed, because a penis lacks,

---

8. As I noted in chapter 1, achieving the American Dream has historically required learning how to exploit Black people in pain; thus, audiences who see Black bodies in pain do not learn anything about the people experiencing the pain; instead, they learn how those bodies can be exploited to achieve the American Dream.

among other things, a consciousness, it cannot fall in love with someone, nor can it feel the love of others or be loved by others; therefore, to represent Black males as penises is to imagine them as unloved, unloving, and mindless. That representation of Black maleness not only engenders not-ness monsters, but it also excuses their sexual abuse of Black males. Excusing the violence of not-ness monsters is an issue that Lexi Davis addresses in "Are You My Daddy?" (2007), where she asks readers to consider the following question: Are there scenarios in which not-ness monsters are justified in terrorizing certain types of Black men, specifically Black men who internalize the myth of the hypersexual Black male? As we shall see, Davis's story suggests that answering that question largely depends on what is considered the real and imagined consequences of internalization.

Are There Heroic Not-Ness Monsters?

According to Michael Pass, Ellen Benoit, and Eloise Dunlap, the history of American masculinity encompasses five historical periods: "Agrarian Patriarchal (1630–1820), Commercial (1820–1860), Strenuous Life (1861–1919), Compassionate Providing (1920–1965), and the period after 1965" (166). While the first four periods "did not privilege black men as a group on a societal level," the post-1965 period represents the moment when "black men's masculinity is acknowledged on the societal level—and then only to define it as pathological and deviant" (166). Indeed, 1965 is the year when Daniel Patrick Moynihan's infamous depiction of poor and working-class Black American families as institutions of emasculated men and matriarchal women was published as *The Negro Family: The Case for National Action.* While Moynihan admits that slavery, the end of Reconstruction, Jim Crow, and anti-Black urbanization "worked against the emergence of a strong father figure" (16), he also argued that Black children without fathers, unlike their White counterparts, "flounder . . . and fail" because "White children without fathers at least perceive all about them the pattern of men working" (35). Although Moynihan acknowledges the educational, occupational, and economic advantages that the White family, "despite [its] many variants," has over Black families (35), he contends that the emergence of "strong" Black fathers will magically overcome the material and symbolic forces that privilege White families over Black families. As Candice M. Jenkins puts it, "Moynihan's report generated significant controversy not simply because of [his] claim about black matriarchy . . . but because his work appeared to emphasize not structural racism and socioeconomic disadvantage as the cause of these issues within the black family but rather something dysfunctional inherent to black culture itself" (83).

Ironically, as Roderick Ferguson notes, while Black nationalist groups in the early post–civil rights era contested Moynihan's argument that the state should be the "appropriate catalyst to masculine agency,"[9] they did agree with his thesis, inherited from E. Franklin Frazier, that Black men need to resume their role as patriarchs to overcome the "emasculating effects" of a matriarchal family structure (123). Such thinking led to what I refer to as "paternal Pan-Africanism," which "not only agreed with Moynihan's depiction of the so-called emasculated man-matriarchal woman problem but also argued that a cultural return to Africa could solve that problem" (*Paradox* 94). Even though, as Candice Jenkins points out, recent scholarship "continues to refute" stereotypes about the Black family's "brokenness or pathology" (85), "the trope of black family 'pathology' popularized by Moynihan continues to circulate in the United States, particularly in political commentary about black families from both ends of the political spectrum" (83). As we shall see, Lexi Davis's "Are You My Daddy?" is a comedy-horror story that highlights the problem with working-class Black folks adopting Moynihan's depiction of Black upward mobility.

"Are You My Daddy?," according to Brandon Massey's introduction to *Whispers in the Night*, "dishes up a load of laughs" as it follows "a young black man who just can't get away from the responsibility of serving as a child's father—a kid gifted in ways that'll make your head spin" (3).[10] The young Black man is Chris "Crisp Dollar" Duckett, the CEO and owner of a leading Los Angeles–based music promotion company and "bachelor extraordinaire" (L. Davis 65–66). Chris had been dating Shamir, the kid's mother, for two months, and she never mentioned that she had a child, so Chris was shocked when he wakes up in Shamir's bed to find Nehemiah,

---

9. Moynihan posited that the masculinization of Black males had to come from outside Black American culture (Ferguson 122). As he saw it, the US armed forces, despite its history of social and institutional racism, could serve as that outside influence because he believed that the military was not only a world where "the category 'Negro' and 'white' do not exist," but it was also an "utterly masculine world," a world "run by strong men of unquestioned authority" (Moynihan 42).

10. Before writing "wickedly entertaining, humorous stories" rooted in the paranormal, Lexi Davis wrote "hard-edged horror," which "ended after she scared herself a few times" (https://goodreads.com). In this light, her story's inclusion in *Whispers in the Night* (2007), the third volume of the *Dark Dreams* series, represents her transition from horror to paranormal humor.

her "special" son, asking him the question that will terrify Chris for the rest of his life: "Are you my daddy?" The significance of Shamir's omission is that Chris refuses to date women who have kids or want them, as he reiterates to her after she claims that he did not ask her if she was a mother: "I *told* you, no *kids*. I got too much going on. Kids are complications. I can't even kick it with a woman who has kids, and I for damn sure don't want none of my own" (63). While Shamir confesses that she did not think her parental status mattered to Chris because they have a good relationship, implying that he could "kick it" with a single mother, Chris reminds her that the relationship is good because he believed that she did not have kids. Although Chris tries to distance himself from Shamir, he always finds himself back at her house with Nehemiah asking him to be his daddy. When Chris accepts Shamir's offer for "make up sex," Nehemiah magically appears in the bedroom offering Chris a proposition: He will agree to be Nehemiah's daddy or lose his testicles. Chris discovers that Nehemiah likes making "pea-*nut* butter" from the men's testicles who dated his mother but left her because they did not want to be his daddy (82). Chris's story ends with his marriage to Shamir, and their several children, all boys who look like Nehemiah and have their brother's special quality, asking Chris every night if he is their daddy and with Chris always responding, "Hell yes, I'm your daddy" (83).

While "Are You My Daddy?" is critical of Black men who internalize the myth of the hypersexual Black male because they reduce themselves to their penises, I argue that Nehemiah's not-ness monstrosity is engendered by Black folks who have internalized Moynihan's patriarchal approach to Black progress. Like Davis's debut novel, *Pretty Evil* (2005), which "serves as a warning to all proclaimed 'playas' who like to live fast, but dangerously" (https://goodreads.com), Chris's first-person narrative functions, in part, as a warning to Black men who have internalized the myth of the hypersexual Black male. Indeed, Chris's response to Shamir's hilarious accusation that he lied to her alludes to the costs that Black men can incur attempting to live up to that myth:

"You deceived me," I said, self-righteously indignant.
  "You deceived me, too."
  "I ain't lied about nothing."
  "You said you could last a whole hour." (L. Davis 65)

In response to Shamir making fun of his hilarious claim about his sexual stamina, Chris tells us not to believe that "lie about not lasting an hour. The girl was out of her mind. She lost track of time. Believe that" (66). Chris's need to inform readers that Shamir is lying about his sexual stamina indicates that one of his major fears is to be perceived as not living up to the myth of the hypersexual Black male. While Chris's fear implies that he has benefited from being perceived as hypersexual, he provides no examples in his public or private life in which he is viewed as such. In fact, Chris's decision to have make-up sex with Shamir highlights how self-destructive the myth of the hypersexual Black male is for Black men, since that myth assumes that Black men's "horniness" always overrules concerns about their "pride" as well as their safety: "Every muscle in my body wanted to hang up on her lying behind for tricking me—except one, and it was already standing at attention" (73–74). Thus, being a hypersexual Black man sometimes requires a willingness to endanger one's life to satisfy one's penis, as evidenced by Chris's willingness to go a "bad area" of the city, where he might encounter "thugs" and the "little alien gangsta" that is Shamir's "spooky-ass snot-nose kid," because he believes that make-up sex with Shamir is going to be "off the chain" (74).

While Chris is critical of himself and other Black men who are attempting to become mythically hypersexual, he is equally critical of Black folks who have internalized Moynihan's conception of Black men. For instance, Chris reveals on his way to a date with Rachel, a woman he met two weeks prior to his encounter with Nehemiah, that Black women's attraction to him is due to his class not his imagined sexual stamina: "how many single, fine, designer suit-wearing young brothers with serious bank roll and no baby-mama drama were pulling up in a style like mine to take her out?" (72). The link between Chris's "serious bank roll" and his lack of "baby-mama drama" reveals his realization that his attractiveness and upward mobility are the result of being single and childless; therefore, having a family would end his life as a "playa," a life he thoroughly enjoys, and transform him into Moynihan's Black father, a figure that he has done everything in his life not to emulate. Yet, as represented by the ease with which Nehemiah, without providing any evidence except for his claim, convinces strangers that Chris is an absent father (66–67; 70–71), Chris's image of himself, like all Black men viewed through the lens of Man-Not-ness, is denied, negated, and determined by the fears and desires of others who are, in this case, the Black American community. For example, while Nehemiah recognizes that he is lying about Chris's parental status, he strongly believes that Chris is like his missing-in-action father and the other "horny dudes" that slept with Shamir and refused to be his daddy: "you got what you want from my mama! Now you wanna leave. Can't stick around, not even to play checkers. You selfish son of a bitch!" (80). As Nehemiah sees it, Chris is sexually exploiting his mother and is, therefore, one of many "dickheads" who has made Shamir "feel bad and look bad" after leaving her (80–81). For Nehemiah, in other words, Chris is indistinguishable from Moynihan's Black father and, as such, deserves the same fate as other victims—having his testicles mashed into peanut butter if he chooses not to be Nehemiah's daddy.

According to the logic of Nehemiah's ultimatum, Black men who have sex with Black women and do not want children are made from the same ideological cloth as the absent Black father. However, while Nehemiah calls Chris a dickhead, a reference to Chris's internalized hypersexuality, he ignores or devalues the role that he and Shamir play in her feeling and looking bad. In addition to Shamir lying to Chris about Nehemiah's existence, Nehemiah is responsible for helping Shamir attract potential fathers by transforming her real self, "the trapped-in-the-closet, overweight, curlers-in-the-hair Shamir," into her desired and desirable self, "the young, hot Shamir" with whom Chris and the other Black men will become sexually obsessed (82). Thus, Nehemiah's anger and violence, as Chris points out, is not due to Black men sexually exploiting his mother but due to his investment in Moynihan's heteropatriarchal assumptions about Black progress. Like Moynihan, Nehemiah believes that having a daddy is the only way that he and Shamir can escape the "bad area" that they live in; however, that belief has been continuously discredited throughout his lifetime, given the "thousand screams and pain-filled moans" that blasted from the "big jar" of testicles labeled "NEH'S PNUTS" (82). Yet, instead of using his special powers to help Shamir feel better about herself by expanding her career as a hair stylist and increasing her income so that she can *choose* a mate rather than always waiting to be *chosen,* Nehemiah attracts, via the "young, hot Shamir," Black men who do not want to be his daddy and then harms them for not wanting this role. In this light, Nehemiah functions as the horrific embodiment of Black people who believe that Black men who are single and childless lack *proper* masculinization and are, therefore, threats to Black working-class progress. To squash those threats, as posited by Nehemiah's method for making peanut butter, these Black men must be castrated to ensure that they will be *"nobody's* daddy" (82), that they will be unable to reproduce their conceptualization and performance of Black masculinity.

The warning offered by Davis's "Are You My Daddy?" is the same as that offered by her *Pretty Evil*: "You don't really know who or what you're taking home with you. One night of thrills could cost you a lot" (L. Davis qtd. in https://goodreads.com). Indeed, the pain that Nehemiah inflicts onto Black men's testicles symbolizes the price that Black men pay for people's investment in Moynihan's conceptualization of Black progress as a heteropatriarchal project. That project, which requires "strong" Black fathers but not a change to the material and symbolic forces that devalue them, is depicted as detrimental to Black men who do not want to be husbands and fathers because these men are viewed as dysfunctional and destructive. Even though Chris is upfront about his no-child policy, his desire to have sex without children is read by Nehemiah as a form of sexual exploitation, implying that sexual intercourse between Black people should be for procreation only since premarital straight sex always harms women because they are always susceptible to becoming single mothers. In addition to his problematic assumption that Shamir *needs* a Black husband to make her look and feel good, Nehemiah relies on Moynihan's view of what Black men are and how they should be to justify terrorizing Chris and other Black men who are and want to remain single and childless. Thus, Chris and Nehemiah are the answer to the questions alluded to at the end of my discussion of George's "Good 'Nough to Eat": how do we identify Black men who have internalized the myth of the hypersexual Black male, and what are the consequences of their internalization? While Chris can be read as representing an ambiguous outcome of internalization, given his explanation for why he does not want kids, Nehemiah represents one of the dangerous and disgusting outcomes—justifying the social and physical castration of childless Black bachelors by demonizing them as *the* reason why the working-class Black family is unable to foster upward mobility in its youth, especially its boys.

Not-Ness Monstrosity and American Manhood

Kamesha Spates and Brittany C. Slatton note that manhood in contemporary America is "fundamentally constructed around perceptions of whiteness and heterosexuality" in which straight White men are stereotyped as "financial providers and protectors" and Black masculinity is "closely associated with perceptions of dangerousness, unreliability, criminality, and an inability to serve in supportive or protective capacities" (3). The horrors produced by that understanding of American manhood and Black men's place in it are embodied by the not-ness monsters in the short stories by Richard Wright, Robert Fleming, Rickey Windell George, and Lexi Davis. Indeed, in Man-Not-ness thinking, as Curry argues, the Black male is "made into horror," and the fear of the Black male is "not solely racial antipathy; it also includes a very real sexual appetency" (*Man-Not* 34). Thus, in addition to sexually terrorizing and harming Black boys and men because of their desire and distaste for the Black male body, the monsters of not-ness in these stories are disturbing because they believe that their violence is morally valid and socially necessary. For instance, Saul and Neptune are harmed because they do not live up to the myth of the hypersexual Black male. Indeed, by failing to live up to that myth, Saul and Neptune prevent Maybelle and Miz Gertrude from achieving orgasms because they do not provide ideo-pleasure, since Saul and Neptune expose Maybelle's and Miz Gertrude's presumptions about Black men to be blatantly false. Thus, for the not-ness monster, a Black male who refutes or rejects the myth of the hypersexual Black male is a threat to America's racial social order because he is rejecting his predetermined place in that order as well as the order itself. Such a threat transforms the not-ness monster's desire for the mythical hypersexual Black male into hatred and violence.

Whereas Saul and Neptune are harmed because they do not live up to the myth of the hypersexual Black male, Kelly and Chris are terrorized because they are perceived to be reaffirming that myth or attempting to live up to it. On the one hand, Kelly is raped and castrated by the football team and the cannibal females, respectively, because they desire his unusually large penis, which is perceived to be always hard, always willing, and always dangerous. On the other hand, Chris is terrorized by Nehemiah because Chris thinks of himself as a hypersexual Black man who wants to remain a childless bachelor, which is read as a threat to Black working-class progress. While the monsters seem to imagine their abuse of Kelly as guiltless pleasure and Nehemiah's terrifying ultimatum to Chris is treated as socially necessary, both instances demonstrate that appearing to live up to the myth of the hypersexual Black male is just as dangerous for Black men as failing to meet that myth's demands.

In that no-win scenario, Black males are always vulnerable to how others define them and to the violence that is spawned by those definitions. Thus, although "an integral part of black male identity formation often includes attempts to counter these conflicting and impossible definitions of manhood" (Spates and Slatton 2), it is also the case that an integral part of not-ness monstrosity is attempting to deny Black men any power in having the final say in how they define their Blackness and maleness. That denial not only makes it difficult for Black boys and men to debunk the dangerous and disturbing myth that Black males are priapic, hypersexual, and prone to commit rape, but it also, as I discuss in chapter 4, highlights the important role of what Christina Sharpe calls "anagrammatical blackness," which refers to the ways in which the meaning of a word changes when Blackness is placed next to it, plays in Black American horror fiction. Indeed, as we have seen, Black bodies in pain are guiltlessly produced and consumed by human monsters whose anti-Black hatred and violence is driven by self-generated fears evoked by terms such as Black male, Black female, Black sexuality, Black family, and Black progress. The next chapter will give us the opportunity to see what happens in Black horror stories where *serial killer, serial killing,* and related terms abut Blackness.

CHAPTER 4

The Monsters of Serial Killing

Serial killing has a recorded history in Western culture that dates to the 1400s (Knight 1190), yet, as I noted in the introduction, the fictionalization of Ed Gein and his horrific acts by Robert Bloch and Alfred Hitchcock in 1959 and 1960, respectively, ushered in the age of the murdering maniac in American popular culture, whose most enduring representation is the serial killer. Unlike the human monsters of teratology, who are defined by their physiological abnormalities, the serial killing monster in popular culture, especially the horror genre, is the product of an abnormal mind. Representing two "warring discourses" in one body, the serial killer is a human monster whose "severe mental disability" results in committing acts that are "beyond the ken of human experience," making the serial killer a person who "cannot be treated and rehabilitated, only destroyed" (Poole 158). One point that stands out in popular culture's untreatable serial killer is the assumption that people with severe mental illnesses that compel them to harm and terrorize people are monsters. The problem with that assumption is that it not only dehumanizes and demonizes those who suffer from severe forms of mental illness, but it also lacks credible support.[1] According to Zelda Knight, for example, while serial killers are terrifying because they "enjoy" killing people, they are disturbing because their behavior "highlights a small but troublesome group of people in society who engage in acts of insanity and terrorism but who are not insane" (Knight 1189–90). Similarly, the FBI has pointed out that serial killers, regardless of motive, kill because they want to; however, "the exception to this would be those few killers suffering from a severe mental illness" (18). Like Knight and the FBI, the Black American horror stories examined in this chapter—R. J. Meaddough III's "The Death of Tommy Grimes" (1962), Chesya Burke's "Chocolate Park" (2004), Michael Boatman's "Our Kind of People" (2006), and Dia Reeves's *Slice of Cherry* (2011)—propose that serial killing monsters are dangerous and disgusting because they are sane.

I argue in this chapter that the works by Meaddough, Burke, Boatman, and Reeves expose another problem with popular horror's untreatable serial killer—the killer's violence, rather than the thinking and desires behind that violence, is the issuing source of horror. By removing insanity as possibility for the serial killer's actions, their works propose that motive and victim selection are key factors in determining the humanity or monstrosity of a serial killer. According to the FBI, there are at least seven general categories of motivation associated with serial killing (i.e., "Anger," "Criminal Enterprise," "Financial Gain," "Ideology," "Power/thrill," "Psychosis," and "Sexually-based"), and a serial killer may have multiple motives for killing people (17–18). While the fictional serial killers examined in this chapter have different motives for killing, none fall into the category of psychosis, "a situation in which the offender is suffering from a severe mental illness and is killing because of that illness" (18). As Samuel Adjorlolo and Heng Choon (Oliver) Chan point out, since a key feature in aggressive behaviors, such as serial killing, is intention, we should see serial killing as "a conscious act in which the perpetrator actively conceives and acts on his/her intentions, including the choice of victim, victim body disposal method and location, time of the day to commit the offense, and ways used to evade police detection and delay body discovery" (489). Indeed, since the fictional serial killers

---

1. As the Federal Bureau of Investigation (FBI) noted in its *Serial Murder: Multi-Disciplinary Perspectives for Investigators* (2008): "Much of the general public's knowledge concerning serial murder is a product of Hollywood productions. Story lines are created to heighten the interest of audiences, rather than to accurately portray serial murder. By focusing on the atrocities inflicted on victims by 'deranged' offenders, the public is captivated by the criminals and their crimes. This only lends more confusion to the true dynamics of serial murder" (2–3).

examined herein were not forced by others to murder people, their decision to kill is intentional, as is their choice of victims. Given their emphasis on motive and victim selection, the texts by Meaddough, Burke, Boatman, and Reeves call for a definition of the serial killer that does not focus on the number or type of deaths committed by the killer at the expense of why the killer kills and whom they decide to kill.

Even though serial killing has a long history in Western culture, Emma E. Fridel and James Alan Fox note in 2018 that "serial murder is one of the least understood terms in the literature of criminology and psychology" (505). For example, while Fridel and Fox focus on addressing the minimum victim threshold for serial killing and recommend "the use of three victims for the minimum threshold" (510), Adjorlolo and Chan argue for a definition of serial murder that "deviates from prior research definitions by taking into account not just the number of murders, but also the legal and scientific requirement for associating murders to suspects" (490). As they see it, a serial murder is defined by three key elements: "(1) Two or more forensic[ally] linked murders with or without a revealed intention of committing additional murder, (2) the murders are committed as discrete event(s) by the same person(s) over a period of time, and (3) where the primary motive is personal gratification" (490). Adjorlolo and Chan's definition of serial murder aligns with the definition of the serial killer offered by Richard Wayne Charlton and Jaco Barkhuizen in *The Encyclopedia of Criminology and Criminal Justice* (2014): "a person who kills two or more victims, usually strangers, at different times and at different locations, with a cooling-off period between the murders. The motive is psychological (intrinsic). The victims might be tortured, sexually abused and/or mutilated, and the serial killer might also participate in necrophilia and cannibalism. The killings are intensified by a fantasy element unique to each killer, and the act of serial homicide is behavior that expresses a personal need of the offender" (par. 3).

In each of the definitions above, the serial killer's "personal gratification," "personal need," and unique "fantasy element" are as important as the number of victims killed or how they were murdered. Moreover, according to the FBI, in addition to helping investigators narrow their focus and potential subject pool, attempting to discern the motivations for serial murders enhances the investigator's understanding of a serial killer's selection of victims (17):

> An offender selects a victim, regardless of the [motivation] category, based upon availability, vulnerability, and desirability. Availability is explained as the lifestyle of the victim or circumstances in which the victim is involved,

that allow the offender access to the victim. Vulnerability is defined as the degree to which the victim is susceptible to attack by the offender. Desirability is described as the appeal of the victim to the offender. Desirability involves numerous factors based upon the motivation of the offender and may include factors dealing with the race, gender, ethnic background, age of the victim, or other specific preferences the offender determines. (18)

While desirability is what links the motives for killing people with the pleasures of killing people, that link can also be tied to availability and vulnerability in that the ease or difficulty of accessing and overpowering victims can incite desire and function as justification for motive. Thus, although the search for a motive may not be helpful in identifying a serial murderer or could derail the investigation by wasting resources on such discovery (17), motive is nevertheless crucial to understanding the joy that serial killers receive from killing people and why they choose specific people to be their victims. As I show throughout this chapter, motivation is the line that separates serial killing humans from serial killing monsters in the works of Meaddough, Burke, Boatman, and Reeves. Indeed, one point that each of these stories makes is that generating bad deaths does not transform serial killers into monsters; rather, the beliefs and fantasies behind the bad deaths, partly reflected in their victim selection, are responsible for their human-to-monster transformation.

Anagrammatical Blackness and the Anti-Black Serial Killer

Published a few years after Bloch's *Psycho* and Hitchcock's cinematic adaption of Bloch's novel, Meaddough's "The Death of Tommy Grimes" is a fictional serial killer narrative that anticipates a trend that will become increasingly popular by the twenty-first century—telling serial killing stories from the perspectives of the serial killers (see Murphy 126). Meaddough's story follows an adolescent Tommy and his father, whom he refers to as Pa, on an early morning hunt in a Mississippi forest. Tommy has never liked to kill anything, and Pa has expressed disapproval of Tommy's apprehension to kill: "Tommy, damnit, a man *always* dies a little when he kills something, but it just plain has to be done. Some animals just ain't no damn good and got to be *killed*" (Meaddough 408). What propelled Tommy to overcome his fear of killing and join the morning hunt with Pa is his desire to become a man like Pa, a desire captured by the narrator's interpretation of Tommy's feelings of excitement and dread as he prepares for his first kill: "*Soon they would be calling him Tom Grimes like his father. Soon he would be able to go into the Hut and drink liquor with the rest of the men. Soon the waiting will be over. Soon he would be grown*" (411). When Tommy finally makes his first kill, he is initially horrified because he thought that he accidentally killed Pa, but he soon learns that he has killed a young Black man. After Pa and Tommy make the mile-long journey to the Hut, Tommy learns that Pa and the men at the Hut are hunters who prey on Black men. Thus, Tommy's murder of a Black man represents not only his death as a boy and a human, but also his birth as a White man and a monster, a birth that suggests a disturbing link between White manhood and anti-Blackness.

I argue that "The Death of Tommy Grimes" not only problematizes the role that family often plays in twenty-first-century narratives about fictional serial killers, but it also depicts "anagrammatical blackness," which Christina Sharpe defines as an "index of violability and also potentiality" (*In the Wake* 75), as shaping the ideological motive of the story's anti-Black serial killers. In the literal sense, anagrammatical Blackness refers to the moments when a word, phrase, or name is created when Blackness abuts another word, while anagrammatical Blackness in the metaphorical sense refers to moments when "grammatical gender falls away and new meanings proliferate" as a result of attaching Blackness to certain words (76). In other words, the metaphorical understanding of anagrammatical Blackness speaks to "blackness's signifying surplus: the ways that meaning slides, signification slips, when words like *child, girl, mother,* and *boy* abut blackness" (80). As I show in this chapter, the serial killing monsters in "The Death of Tommy Grimes" represent the horrors that emerge when anagrammatical Blackness informs these monsters' ideological motives.

Poole notes that the serial killing monsters in American popular culture (e.g., Norman Bates, Leatherface, Michael Myers, Jason Voorhees, Buffalo Bill, Hannibal Lecter, Patrick Bateman, Dexter, Big Driver, and Bob Anderson) tend to be White men who "share a common tale of family dysfunction" (176), and they are often portrayed as monsters "who threatened not only the lives but also the values of middle-class Americans" (156). Although Tommy, his father, and the Hut men are White, they are not the products of dysfunctional families or viewed as a threat to White middle-class lives and values. Indeed, although Pa is disappointed that Tommy is scared to kill, he did teach Tommy, with great care, "how to track animals and how to lead quail, and how to lean into the rifle to take up the recoil. And Pa showed him how to lie quiet so the forest forgot he was there and Nature went on about her business" (Meaddough 409). Moreover, the night before

Tommy's first hunt with his father, Pa is so convincing in his description of the forest's diversity of flora and fauna as a "beautiful thing" that Tommy begins to question if he wants to disturb the forest's beauty by hunting (410). As suggested by these examples, Pa is not an abusive, insane, or disinterested father, and the life lessons that he teaches Tommy are aimed at making Tommy a man who is self-sufficient, respected by his peers, and in harmony with nature. Since Pa has not been overt about his anti-Black beliefs, Tommy is surprised, as well as readers, to learn that the life lessons Pa has taught him were also meant to be lessons on how to hunt and kill Black men. Indeed, Pa's lessons are responsible for the lack of guilt and horror Tommy feels after Pa orders him to look at the victim: "So he looked, and then it wasn't so bad" (413). Tommy's response not only reveals how Pa's lessons prepared him to view killing a Black man as not "so bad," but it also indicates that the reason why Tommy will follow in Pa's footsteps and become an anti-Black serial killer is not due to being raised in a dysfunctional family; rather, it is due to ideology, what the FBI describes as "a motivation to commit murders in order to further the goals and ideas of a specific individual or group, [such as] terrorist groups or an individual(s) who attacks a specific racial, gender, or ethnic group" (18).

I noted earlier in this chapter that desirability plays a major role in a serial killer's selection of victims and is shaped by the killer's motives and the pleasures that the killer receives from killing. Indeed, Pa's glowing declaration to the men at the Hut that Tommy has become a man highlights the dangers of anagrammatical Blackness:

> "Boys, I wanna tell you my boy became a man today. Yessir, killed his first n——."
>   "No!" a man said. "Who?"
>   "Swamp-buck got away from the chain gang yes-tidy" (Meaddough 413).

Tommy's murder of a Black man and Pa's celebration of it represent the horrors that can occur when words such as *man* and *freedom* abut Blackness in the mind of an anti-Black serial killer. In his reference to the dead Black man as a "n——" and "Swamp-buck," Pa disassociates *man* and *freedom* from *Black man* and *Black freedom* to justify his son's crime as well as his own. As Tommy recalls, Pa's explanation for the need to kill Black people alludes to the fear that, as I discuss in chapter 1, many White folks during Jim Crow had of free Black men: "Pa said that man preyed on himself, whatever that meant, but everything had a place, and when they got out of place they upset the balance" (411). Like the farmer's wife in Du Bois's "Jesus Christ in

Texas," Pa believes that a Black man escaping the chain gang could never be a victim of Jim Crow's racially unjust system precisely because the "place" designated for him in that system is the chain gang. Since White life during Jim Crow relied on the subjugation of Black freedom, Black humanity, and Black progress, killing Black men is not a sporting contest for Pa; rather, it is serious work that must be done to protect White life.

While Pa asserts that he is metaphorically dead due to hunting and killing Black men, he also portrays his "death" as a heroic sacrifice: "Man kills once and he starts to get callous. Next time it ain't so hard. Then you get so's you make a decision that something's got to die and you kill it, just like that. Then you dead, boy. You got no feeling no more so you just as good as dead. You just ain't had time to lay down" (411). Even though Pa acknowledges that Tommy's humanity died when he became a "man," that death, as indicated by Pa's approach to keeping the forest's beauty intact, was necessary to protect White people from Black freedom:

> It *is* nice, boy, real nice, but things got to be done to keep it that way. Fox eats a rabbit, he keeps the rabbit population down, else they'd overrun the land. Same here. You hunt 'cause you hungry and got to eat, that's one reason. Then you might hunt for sport—pit your mind against animal cunning—'course I don't hold much with that, but some do. Some do. But there's some varmints that do damage and just plain got to be killed. (410)

Pa's reference to Black people as troublesome wild animals who must be killed because they "do damage" to the niceness of White life not only reflects his disassociation of *human* from *Black human*, but it also serves to beautify Jim Crow and its anti-Black violence. In this light, Tommy's murder of a Black man is not the only reason why Pa is proud of Tommy. Pa is also proud of Tommy's not-so-bad response to killing a Black man because it is a sign that Tommy will follow in his footsteps. Indeed, Tommy "smiled happily" as he drank the liquor Pa ordered for him, realizing that he finally "belonged," that he is now, as the man at the Hut told him, "a real live honest-to-goodness 'fore God man" (413). However, the White man Tommy has become is one who has forsaken his humanity, implying that a White boy does not need to be raised in a dysfunctional family to become an anti-Black serial killer, but he does need a belief system in which anagrammatical Blackness exists and functions as an index of violability rather than one of potentiality. Like "The Death of Tommy Grimes," Burke's "Chocolate Park" is concerned with the motives that produce anti-Black serial killers; however, Burke's story focuses on those killers who are Black.

The Business of Anti-Black Serial Killing

Set in the 1990s, Burke's "Chocolate Park" focuses on a grieving mother and a family of sisters living in an inner-city housing project. While the family of sisters—eighteen-year-old Ebony, fourteen-year-old Sable, and twenty-year-old Coco (who has become a crack-addicted sex worker named Chocolate)—is learning to cope and survive after their mother's death, Lady Black is the grieving mother who lost her son Jacob to drug addiction and is seeking to punish the drug dealer who killed him. In addition to being neighbors in the same housing project, what links Lady Black to the family of sisters is Torch, a sadistic drug dealer who rapes Sable, abuses Coco, and kills Jacob. The story ends with Ebony and Sable leaving the housing project after Sable kills Coco and with Lady Black killing Torch, whose birth name is Eddie Roberts, through her use of "black magic" or what the narrator calls "the fine art" (C. Burke 58). Burke's story, on the one hand, honors and revises what Kinitra D. Brooks refers to as "folkloric horror."[2] According to Brooks, "Chocolate Park" follows "the black feminist literary tradition of tackling difficult subjects that affect black women's lived realities—but actively use[s] horror and supernatural elements to highlight the ways that African spirituality offers both problems and solutions" (109). More specifically, Brooks argues that Burke "actively celebrates the epistemological benefits of traditional African religions by constructing several intense scenes in which she rights the wrongs of the project's predators by enacting spiritual justice" (110).

On the other hand, as I demonstrate in this chapter, "Chocolate Park" is also an example of what Bernice M. Murphy calls "victim-centered narratives" of fictional serial killers, one that problematizes the myth that all serial killers are White males by showing how the promise of status and money can transform some Black people into anti-Black serial killers. According to Murphy, victim-centered narratives revolve around "prospective victims and other innocent parties who are pulled into the serial killer's chaotic wake" (121). Unlike "procedural narratives," which feature "FBI agents/profilers/cops whose investigations of the darkest facets of human nature

---

2. Brooks identifies the following as the four facets of folkloric horror: (1) "folkloric horror highlights knowledge systems grounded in the cosmologies of natal African religions such as Vodou, Obeah, and Santería"; (2) folkloric horror accepts "spiritual possession as a valid ontology and valued epistemological tool"; (3) "folkloric horror privileges the experience of the spiritual bildungsroman, the discovery of a young woman's powerful self while under the tutelage of spiritual mentors and elders"; and (4) folkloric horror "center[s] itself on the realization and celebration of the black spiritual feminine to achieve a revised literary articulation of the Mambo, the Santera, and the Obeah woman" (102–3).

are interspersed with scenes in which the brutal mechanics of violent death take centre stage" (119), victim-centered narratives "focus more intently on the horror of everyday life horrifically disrupted by the violent Other" (122). Indeed, for Lady Black and the family of sisters, living in their project building is an everyday horror, a place "not suited for rats" but that is nevertheless filled with rats and people who are restricted to "long, hard workdays for very little money" (C. Burke 58). For its "overworked" residents, the horror of project life is its extremely limited paths of escape, given that the housing projects is a place "where you could get in, but getting out was a son-of-a-bitch" (58). Consequently, if one cannot escape the projects, then one is forced to deal with the "resident rats" of the projects such as the pedophile Fast Charley, whose attempts at grooming Sable are thwarted by Lady Black (59), or the anti-Black serial killer Torch, who horrifically disrupts the lives of Lady Black and the family of sisters by killing Jacob and raping Sable.

Torch's motivation for violence challenges an assumption about the serial killer that tends to be present in twenty-first-century fictional serial killer narratives, including the procedural and victim-focused categories—the serial killer is a "criminal threat which embodies disorder, irrationality and chaos" (Murphy 118). That image of the serial killer reiterates the myth that "serial killers have either a debilitating mental condition, or they are extremely clever and intelligent" (FBI 5). According to that myth, the only or primary reason why serial killers enjoy committing murder is due to a severe mental illness, implying that sane people would not enjoy murdering people or that society is essentially blameless for why serial killers exist. In contrast to the insane-evil genius myth that pervades twenty-first-century fictional serial killer narratives, Burke's depiction of Torch, like Meaddough's depiction of Pa, reveals the real-life horrors that are produced by sane serial killers who live in a society that encourages their behavior. Indeed, Torch embodies the order and rationality of what the FBI refers to as the "Criminal Enterprise" motive. Defined as "a motivation in which the offender benefits in status or monetary compensation by committing murder that is drug, gang, or organized crime related" (FBI 18), criminal enterprise represents those worlds where business and serial killing meet, where killing is required to elevate one's status and increase one's profits. Thus, Torch kills Jacob not because he disliked Jacob but because the business of drug dealing demands that he kills those who steal from him, even if he is responsible for their addiction to his drugs and the theft that results from that addiction: "Jacob hadn't been the first employee he'd had put down for stealing from him. And he hadn't been the last. But he was the only one that Torch had regretted" (C. Burke 68). Although Torch "regretted" killing Jacob, "if he had let the boy live, he would have been taken as a pussy. His competitors and junkies would have tried to run all over him" (68). In this way, Torch is like Pa, since both kill because they feel that they must, not because they want to.

Another way in which Torch and Pa are similar is their selection of victims. Indeed, both select Black victims whom American society has deemed as expendable—poor and working-class Black folks. While Pa's anti-Black serial killing is supported by Jim Crow laws and social practices, Torch's is supported by America's "War on Drugs" that began in the 1970s but was amplified by the presidential administrations of Reagan, Bush, and Clinton during the 1980s and 1990s. For example, Angela Y. Davis pointed out in 1998 that "women are far more likely than men to be imprisoned for a drug conviction. . . . Decriminalization of drugs would greatly reduce the numbers of incarcerated women, for the 278 percent increase in the numbers of black women in state and federal prisons (as compared to the 186 percent increase in the numbers of black men) can be largely attributed to the phenomenal rise in drug-related and specifically crack-related imprisonment" (276). Similarly, for more than three decades after that War on Drugs began, as Michelle Alexander notes, "images of black men in handcuffs have been a regular staple of the evening news" (226), and media images such as those, along with political rhetoric, popular culture, and incarceration rates, have convinced many Americans that Black men (and Brown men) are justly imprisoned: "These racialized narratives tend to confirm and reinforce the prevailing public consensus that we need not care about 'those people'; they deserve what they get" (227). Given the above, it is disturbingly not surprising that Black people, by 2001, comprised thirty-six percent of the people "in prison, on probation, and on parole," while accounting for roughly twelve percent of the US population (Russell-Brown 8). As Alexander puts it, "Despite the jaw-dropping impact of the 'get-tough' movement on the African American community, neither the Democrats nor the Republicans revealed any inclination to slow the pace of incarceration" (71).

Thus, Torch preys on and kills Black people whom the War on Drugs has declared as ready for imprisonment or removal from society—those living in the housing projects of urban America. His response to those who would argue that drug dealing and burning people are morally wrong, destructive to those in the projects, and simply inhumane is reflective of the rationale that supports that war. As Torch sees it, "Those who he dealt with were already at the bottom of the human trash-heap, had usually surpassed help, and were destructive to only themselves" (C. Burke 70). Implicit in Torch's logic is a distinction between he and Pa—although both are anti-Black serial killers, Pa's selection of Black people as victims is shaped by a desirability rooted in anagrammatical Blackness, whereas Torch's selection is shaped primarily by an availability and a vulnerability rooted in the acquisition of status and money. In other words, Torch does not kill Black people in the projects because they are his desired victims; rather, he kills them because the War on Drugs has made them easily accessible and always vulnerable to his violence by confining his business operations to the inner city.[3]

Another way in which Torch and Pa differ is via the types of pleasure they receive from killing their Black victims. While Pa's pleasure is ideological, Torch's pleasure derives from his sexualization of his acquisition of status and money. For instance, after using a hammer to break Jacob's kneecaps and ten fingers as he begged for his life, Torch shot Jacob in head and "set the body on fire and watched it burn for as long as he could" (68). While Torch claims that his murder of Jacob was about business, watching the body burn indicates that he derived pleasure from setting Jacob ablaze. Torch's threat to Coco, who also stole drugs from him, combines the act of making money with the pleasure of burning people: "I'll burn my money out of your ass, if I have to" (51). Even when Torch is not burning people, he sexualizes the violence he uses for business. For example, after Torch and his "employees" gang raped Sable because Coco owed him money (55), he confesses to himself that he enjoyed the brutality he inflicted on Sable: "Pleasure had been the young girl from across the street. Chocolate's sister. Even he had to admit that, if he had a vice, it was women. Virgins" (69). While Torch enjoyed raping Sable and hopes to rape Ebony in the near future, his warning to Sable speaks to the role that making money plays in shaping his enjoyment: "Tell Chocolate, I want my money, Or the next time I'll kill you, bitch" (55). Thus, while Torch's motivation to kill appears to fall in the category of sexually based murders, which means that his sexual needs/desires drive him to kill (FBI 18), the only time he kills or commits bodily violence is when he stands to lose money or status. Given Torch's motivation, one

---

3. Alexander succinctly explains this confinement in the following passage:

> The enduring racial isolation of the ghetto poor has made them uniquely vulnerable in the War on Drugs. What happens to them does not directly affect—and is scarcely noticed by—the privileged beyond the ghetto's invisible walls. Thus it is here, in the poverty-stricken, racially segregated ghettos, where the War on Poverty has been abandoned and factories have disappeared, that the drug war has been waged with the greatest ferocity. SWAT teams are deployed here; buy-and-bust operations are concentrated here; drug raids of apartment buildings occur here. Black and brown youth are the primary targets. (156)

wonders if he would enjoy or even commit his acts of horror if he believed that his money and status were always secure.

As a victim-centered narrative, "Chocolate Park" focuses on how Lady Black and the family of sisters struggle to survive project life and Torch's physical and psychological violence. However, by depicting Torch as a serial killer who is Black and sane, Burke resists the temptation to continue the myth found in most twenty-first-century fictional serial killer narratives— the belief that all serial killers are White males. As suggested by Burke's depiction of Torch, the racialization of the serial killer as White is a form of race realism in which it is believed that one's race determines the types of killing one will commit. Indeed, Torch reminds us of the FBI's findings on race and serial killing: "Contrary to popular belief, serial killers span all racial groups. . . . The racial diversification of serial killers generally mirrors that of the overall U.S. population" (4). While Burke's depiction of Torch as Black and sane does not interrogate the myth that all serial killers are male, which I will take up in my discussion of Dia Reeves's *Slice of Cherry*, it does disrupt the narrative practice of using mental illness as the primary reason why serial killers, including the Hannibal Lecter–like evil geniuses, commit murder. Like Pa, Torch kills not because he is an evil genius or mentally ill but because he must and wants to. As Torch sees it, to acquire and keep the status and money that he has earned from his criminal enterprise, he had to become a serial killer. While Torch derives pleasure from burning, raping, and killing people, that violence is always tied to protecting his status and profits. Moreover, Burke's depiction of Torch emphasizes the role that the state plays in how serial killers chose their victims. Torch's victims are Black not because he desires Black victims but because the War on Drugs has confined his criminal enterprise to an inner-city Black community and has defined its residents as humanity's "trash-heap," making the residents of that community easily accessible and susceptible to his inhumane violence. Like "Chocolate Park," Boatman's "Our Kind of People" depicts a Black serial killer who views poor and working-class Black folks as part of the trash-heap of humanity. However, Boatman's anti-Black serial killer, unlike Torch, is a member of the Black elite and includes his class of Black folks in humanity's trash-heap.

Anti-Black Serial Killing and the Anger of the Black Elite

Boatman's "Our Kind of People" can be read as a fictional response to Lawrence Otis Graham's *Our Kind of People: Inside America's Black Upper Class*

(1999). Graham states that the goal of writing *Our Kind of People* is to provide a "chronicle" of the Black American elite, "a community that [has been] hidden from so many people" (xviii). Graham, who is a member of this hidden and inward-looking community, believed that a book about the Black elite would be "interesting," since it tells the story of a community whose "history of thriving in the awkward position between two worlds—one black and one white"—has led to them being "misunderstood" by both racialized groups (xvii–xviii). As Graham sees it, a large part of this misunderstanding is based on the "pride and guilt" that shapes this community's Blackness:

> On one level, there are those of us who understand our obligation to work toward equality for all and to use our success in order to assist those blacks who are less advantaged. But on another level, there are those of us who buy into the theories of superiority, and who feel embarrassed by our less accomplished black brethren. These self-conscious individuals are resentful of any quality or characteristic that associates them with that which seems ordinary. (18)

Thus, according to Graham, while the Black elite is proud of its history of success in a nation that has historically suppressed Black success, as well as its role as savior for the "less advantaged," many of its members feel guilty because they do not to want to be lumped together with the less advantaged. The potential consequences of the pride-guilt tension that shapes the elite Blackness described by Graham is horrifically represented by Boatman's "Our Kind of People."

Like "The Death of Tommy Grimes," "Our Kind of People" is a fictional serial killer narrative that is told from the perspective of the killer. Set in contemporary New York City, Boatman's story documents the last night of life for Marcellus Craft, an anti-Black serial killer who is the son of upper-middle-class Black professionals. Marc, as Marcellus is called by the narrator, was raised in a "respectable" Connecticut neighborhood that was "miles distant from the urban nightmares of places like Stamford and New York." After graduating from Yale's law school, Marc attained a "lucrative position" at a top Manhattan law firm, which allowed him to buy a spacious apartment in one of the most expensive neighborhoods in New York City (Boatman 126). Marc's background is noteworthy because his last night of life begins with the end of a date with a Black woman who is also part of the Black elite. She is not only the daughter of a "prominent black judge," who happens to be a long-time friend of Marc's father, and hails from "one of the better black families in her upper Westchester County town," but is also a "former Miss Black New York [and] an accomplished young physician"

(123–24). The young woman seems like the perfect partner for Marc, since both are the "right kind of people," as his mother told him on his voicemail, but the narrator, conveying Marc's feelings about the young woman, refers to her as "Miss Wrong" and "the waste." Marc rejects the young woman's request for him to come into her apartment because, as he thinks to himself, *"if I come inside, I'll cut your head off"* (123). Although Marc's desire to kill Miss Wrong is motivated by the pleasure that he receives from killing, it is also motivated by his disdain for his "kind of people," which is also represented by his desire for Lady Love, a nonhuman monster who takes the form of a homeless White woman and gives birth to Marc's *children*, creatures who commit patricide upon their birth.

I argue that Marc's serial killing is not motivated by what Ann duCille refers to as an "embarrassment of riches,"[4] but by an anti-Black anger born out of Du Bois's talented tenth ideology, what I am calling "Old Tenth" ideology. In "The Talented Tenth" (1903), Du Bois argues that Black people, like all other racialized people, are going to be "saved by [their] exceptional men," who will have the proper education to "guide the Mass away from the contamination and death of the Worst, in their own and other races" (133). While Du Bois insists that the Black elite will help the Black non-elite, he also supports an idea promoted by Andrew Carnegie in "The Gospel of Wealth" (1887)—that being civilized means embracing economic inequality:

> The contrast between the palace of the millionaire and the cottage of the laborer with us to-day measures the change which has come with civilization. This change, however, is not to be deplored, but welcomed as highly beneficial. It is well, nay, essential for the progress of the race, that the houses of some should be homes for all that is highest and best in literature and the arts, and for all the refinements of civilization, rather than that none should be so. (par. 1)

---

4. According to duCille, the "embarrassment of riches" is a discourse about Blackness and class that represents a form of internalized racism in which middle-class Black intellectuals feel guilty about their economic success because such success somehow makes one less Black because they are economically separated from "the people" (28). Indeed, duCille makes a compelling case for why the embarrassment of riches discourse limits Black possibility and supports anti-Blackness: "The real power of whiteness—the actual evidence of internalized racism—is how readily many African Americans have accepted the notion that authentic blackness is first and finally vernacular, impoverished, illiterate" (29). Thus, unlike the guilt that haunts Graham's Black elite, a guilt engendered by the desire to distance itself from the Black non-elite, the guilt produced by the embarrassment of riches discourse is borne out of the Black elite's desire to be viewed as part of Black non-elite.

Carnegie's understanding of civilization calls for those who are the most marginalized to accept their marginalization as their contribution to humanity's progress. Du Bois makes a similar demand of the Black non-elite in "The Talented Tenth": "Can the masses of the Negro people be in any possible way more quickly raised than by the effort and example of [a Black] aristocracy of talent and character? Was there ever a nation on God's fair earth civilized from the bottom upward? Never; it is, ever was and ever will be from the top downward that culture filters. The Talented Tenth rises and pulls all that are worth the saving up to their vantage ground" (139).

Du Bois revised his racial uplift discourse in "The Talented Tenth Memorial Address" (1949) because he was criticized, and he believed rightly so, for "building an aristocracy with neglect of the masses" (159). Yet, he argues in that address that only a few "educated and specially trained experts in the main branches of science and the main categories of human work," whom he called the "one one-hundredth," could uplift the race (168). Nevertheless, as Du Bois saw it, what separated the talented tenth from the one one-hundredth, whom Joy James refers to as the "New Tenth," is that the New Tenth would develop an "international perspective" on Black agency and leadership by acknowledging that the "'races' are only cultural groups" and that "political coalitions are essential" to uplifting all Black people (James 24–25). Unfortunately, as Boatman's story highlights, the New Tenth approach to uplift did not become the dominant ideology of the late twentieth-century Black American elite; rather, an updated version of Du Bois's Old Tenth ideology dominated this group's understanding of uplift. Indeed, this version of the Old Tenth ideology, according to Angela Dillard, focuses "less on structural barriers to advancement and more on the glories of self-help, personal responsibility, moral fiber, and, of course, good old-fashioned hard work" (33). In other words, late twentieth-century concept of uplift insisted that Black ambition is all that is really needed to get through the structural barriers that keep Black people from fully integrating into mainstream America. The problem with that "highly individualistic reading" of uplift, as Dillard notes, is that it ends up reproducing "the racial (and potentially racist) assumptions of white cultural superiority, the masculinist assumptions of patriarchal authority, and the elitist assumptions that progress for the 'talented tenth' would automatically signal progress for the race as a whole" (34). Thus, if anger is, as the FBI contends, "a motivation in which an offender displays rage or hostility towards a certain subgroup of the population or with society as a whole" (18), then we can read Marc's anti-Black anger as a warning about the dangers of the Old Tenth's elitist, masculinist, and racialist/racist assumptions about Black progress—they can lead one to think that hating Blackness is a requirement for Black uplift.

Marc's background and desire to kill Miss Wrong, on the one hand, suggests that his anti-Black anger is directed at the Black elite. For example, before showing the hunting knife to a young Black man whom he is about to kill, Marc looked the young man "directly in the eye," a ritual that Marc "passed on to his victims before they died." This practice or "lesson," as the narrator describes it, was taught to Marc "at the ends of the Admiral's fists" in which Admiral would demand that the young Marc "look [him] in the eye" while he was being beaten (Boatman 127). After beating the young Marc, Admiral would tell his son that such violence is necessary if he is going to help uplift the race: *I don't hit you because I hate you, boy*, his father's rage whispered. *I hit you to make you strong. You're to be a credit to the race, Marcellus* (126). Admiral's approach to instilling Old Tenth doctrine into Marc suggests not only that there are so many problems with that doctrine that one must be forced into believing in it but also that its masculinist assumptions about the need for patriarchal authority wrongly assumes that developing phallocentric mastery over Black bodies is the only way to be a Black male who is a credit the race (see Scott 149). In other words, Old Tenth ideology did not lead to a liberated Black male identity for Marc, nor did it encourage Marc, as Admiral hoped, to help uplift the race; instead, it encouraged him to become an anti-Black serial killer.

Marc's interactions with the Black non-elite, on the other hand, reveal that his anti-Black anger is not class specific and is, therefore, directed at Blackness itself. Indeed, while Marc seems to enjoy displaying his mastery of "the art of subtle intimidation" when engaged in negotiations with "adversaries who counted their worth in the billions" (Boatman 127), adversaries whom we are to assume are mostly White or non-Black, the narrator makes it clear that Marc, like Pa, only enjoys killing or terrorizing Black people. For example, while riding the subway to meet Lady Love after leaving Miss Wrong, Marc is confronted by a group of young Black men who refer to him as one of the "stupid-ass f——ts" on the train. The homophobic slur and threat do not bother Marc because he believes that he is "different from them, *better* than them." When the group's leader, whom I mentioned earlier, approaches Marc in attempt to intimidate him, Marc asks the "big, ebony-skinned" young man who has a "scraggly beard and the eyes of a corpse" a disturbingly insightful question: "Do you read?" (127). Implicit in Marc's question is that illiteracy and homophobia are signs that someone is part of the *worst* of the race. Indeed, when the narrator tells us that Marc has "murdered men more desperate than this one and sung along at a Broadway musical twenty minutes later" (126–27), it is also telling us that Marc did not think these "desperate" Black men could be helped because their illiteracy made it impossible for them to ever be, as Admiral would put, a credit to the race. The point that Boatman seems to be making in depicting Marc's anti-Black anger as transcending class is that the racial self-hatred engendered by Old Tenth ideology encourages the Black elite to challenge what Graham refers to as one of that elite's important "traditions"—the practice of emulating Whiteness, but not marrying or having babies with White people (15).

Graham's recollection of his maternal great-grandmother's advice to him and his brother about playing in the sun reveals some of the ways in which the Black elite attempted to lighten the race without Whitening the race:

> I recall summertime visits from my maternal great-grandmother, a well-educated, light-complexioned, straight-haired black southern woman who discouraged me and my brother from associating with darker-skinned children or from standing or playing for long periods in the July sunlight, which threatened to blacken our already too-dark skin.
>
> "You boys stay out of that terrible sun," Great-grandmother Porter would say in a kindly, overprotective tone. "God knows you're dark enough already." (1–2)

As Great-grandmother Porter saw it, Black people can be lightened without marrying White, but they must take proactive measures to prevent their offspring from becoming too dark, such as keeping the kids out of the summer sun or marrying a Black person who has straight hair and light skin. According to Boatman's depiction of Lady Love, the problem with the Black elite's focus on lightening the race without Whitening the race is that such a focus can result in a racial hierarchy among the elite's straight men in which the *wrong* White woman becomes more desirable than the *right* Black woman.

Although Lady Love is not Marc's educational or economic equal and is the antithesis of the White elite's *right kind* of White woman, he thinks she is "beautiful":

> Her skin was the color of a cadaver's sclera, her hair the color of ravens' wings, encrusted with filth. Dirty black spikes leaped out from her head like a shout of exaltation.
>
> Her eyes were the color of summer skies, piercing in a face nearly black with blood and dirt. Her jaw had been paralyzed on one side by a stroke or birth defect. Her mouth hung open, her face fixed in a silent shriek. (128)

In addition to representing the color hierarchy in which the *wrong* White woman becomes more desirable than the *right* Black woman, Marc's identification of Lady Love as beautiful also implies that she, not Miss Wrong, who is referred to as "the waste," can guarantee him children who are not too dark. However, after impregnating Lady Love, which involved her grabbing him with "hands and mouth and things he couldn't see, *wouldn't* see, things that caressed him wetly, pierced him, sank talons into his flesh and hooked him to her" (129), Marc learns that his hatred of Blackness and obsession with Whiteness has resulted in him fathering his own gravediggers. Indeed, that hatred and obsession manifest in his offspring, "squirming tuber[s] of bio-matter" that are "the deep red color of heart's blood" and possess "a circular row of needle-sharp teeth." When Marc notices that one of the squirming tubers has "Admiral's eyes," he tries to escape from Lady Love and their monstrous brood, an attempt that fails because "something like a tentacle extended out of the Lady's torso" to pull Marc toward her and their children so they can eat him (130).

What is noteworthy about the Admiral-eyed tuber is that it suggests, among other possibilities, that Admiral also had sex with Lady Love, implying that the Black elite's tradition of racial lightening has always been about, despite claims to the contrary, marrying White or having racially mixed babies. For example, although Marc has checked all the boxes that are required for a Black man to be a credit to the race, Admiral would constantly remind him that the *"race must be perpetuated, elevated"* with a woman who is *"the right kind of people"* (126), while his mother would tell him that *"love is for fools and dreamers,"* an emotion that their kind of people cannot invest in because they are *"bound by a greater responsibility"* (125). Such thinking explains why Admiral "had beaten [Marc] unconscious the one time he'd dared to bring a white girl home from college" (125)—White women are not the right kind of people and, therefore, fathering biracial children is not elevating the race. In other words, although Admiral's approach to making Marc a credit to the race requires cultural Whitening, his beating of Marc indicates that he does not condone marrying White. Thus, the Admiral-eyed tuber questions if racial emulation can occur without the desire for miscegenation, given that the racial self-hatred engendered by the Black elite's tradition of racial lightening encourages its straight males, even those claiming to be anti-interracial in dating and marriage, to seek White partners.

While Marc's pursuit of Lady Love is an act of rebellion against his parents' attempt to find him a wife, it also represents one of the unexpected outcomes of the Old Tenth tradition of emulating but not marrying White— the birth of a Black elite that sees physical Whitening, after cultural Whitening, as the next step in the movement to uplift the race. Admiral's mantra concerning Marc's future children, which Marc recalls as he is being eaten by Lady Love and the squirming tubers, alludes to the consequences of the Old Tenth's notion of uplift: *"We raised you up to produce something new, Marcellus. Your children will conquer the world. But they'll have to be the right kind of people. Our kind of people"* (130). What makes these creatures "new" or different from Admiral or Marc is that they suggest that the final step in the Old Tenth approach to Black progress is the erasure of all physical traces of Blackness from the Black elite. Thus, Marc's last thought before his death, *"Mission accomplished"* (130), is a warning for the twenty-first-century Black elite—if uplifting the race continues to mean culturally and/or physically lightening the race, it will always produce an anti-Black anger that can turn Black elite men into serial killing monsters.

Black Female Serial Killers and the "Helping People" Motive

Despite the increase in fictional depictions of female serial killers, fictional serial killing stories "still overwhelmingly revolve around 'rogue males' who target women and children and cannot (or choose not to) restrain their most savage impulses" (Murphy 118). There are several reasons why that disparity exists, and these reasons are essentially the same as the reasons why there is a relative dearth of scholarship on real-life female serial killers. For instance, since most fictional serial killer narratives have been inspired by known serial killers and/or their crimes, the dearth of female serial killer narratives is partly due to the public's lack of knowledge about real-life female serial killers. As Marissa A. Harrison and her colleagues note,

> The public is not typically aware that female serial killers (FSKs) have indeed committed murders in the United States (US) for about as long as the US has been a nation. As an example, from 1802 to 1829, Martha 'Patty' Cannon, called a 'she demon' by newspapers of the time, killed men, women, and children by beating, shooting, and burning them. She also kidnapped and sold people into slavery. ("Female" 383)

In addition to the public's lack of familiarity with real-life female serial killers, the rarity of fictional female serial killer narratives is also due to the "general misconception that women in our society are, by their very nature, incapable of multiple murders," even though roughly sixteen percent of serial killers are women (384). According to that misconception, female serial killers do not even exist and, therefore, girls and women who kill multiple people over a period of time are something else besides serial killers.

Another reason why female serial killers and fictional narratives about them are rare is that these killers do not usually commit bad deaths. For example, in their discussion of the limitations of their study, Fridel and Fox note that female serial killers "rarely torture, take totems, or kill for sexual reasons, regardless of victim count" (512). Amanda L. Farrell, Robert D. Keppel, and Victoria B. Titterington point out that the way in which female serial killers tend to murder their victims partly explains why they have historically received little scholarly attention: "Women tend to kill quietly, preferring not to butcher and maim. It is unlikely you would find a woman sexually assaulting a corpse or engaging in cannibalistic or vampiric activities" (270). This suggests that how female serial killers murder their victims is viewed as less transgressive and, therefore, less sensational than how their male counterparts kill. Harrison, Susan M. Hughes, and Adam Jordan Gott argue that the *noms de guerre* of female serial killers tend to be gendered due to how our culture imagines female violence: "although not statistically significant, it is arguably meaningful that over three quarters of men had nicknames that underscored their gruesome modi operandi (e.g., 'The Bind, Torture, Kill Strangler'), versus slightly more than half of FSKs' nicknames" ("Sex" 305–6). They go on to say that while this emphasis on the female serial killer's sex might be due to law enforcement and/or the media feeling compelled to highlight the killer's gender in a case, that emphasis may also be due to the possibility that "people view the crimes of women as less severe even when the outcome is the same" (306). Thus, we can consider the public's lack of familiarity, gender expectations, and view of female violence as some of the reasons why fictional depictions of female serial killers continue to be rare.

Reeves's *Slice of Cherry* not only contributes to the disruption of the myth that all serial killers are White and male, but it also interrogates some of the findings on female serials killers as well as their fictionalization. Set in the fictional town of Portero, Texas, at the beginning of the twenty-first century, *Slice of Cherry,* like "The Death of Tommy Grimes" and "Our Kind of People," is a fictional serial killer narrative told from the perspective of the serial killer, except the serial killers featured in Reeves's novel are Black female teenagers. The novel focuses on the lives of Kit and Fancy Cordelle after their father, the infamous Bonesaw Killer, is caught and sentenced to death for torturing and killing at least fifteen people. Although the sisters and their mother Lynne have been shunned by nearly everyone in Portero because of Bonesaw's crimes, the sisters are not upset with Guthrie, Bone-saw's actual name, because of what he did, but because he "had been rash" and was caught (Reeves 3). Indeed, Kit and Fancy enjoy killing just as much as Guthrie, but Fancy is worried that Kit's impulsiveness can put her in the same situation as their father, as she explains to Franken, the young man whom Kit will torture for weeks before Fancy kills him: "Daddy's locked up, so we never see him. Madda had to start working twelve-hour shifts to support us, so we never see her, either. If Kit kills you, they'll lock her up too, and then I won't have nobody. That's the only reason you're alive. Because if I thought I could do it and not get busted, I'd kill you myself" (20). With the help of Cherry du Haven, the girls' slave ancestor who returns as a ghost on every Juneteenth to grant wishes to all the good Black children in Portero, Fancy discovers a solution to satisfying her and Kit's desire to kill without going to jail—the "happy place." Invented by Fancy and made real by a kinetoscope gifted to her by Guthrie, the happy place is a fantasy world where the sisters can kill their victims and dispose of their bodies without ever being discovered by law enforcement. However, unlike their father, whose motives for killing were a "mystery" (40), Fancy and Kit hunt and kill the "bad guys" (184), a motive inspired by Fancy's interpretation of Cherry's advice to her: "I told you what Cherry said. About how we need to help people. I figure she means we should protect them from pervs like the old man. Criminal types" (175).

As serial killers who "help people," Fancy and Kit allow us to consider a question that Pa, Torch, Marc, or even Guthrie does not allow us to consider: Should we condemn or condone serial killers who murder *bad people*? While defining what constitutes a bad person is needed to answer that question, the question itself asks us to think about the role that morality plays in how we think about serial killers, their motivation, and their victims. Reeves's depiction of Fancy and Kit, I argue, suggests that serial killers who kill bad people should be socially pardoned so long as they are helping people who have been wronged. As serial killers for the socially marginalized, Fancy and Kit not only deviate from fictional depictions of serial killing women, but they also problematize the ways in which the scholarship has profiled female murderers.

In her discussion of recent popular fiction featuring female serial kill-ers, Murphy notes that the killers in these texts are women who exploit society's expectations regarding "appropriate" behavior and whose back-ground stories are partly shaped by childhood and/or sexual abuse (128). While Reeves's depiction of Kit and Fancy critiques American culture's expectations of women, it also revises popular fiction's portrayal of the serial killing female by not including abuse as part of Kit and Fancy's background. That revision not only suggests that women can kill for reasons other than revenge or addressing personal abuse, but it also disentangles crime from the Black family. Indeed, Kit complains of an "emptiness" that she has been feeling ever since Guthrie's imprisonment (Reeves 58), and Fancy misses her father so much that she wants to use the doors of Portero, portals that lead to other dimensions or places in the universe, to "rescue" Guthrie by going back in time to persuade him to stop killing (50). In fact, Kit and Fancy were shocked to discover that their father is the Bonesaw Killer, the same man who had "taught them how to make kites and teepees, who had taken them fishing and mushroom-picking" (11). The sisters' love for their father speaks to a childhood not defined by abuse but by normality, and their fictional family is like the real-life families of several male serial killers.[5] In other words, the sisters' love for their father indicates that Black parenting is not the reason why Kit and Fancy are serial killers; rather, they are serial killers because they want to be. Moreover, the sisters' desire to be serial killers challenges the racialized distinction between female murderers and female serial murderers.

According to Farrell, Keppel, and Titterington, the "profile of the modern female murderess" provided by scholars is a woman who is "likely to be single, approximately 31 years old, an African-American, a mother, possessing less than a high school education, and has a prior arrest record." They further note that some scholars have found that "women who are likely to be violent are more likely to be younger, an African-American, unemployed, and have a prior criminal record" (271). Unlike the modern female murderess and the typical violent woman, Farrell, Keppel, and Titterington report that female serial killers in the US tend to be White, usually work alone, are mostly active in the South, and usually lack a previous criminal record (271–72). Harrison and her colleagues offer a similar profile of the typical female serial killer in the US: "She is likely White, has been married, and

---

5. For example, the FBI notes that "Robert Yates killed seventeen prostitutes in the Spokane, Washington area, during the 1990s. He was married with five children, lived in a middle class neighborhood, and was a decorated U.S. Army National Guard helicopter pilot" (3). Gary Ridgeway, known as the Green River Killer, "confessed to killing 48 women over a twenty-year time period in the Seattle, Washington, area. He had been married three times and was still married at the time of his arrest. He was employed as a truck painter for thirty-two years. He attended church regularly, read the Bible at home and at work, and talked about religion with co-workers" (3). Finally, Dennis Rader, the infamous BTK killer, "killed ten victims in and around Wichita, Kansas. . . . He was married with two children, was a Boy Scout leader, served honorably in the U.S. Air Force, was employed as a local government official, and was president of his church" (4).

perhaps has had multiple marriages. She is probably in her 20 or 30s, and may be middle class, Christian, of average intelligence, and likely of average or above-average attractiveness. She is likely legally employed and may be a health-care worker or hold another stereotypically feminine job" ("Female" 400). Although the racialization of the modern female murderess as Black and the female serial killer as White is supported by statistics, the reason for this racialization appears to be devalued by scholars. As Farrell, Keppel, and Titterington put it, several studies suggest that "gender and racial, ethnic, and cultural factors may somehow influence each other to either exacerbate or mitigate traditional roles, but little discussion is provided as to this effect in the context of homicide" (271). Since race is a social construct and not a biological fact, the racial disparity between the modern female murderess and the female serial killer is not a product of the racialized bodies of Black and White women; rather, it is a product of how those bodies are viewed and treated by society. Thus, by not explaining the effects of racism on the racial disparity between the modern female murderess and the female serial killer, these profiles function as examples of race realism in which it is presumed that racial differences determine why the female murderess tends to be Black and the female serial killer tends to be White.

Reeves's depictions of Kit and Fancy not only question the racialized profiles of the female murderess and the female serial killer, but they also suggest that eliding the issue of race as it pertains to female killers gives the impression that Black women are less likely to be serial killers simply because they are Black. In other words, Kit and Fancy challenge an assumption that is implied by the absence of discussions of why female serial killers tend to be White—that Black females lack the ability to carefully plan murders, to be slow and methodical in how they kill, or to murder vulnerable populations by exploiting their positions as people responsible for caring for those populations, traits that distinguish female serial killers from other women who murder (Farrell et al. 269). Indeed, while Kit embodies the qualities of disorder, irrationality, and chaos that are associated with fictional serial killers, she also acknowledges, though begrudgingly, that Fancy is the more rational of the two. For example, after Kit and Fancy decide to hunt and kill bad people, they immediately began to discuss how they would determine who is bad enough to kill. As Kit saw it, since they are "predators," who "can always sniff out prey," their "killer instinct . . . negates the need to think" (Reeves 184). However, Fancy quells Kit's impulsiveness and "easy-peasy" approach to finding bad people by telling her they have to "think this through" to avoid killing the wrong people and going to jail (184–85). Moreover, when Fancy brings Datura Woodson to the happy place to be killed for torturing her pre-adolescent sister Selenicera, Kit becomes upset because Fancy did not allow her to stab Datura to death at the Woodson home, nor is she allowed to kill Selenicera in the happy place. Fancy reminds Kit that killing Datura at her home would be inconvenient and potentially costly: "I don't feel like scrubbing that woman's blood out of my clothes, like I had to with those transies and the old man. It took forever. And think of all the evidence you'd leave behind" (256).[6] At the same time, killing Selenicera is unnecessary because she is the one who has been wronged and because the "happy-place people," who must obey Fancy's commands, allow Kit and Fancy to "kill people without stabbing them or getting [their] hands dirty" (269).

Kit and Fancy not only challenge the notion that emerges from the lack of discussion on race and female serial killing—that Black females lack the mental capacity to plan murders and methodically kill their victims—but they also deviate from the profile of the typical female serial killer in that they are Black, unmarried, not religious, of above average intelligence, and work with a partner. At the same time, Kit and Fancy are unlike the modern female murderess in that they do not have children or previous criminal records. Moreover, as exhibited by their murders of the old man, transies, and Datura, Kit and Fancy also challenge the victim-selection process attributed to female serial killers. For instance, Farrell, Keppel, and Titterington found in their study that it is possible to categorize female serial killers into two broad groups: "The occupational female serial murderer meets, targets, and gains access to her victims through her career, whereas the hearthside female serial murderer interacts and accesses victims through personal contact" (285). What is noteworthy about both categories is that they suggest that, as Harrison, Hughes, and Gott argue in their study, female serial killers are "theoretical 'gatherers' of victims," whereas male serial killers are "theoretical 'hunters' of victims" ("Sex" 296). Unlike male serial killers, who "more frequently kill strangers they stalk, traveling distances to 'hunt' and kill," female serial killers "more frequently kill those around them, figuratively 'gathering' victims who are familiar to them, staying in one place to kill" (296). In contrast to the research on the female serial killer's victim-selection process, Kit and Fancy are neither occupational nor hearthside serial killers, nor do they kill people whom they know or stay in one place to do their killing. Indeed, the sisters' selection of victims and methods of killing are very much like that of the typical male serial killer. As I noted

6. "Transies" is not a derogatory term for transgender folks but a shortened version of transients. As the narrator explains, transies are how "Porterenes thought of outsiders who wandered into their town, because they almost never stayed long" (Reeves 189).

earlier, Kit and Fancy see themselves as "predators" on the hunt for bad people whom they never met, and their hunt requires them to go to the homes of the bad people.

Another important way in which Kit and Fancy differ from the typical female serial killer is their motivations for killing. For example, although Kit alluded to the possibility that she and Fancy should kill to help people, Fancy is not motivated to do so until she meets Cherry. In response to Fancy admitting that killing makes her a *"little* happy" but is not filling the hole left inside her and Kit after their father's imprisonment, Cherry offers the following explanation: "Maybe because you don't use it to make others happy. A world of people could use your help" (Reeves 134). Cherry's response implies that Bonesaw and the sisters are hated by the folks in town because they are too "selfish" with their "gifts," one of which is their ability to find happiness in killing (133). This explains why Cherry disapproves of Fancy's willingness to kill Franken to keep the Cordelle women eternally together—she is killing to make only herself happy (131). Cherry's advice to Fancy not only highlights the major role that motive plays in determining whether people empathize with a fictional or real-life serial killer's actions, but it also offers a motive that is not associated with most female serial killers—morality. While motive is not an ideal means of classifying female serial killers because it is often shaped by the researcher's or the investigator's subjectivity (Farrell et al. 284), there are differences between male and female serial killers regarding why they kill. As Harrison, Hughes, and Gott show in their study, "FSKs were 3 times as likely as MSKs to kill for profit/resources. In line with the 'gatherer' hypothesis, female serial killers seem to be gathering resources as a result of their killings" ("Sex" 305). Unlike female serial killers and their male counterparts, who are more than ten times as likely to have a sexual motive for their serial killing (305), Kit and Fancy are like the fictional Dexter, "the apotheosis of the 'serial killer as vigilante' idea" who is "mainly ridding the world of deeply unpleasant characters we do not approve of ourselves" (Murphy 126–27).

Thus, Cherry's advice to Fancy suggests that killing for selfish reasons is how serial killers become monsters, implying that ridding the world of "deeply unpleasant" people is morally valid and one way in which serial killers can retain their humanity. In other words, Kit "volunteer[ing]" her and Fancy's serial killing gifts to help people, particularly those who "won't ask for help" (Reeves 184), is about humanizing their killing: "It's not about being saints or sinners or good or bad, Fancy. It's about both. You know? About being complete" (264). Being "complete," for Kit, means that the happiness they derive from killing has been humanized and morally validated by themselves and others through their selection of victims. For instance, among the fan and hate mail they receive due to being the daughters of the Bonesaw Killer, there is the suggestion that, as stated in one letter, serial killers who kill bad people are not monsters: "I don't get why Guthrie killed nice people when there's so many jerks out there who deserve it way more" (176). As implied by the author of the letter, if Guthrie had killed only bad people, he might not have been sentenced to death row. Kit and Fancy seem to receive the same message from Lynne after she learned what her daughters have been doing when she was not around them: "You girls *be careful*" (505). Lynne's response, on the one hand, suggest that she wants her daughters to be, as most mothers would, "happy and healthy" (505); on the other hand, her response suggests that she approves of her daughters' serial killing since they are, unlike their father, helping people. Implicit in the fan letter and Lynne's advice is the notion that serial killers become monsters not because of how they kill or how many they kill but because of whom they kill and why. While proposing that serial killers can be *good* people if they kill *bad* people, the fan letter and Lynne's advice also suggest that the public or members of a community might not help investigators catch a serial killer who is believed to be helping the community or society. In this light, *Slice of Cherry* is not only a meditation on the Black female serial killer, but it is also a request for us to think about the material conditions and ideological hegemony within a society or community that allows for some serial killers to be viewed as champions of justice and others as monsters.

Good and Bad Serial Killers

In addition to questioning popular culture's image of the serial killer as an insane monster, the sane serial killers depicted in the horror stories by Meaddough, Burke, Boatman, and Reeves suggest a distinction between *good* and *bad* serial killers that highlights the importance of intentionality. Although the bad serial killers—Pa, Torch, and Marc—are male and the good serial killers—Kit and Fancy—are female, one's sex is not the reason why a serial killer becomes a monster.[7] According to the stories, a serial killer's goodness or badness is determined by their motives and choice of victims. Indeed,

7. While being male or female does not guarantee that a serial killer will become a monster, it is worth noting that the male serial killers (i.e., Pa, Torch, and Marc), unlike the female serial killers (i.e., Kit and Fancy), are anti-Black serial killers because it suggests that male serial killers are more likely than their female colleagues to have racial motives or to racialize their motives for killing.

while Kit and Fancy's approach to killing is like that of the male serial killer, their primary motive for killing, a motive not generally associated with male or female serial killers, is doing what is morally right. Unlike ethics, which addresses questions of human flourishing, morality is, as Appiah defines it, "the constraints that govern how we should and should not treat other people." In other words, issues of morality force us to engage the following question: "What do we owe to other people?" (37). Given that these "constraints" could be economic, ideological, cultural, political, and religious, one could argue that Pa, Torch, and Marc are also motivated by moral concerns. According to that argument, Pa, Torch, and Marc are anti-Black serial killers because the moral codes of Pa's White supremacism, Torch's drug dealing enterprise, and Marc's Old Tenth–based anger make them morally obligated to kill Black people.

The problem with defining the anti-Black serial killing of Pa, Torch, and Marc as morally motivated is that they kill Black people for ethical reasons. While questions of morality, as noted above, are concerned with how we treat others, questions of ethics are concerned with how we achieve a "good life," that is, how does one go about achieving what is needed to have a well-lived life (Appiah 36–37). Thus, while Appiah notes that questions of the good life are "indissolubly social" and "doing what is morally right is one of the constituents of human flourishing" (168), an individual's self-development is the primary focus of ethics since "the fundamental task of ethics is to shape one's own life" (163). This means that even though Pa kills Black people in the name of protecting White life and Marc kills Black people whom he believes are hindering the elevation of Black life, their actions, like Torch's, benefit themselves rather than other people. Indeed, Tommy becomes a monster because of Pa's actions; the project residents near Chocolate Park are in a constant state of terror due to Torch's violence; and Marc's killing of the Black non-elite is not uplifting the race. Thus, Pa's, Torch's, and Marc's motives for killing Black people (i.e., ideology, criminal enterprise, and anger), unlike Kit and Fancy's helping-people motive, are shaped by their individual pursuits of the good life: Pa's status as a White father in Jim Crow Mississippi, Torch's status as a successful drug dealer in Black urban America, and Marc's status as a member of the twenty-first-century Black elite who seeks to be a "credit" to the race.

In contrast to Pa, Torch, and Marc, the Cordelle sisters are portrayed as good serial killers. While Kit and Fancy enjoy killing people, their victims are those who harm or attempt to harm people who are defenseless and have done nothing to deserve such treatment, such as the old man who tried to kidnap and rape Kit and Fancy, the transies who were beating up a scrawny boy they called a "freak," and Datura, the young woman who was slowly killing her younger sister. As indicated by their decision to use their "gifts" to help people who are suffering from the whims of those whom we consider reprehensible, Kit and Fancy represent the serial killer as social justice warrior, and the fan letter and their mother's response to their serial killing suggest that motive and victim selection play an important role in determining whether people will empathize with fictional or real-life serial killers. Indeed, their decision to use their gifts to help others explains, in part, why the sisters do not become anti-Black serial killers, even though some of their victims are Black—they seem to believe that being an anti-Black serial killer is not what is owed to Black people, since becoming such a killer requires revictimizing the racially victimized. Such thinking also explains why the sisters volunteer their "gifts" to helping people after their business venture failed to monetize their gifts—killing for money might lead to helping the reprehensible. Thus, as proposed by *Slice of Cherry*, good serial killers are those who might be viewed by the public as unlikable because of their methods of killing but are not seen as monsters because the same public feels, on some level, that these killers are needed.

The fictional serial killer narratives by Meaddough, Burke, Boatman, and Reeves indicate that all serial killers in Black American horror fiction are not monsters because the horror of serial killing is not located solely in the volume of victims or the brutality in which they are killed. Since motive and victim selection are what determine the difference between *good* and *bad* serial killers, the serial killing monsters in Black horror fiction, unlike popular culture's untreatable serial killer, are dangerous and disgusting not because their acts of violence are beyond the "ken of human experience" but because that violence is inflicted onto those who do not deserve it. In other words, the serial killing narratives in Black American horror fiction insist that what is scary about serial killing monsters (i.e., bad serial killers) is not their methods of killing, since good serial killers could use the same methods, but the possibility that we could be a victim of their violence because their conceptions of the good life require killing certain people for who they represent rather than for what they do.

CONCLUSION

Eliminating Anti-Blackness and Its Monsters

Like all monsters in entity-based horror, the human monsters of Black American horror fiction are both lethal and disgusting. Indeed, the goal of the White rage monster is to ensure that Black people are economically worse off than White people, and the respectability and not-ness monsters believe that Black people cannot be raped because their so-called hypersexuality makes them always willing and wanting. Similarly, the anti-Black serial killers believe that their Black victims are humanity's "trash heap," people who can be guiltlessly exploited, terrorized, or killed precisely because they are perceived to be socially expendable. What makes these monsters lethal is their ability to terrorize Black people with virtual impunity, an ability granted to them, in part, by state-sanctioned policies and practices such as slavery, Jim Crow, the Southern strategy, and the War on Drugs. On the other hand, what makes these monsters disgusting is their anti-Black sadism, the pleasure they derive from inflicting pain on Black people or watching them in pain. In this instance, terrorizing the Black body for these monsters fulfills their mental, aesthetic, and private fantasies (i.e., ideo-pleasures) about defending or aspiring to particular notions of Americanness. In other words, if anti-Blackness is one part of Americanness, then harming and killing Black people becomes ideologically pleasurable for these monsters precisely because they believe that committing acts of anti-Black violence is one way to show that they are *real* Americans. Thus, like the ideo-pleasure that emerges from the customer-product interaction in which a product is ideologically pleasing if it represents the customer's values and aesthetics, the Black body in pain represents the values and aesthetics of the human monsters who produce and consume that pain.

Given that humans are not born with the desire to hate, harm, or kill Black humans, the White rage, respectability, not-ness, and serial killing monsters direct our attention to the role that America's institutions, myths, and cultural practices play in validating Black pain. Despite their various motivations for terrorizing and killing Black folks, the monsters of anti-Blackness embody the horrors that emerge when *Black American* is disassociated from *American*. These monsters and the texts that they populate ask us to think about not only the role that anti-Blackness plays in being or becoming American but also the intellectual resources that Black folks have used or might use in the future to combat these monsters. Since horror helps us to manage our fears, especially those pertaining to the underlying uncertainty of everyday life, and to develop strategies for overcoming them, what can Black horror fiction featuring human monsters tell us about how Black people should deal with the White rage, respectability, not-ness, and serial killing monsters of everyday life? If we compare those stories where the monsters of anti-Blackness avoid death (i.e., Du Bois's "Jesus Christ in Texas," Clarke's "Santa Claus Is a White Man," Meaddough's "The Death of Tommy Grimes," Walker's "The Child Who Favored Daughter," Due's *The Between*, George's "Good 'Nough to Eat," and Davis's "Are You My Daddy?") with those where the monsters are killed (i.e., Wright's "The Man Who Killed a Shadow," Butler's *Kindred*, Burke's "Chocolate Park," Fleming's "The Ultimate Bad Luck," Boatman's "Our Kind of People," Reeves's *Slice of Cherry*, LaValle's *The Changeling*, and Okorafor's *Who Fears Death*), we find that "Afropessimism" and "black aliveness" tend to guide these texts' responses to the question of how to defeat the monsters of anti-Blackness.

In *Ontological Terror* (2018), Calvin Warren argues that the "free black" does not exist, since "it is impossible for any black to be free in an anti-black world" (16). Warren's notion of the free Black person is a foundational tenet of Afropessimism,[1] which Frank Wilderson III describes as a collection of "theorists of Black positionality who share Fanon's insistence that, though Blacks are indeed sentient beings, the structure of the entire world's

---

1. Wilderson informs us that the term "Afropessimism" is a moniker suggested to him by Saidiya Hartman and is different from the term's use in the 1980s, "when many scholars and journalists in Western countries believed that there was no hope for bringing about democracy and achieving sustainable economic development in [sub-Sharan Africa]" (*Red* 346–47n9).

semantic field . . . is sutured by anti-Black solidarity" (*Red* 58).[2] According to this view, since the modern world's notion of the human justifies violence against those deemed not fully human and continues to deny Black people the status of human, Blackness cannot be "disaggregated from social death" (95). Nor can Blackness, as Christina Sharpe contends, be disaggregated from physical death: "ongoing state-sanctioned legal and extralegal murders of Black people are normative and, for this so-called democracy, necessary" (*In the Wake* 7). However, the pessimism of Afropessimism is not just about the existence of anti-Blackness; it is also about "the claims theories of liberation make when these theories try to explain Black suffering or when they analogize Black suffering with the suffering of other oppressed beings" (Wilderson, *Afropessimism* 14). Since current liberation theories do not offer practical solutions to eradicating anti-Blackness because these theories are limited to creating a better or more humane anti-Black world, Black hope and Black agency become Afropessimistic concepts and practices that insist that nothing less than a new world will eliminate anti-Blackness.

Like Afropessimism's pessimism, the Black horror stories where the human monsters survive (i.e., the works by Du Bois, Clarke, Meaddough, Walker, Due, George, and Davis) suggest that anti-Blackness will always be a part of American sociality. One reason for this bleak view of American life is the state's investment in anti-Blackness. For instance, all the White rage monsters in Du Bois's "Jesus Christ in Texas" (i.e., the colonel, businessman, convict guard, and the married farmers) are directly tied to the state, especially its prison system. Similarly, the White rage monster in Due's *The Between* is arrested for his murder of an upper-class Black man, but that monster's history with the judicial system indicates that he may not pay the full legal price for his actions precisely because he received no jail time for his participation in the White terrorist group responsible for killing a Jewish radio host, and his sentence for cracking his girlfriend's skull was reduced by a judge. Implicit in the stories by Du Bois and Due is that the solution to anti-Blackness does not begin with revamping social and institutional practices but with eliminating, as Vargas and Jung posit, "the very notions of the Social and the Human underlying these practices and their constitutive rejection of Blackness and Black people" (8). This helps to explain, as Anthony Paul Farley points out in his discussion of "beaten slaves," the state's uselessness in eradicating anti-Blackness from American sociality: "The beaten blacks, heads bowed, white-over-black, form prayers to the monopolists of

2. In addition to himself, Wilderson identifies Saidiyah Hartman, Hortense Spillers, Frantz Fanon, Orlando Patterson, Joy James, George Yancey, Achille Mbembe, Kara Keeling, Lewis Gordon, Ronald Judy, Jared Sexton, and David Marriot as Afropessimists (*Red* 58).

violence, prayers for legal relief from the violence of dispossession. These prayers create a false god, the state, whom the defeated hope to appease with ever more sickening displays of fidelity to the rule of law and to the future fairness of their masters" (84). As suggested by Du Bois's short story and Due's novel, changing laws and policies will not eliminate anti-Blackness from the judicial system since these laws and policies are built upon a conception of the human that defines Black people as not fully human and, therefore, justifies the state's refusal to answer Black people's prayers.

In addition to the state's investment in anti-Blackness, another reason why anti-Blackness will continue to shape American sociality is that some Black people are anti-Black. For example, although the Black and White monsters in the stories by Du Bois, Clarke, Meaddough, Walker, George, and Davis are invested in anti-Blackness's dehumanization and abjection projects, they differ on which projects to pursue. On the one hand, the White monsters in the stories by Du Bois, Clarke, and Meaddough terrorize and kill Black people to stop Black advancement and ambition, which means, in an anti-Black world, protecting White life. The Black monsters in Walker's, George's, and Davis's stories, on the other hand, terrorize and kill Black people because of issues pertaining to sexuality. Indeed, while the Black father of Walker's story mutilates his daughter's body and beats his wife for their real and imagined relationships with White men, the teenagers and cannibal females who rape and castrate Kelly—the Black male protagonist of George's story—are driven by their hypersexualization of his penis. What motivates the Black monster in Davis's story to terrorize Chris is the belief that Black men who intentionally or unintentionally mimic the mythical hypersexual Black male should be forced into heteronuclear families or lose their testicles. Implicit in these stories is the notion that Black people who have internalized their dehumanization and abjection make it extremely difficult for Black people to resist and eliminate anti-Blackness. Thus, in contrast to Afropessimism's claim that the Black–non-Black binary has replaced the Black-White binary as the "defining antagonism of modernity" (Vargas and Jung 7),[3] the Black monsters in Walker's, George's, and Davis's stories

---

3. This Black–non-Black binary can be seen in what David Theo Goldberg refers to as "racial americanization," which is rooted in the following assumptions and presuppositions: that "homogenized apartness is taken as the deracialized norm," that Whiteness is "the standard" that everyone should aspire to, and that Whites are the "real victims" of antiracism policies and efforts (8–9). Such thinking, as Goldberg points out, helps to explain why "two-thirds of new immigrants to the United States claim to be 'white' on the [2000] U.S. census no matter [their] ethnoracial background." As it turns out, Goldberg continues, being White for these new immigrants means "to be American, with the assimilative logic of 'fitting in,' that is, with opportunity and access, with getting ahead and succeeding" (6).

propose that the Black–anti-Black binary is modernity's defining antagonism, since Black and non-Black people engage in practices of anti-Blackness.

If the survival of the human monsters in the works by Du Bois, Clarke, Meaddough, Walker, Due, George, and Davis suggest that anti-Blackness will always define American sociality, then Black hope and Black agency can only be about questions of reform rather than strategies of eradication. As Farley explains, reform is "a mode of repetition" (103n1), and in anti-Blackness, race is "the endless repetition of [Black people's] unremembered death," which is the "navel of the modern era" (82). This means that, as Vargas and Jung point out, the antiracist hope that emerges from racism in which "racial and other related and intersecting forms of oppression can be eliminated, or at least ameliorated" is "suspended relative to Black life" (8); therefore, Black hope and Black agency in the context of reform represents, respectively, the optimism Black people have in making the anti-Black world better for Black people and the pessimism they have in eradicating anti-Blackness altogether. Indeed, while Black agency describes the articulation of "radically alternative conceptions of what it means to be human and live in society," it is "necessarily and always engaging the fundamentally anti-black world" (Vargas and Jung 9). Thus, those Black horror stories where the anti-Black monsters live or where Black people are punished for killing anti-Black monsters (e.g., Wright's "The Man Who Killed a Shadow") imply that Afropessimism emerges not because Black people have become hopeless or believe that they lack agency, but because the intellectual tools that have shaped Black hope and Black agency have been ineffective in their attempts to eliminate anti-Blackness from American life and occasionally effective in alleviating its negative effects on Black life. In other words, these Afropessimistic horror stories define Black hope and Black agency as anarchistic concepts. According to Farley, anarchy is key to eliminating anti-Blackness: "Anarchy is the end of race, the end of property, the end of the rule of law, the end of the prehistory of humanity. Anarchy is the one big union, the general strike, and the new world within the shell of the old" (87). In their treatment of anarchy as the foundation of Black hope and Black agency, Afropessimism and the Black horror fiction where the human monster avoids death warn us to reject what Warren calls the "humanist fantasy"—an assumption that "masks subjection in emancipatory rhetoric" by claiming that "freedom can be attained through political, social, or legal action" (15)—as the solution to anti-Blackness precisely because it is just another form of reform.

In contrast to Afropessimism's anarchy-based understanding of Black hope and Black agency, the Black horror stories where the human monsters die—Wright's "The Man Who Killed a Shadow," Butler's *Kindred*, Burke's

"Chocolate Park," Fleming's "The Ultimate Bad Luck," Boatman's "Our Kind of People," LaValle's *The Changeling*, Okorafor's *Who Fears Death*, and Reeves's *Slice of Cherry*—offer conceptions of Black hope and Black agency that represent what Kevin Quashie calls "black aliveness." As "an aesthetic imaginary founded on black worldness" in which the expectations of Black people are not Blackness but "beingness" (9–10), Black aliveness suggests that Afropessimism's claims about the universality of anti-Blackness precludes the possibility that free Black people do exist.[4] For instance, Saul of Wright's "The Man Who Killed a Shadow" kills the not-ness monster who attempted to rape him, but her anti-Black necrophilia ensured that his young Black life would end at the hands of the state, either in prison or in a coffin, long before she attempted to sexually assault him. While Quashie agrees with the claim that "every black person lives under the terror of anti-blackness," he is also "cautious of its sayability, since to claim subjection as the definitive fact of black life is to establish a threshold of authenticity, maybe even to imply that there is a certain quality of subjection—a quality of responding to subjection—that confirms black being" (146). Thus, if we read those Black horror stories where the human monster dies through the lens of Black aliveness in which Black people's humanness is not in question, we find that the monster's death implies conceptions of Black hope and Black agency that are rooted in self-defense, a right that all Americans have but continues to be denied to the majority of Black Americans. In other words, the Black aliveness in these Black horror stories is informed by the following logic: if we acknowledge that anti-Blackness is an attack on Black people's beingness, then we must also acknowledge that the monsters of anti-Blackness must be eliminated if Black people's beingness is to be protected and to supersede their Blackness. However, killing the anti-Black monster is not solely about causing that monster's physical death; it also means eliminating the ideologies of anti-Blackness that gave that monster life. This point is reflected in the different meanings assigned to the deaths of the Black and White anti-Black monsters, which represent the different types of racialized monsters produced by an anti-Black world.

---

4. Similarly, Tavia Nyong'o contends in *Afro-Fabulations* (2019) that Hartman's "reparative black historiography" in *Scenes of Subjection*, while offering a "scouring critique of the many ruses of the liberal antiracist imaginary," is partly responsible for the rise of Afropessimism, which he believes represents "a sharp challenge to the broadly relational and intersectional approach" that he favors because Afropessimism "characterizes blackness as a site of accumulation and fungibility, rather than one of identity and resistance" (20).

In the case of the non-Black monsters (i.e., Maybelle in Wright's "The Man Who Killed a Shadow," Rufus in *Kindred*, Miz Gertrude and the peckerwoods in "The Ultimate Bad Luck," Jorgen and Kinder Garten in *The Changeling*, Daib in *Who Fears Death*, and the victims of Kit and Fancy in *Slice of Cherry*), their deaths represent the death of race realism, a pillar of anti-Blackness, and the conceptualization of Black hope and Black agency in terms of racial sameness. Since anti-Blackness is driven by race realism's repulsive insistence that racial injustice and inequality "isn't injustice or inequality . . . because the racial hierarchy is real" (Saini 80), the use of racial sameness thinking in the stories by Wright, Butler, Burke, Fleming, LaValle, Okorafor, and Reeves highlights the fact that humans are nothing more than gradations of the same; therefore, racial injustice and inequality *is* injustice and inequality. Indeed, racial sameness is shown in these stories to be such a powerful ideological weapon that it can allow Black people to evade the state's protection of anti-Black monsters, since each of these monsters are killed by Black people, save for Saul, who avoids death but not imprisonment. Although Miz Gertrude and the peckerwoods are killed by alligators, those alligators help Neptune because he protected the lead alligator from a group of peckerwoods some years earlier. Thus, while the monsters who abused Neptune did not die by his hands, they did die by his decision to defend an alligator against a group of White supremacists, a decision that emphasizes the possibility and necessity of developing Black–non-Black coalitions against anti-Blackness.

Similar to the link between race realism and the deaths of non-Black monsters, the deaths of the Black monsters in Burke's "Chocolate Park" and Boatman's "Our Kind of People" represent the demise of Black racial authenticity, another pillar of anti-Blackness. Given the "impossibility of fixing someone or something as 'authentically black' across time and space," questions about authentic Blackness are political and economic questions (not cultural, biological, or sociological ones) that almost always emerge from "pressures exerted on the black community from without—not from within" (Japtok and Jenkins 45–46). Thus, the search for an authentic Blackness contends that there is more to being Black than having a Black body, that there are certain things that a person with a Black body must think, do, enjoy, or have to be considered authentically Black. The problem with that search is that being Black in the world of race is not determined by what one does, thinks, enjoys, or has but by how one looks; therefore, the only requirement for a person to be authentically Black is to have a Black body. In this light, Burke's Torch and Boatman's Marc are anti-Black monsters who embody the horrors of Black authenticity, the violence inflicted by Black people on Black people for being or not being authentically Black.

In the case of Torch, he sees the poor and working-class Black folks he terrorizes and kills through the lens of anti-Blackness; therefore, he believes that they deserve the pain he inflicts upon them because they are humanity's "trash heap," a conception of the Black non-elite that is considered authentic by the state and expressed by its approach to the War on Drugs. Although Marc is equally hateful of the Black elite and non-elite, his violence has been directed primarily at the non-elite for not being a credit to the race, for not being authentically Black according to the standards of the Black elite. As suggested by the depictions of Torch and Marc, any notion of racial authenticity reflects one's investment in White supremacist thinking and in anti-Blackness, given that racism is not only a philosophy and practice created out of such thinking but is also an aspect of modern world sociality in which anti-Blackness is "an ontological condition of possibility" of that sociality (Vargas and Jung 7). Indeed, the deaths of Torch and Marc imply that for a world to emerge or sustain itself in which beingness, instead of Blackness, is expected of Black people, the search for an authentic Blackness must be terminated, since that search wrongly presumes that Blackness is a club from which Black people can be excluded or expelled due to what they do, think, enjoy, or have.[5]

Even though the Black American horror stories discussed in *Anti-Blackness and Human Monstrosity* offer different answers to questions regarding the mortality or immortality of anti-Blackness, they all seem to agree with a statement attributed to Zora Neale Hurston: "If you are silent about your pain, they'll kill you and say you enjoyed it."[6] Indeed, Black horror fiction can be viewed as a genre that specializes in giving voice to the Black pain produced by anti-Blackness, a cultural logic that insists that Black people enjoy being in pain and that the Black body in pain functions within "a negative symbolic index of social worth defining what an American is *not*" (King 17). In giving voice to Black pain and the anti-Blackness that engenders it, the novels and short stories discussed in this book possess a sensibility that can be found in what Sheri-Marie Harrison calls "new black Gothic," a category of Black horror that refers to twenty-first-century texts

---

5. As I have noted elsewhere, the Blackness club is "a collection of many clubs"; thus, "any conception of blackness that requires one to think and behave in a certain way to be considered authentically black is not only fraudulent and unrealistic, but it is [also] always already a source of conflict" (*Paradox* 175).

6. Though many people cite Hurston as the one who gave voice to that statement, there is a lack of certainty regarding where Hurston made this statement.

that rework gothic traditions ("New" par. 3). As Harrison explains in her discussion of Jesmyn Ward's *Sing, Unburied, Sing* (2017), Jordan Peele's *Get Out* (2017), and Childish Gambino's "This Is America" (2018), the new black Gothic examines how "the exploitative and violent ways black bodies have been used in the service of white supremacy across history continue to linger in the present" (par. 7). For instance, some of the "unifying features" of the new black Gothic, as Harrison observes in the works of Marlon James, are the following:

> a dark humor that is not comedic but is instead horrifying or uncomfortable (sometimes both); a preoccupation with the enduring legacies of various forms of historical racialized oppression (colonization, slavery, and Jim Crow segregation, for example); and a sense of the inescapability of racialized oppression as well as an eschewal of hope for the future. ("Marlon James" 69)

However, new black Gothic texts do not "shy away from this hopelessness"; rather, they are interested in how hopelessness can be used as a tool for teaching "how white supremacy and systemic racism continue to organize American life" (Harrison, "New" par. 23). In this light, the aesthetic of the new black Gothic, as Harrison concludes, "functions in popular black art as a tool for representing black life on its own terrorized terms" (par. 23).

Although several of the stories discussed in this book are not new black Gothic texts because of their publication dates, these stories, like their twenty-first-century counterparts, are interested how certain conceptions of Black hope and Black agency can help eliminate the anti-Black monsters from Black life. Indeed, by depicting the Black hopelessness that emerges from Black pain and teaching how hopelessness can be used to defeat the monsters of anti-Blackness, the novels and short stories examined in *Anti-Blackness and Human Monstrosity* suggest that Black horror fiction, including the new black Gothic, can be viewed as a creative pillar of both Afropessimism and Black aliveness. Although these Black horror stories highlight the differences between Afropessimism and Black aliveness as intellectual weapons in the fight against the monsters of anti-Blackness, they also show that these philosophies of anti-anti-Blackness are in unison in treating reform (e.g., the humanist fantasy) as useless in the fight to eliminate anti-Blackness. Because reform assumes that anti-Blackness is an inevitable reality, Black hope and Black agency in reform's humanist fantasy of Black progress are restricted to making Black life better in an anti-Black world rather than making a world without anti-Blackness. In other words, while

Afropessimism conceptualizes Black hope and Black agency within the context of anarchy and Black aliveness couches them in terms of self-defense, both seem to agree, as suggested by the novels and short stories examined in this book, that destroying an anti-Black world requires non-Black people, not just Black folks, to be invested in eliminating anti-Blackness from that world. For example, the exchange between the Stranger and the colonel's daughter in "Jesus Christ in Texas," Dana's interracial marriage in *Kindred*, Neptune's relationship with the alligators in "The Ultimate Bad Luck," and Emma's decision to become a member of the Wise Ones in *The Changeling* propose that abolishing anti-Blackness from Black life requires demonstrating that anti-Blackness is an attack on the beingness of Black *and* non-Black people.

If the elimination of an anti-Black world is posited as a Black–non-Black project in Black horror fiction featuring human monsters, then we should not be too surprised that these horror stories lack depictions of Black people migrating to worlds absent of anti-Blackness. While some of the Black horror stories discussed in this book do depict Black migration as one way for Black people to escape an anti-Black world (e.g., the stories by Du Bois, Burke, Butler, and Fleming), the places where they migrate are also defined by anti-Blackness. According to these stories, which appear to take a page out of Afropessimism, a world absent of anti-Blackness does not exist; therefore, migration does not solve the anti-Blackness problem. If we consider those Black horror stories where migration is not an option for its Black characters, we find, from the perspective of Black aliveness, that they are making the claim that a world free of anti-Blackness cannot come into being if the Black and non-Black people attempting to create it are unable to free themselves from anti-Blackness thinking. Despite their different approaches, Black horror stories where Black migration as a solution to the anti-Blackness problem is omitted or is depicted as a failure imply that ideological migration is more important than its geographic counterpart in finding a world not defined by anti-Blackness. This emphasis on ideological migration evokes a Black American philosophical tradition that not only claims that a liberated Black mind is the most valuable form of freedom, but it also insists that the Black body cannot experience full freedom until its mind is free (Gilroy, *Against Race* 185). According to that tradition of Black thought, migrating to a place absent of anti-Blackness is not a solution for Black people if those who are leaving have internalized the ideologies of anti-Blackness such as race realism, Black racial authenticity, and the "globally shared" conception of the human that are, according to Vargas and Jung, "the source of Black people's dehumanization, suffering, and death" (9). In this light, the absence or critique of Black migration as an anti-anti-Blackness strategy in Black horror fiction can be read as an argument for thinking about one's migration from an anti-Black world as one's migration from an anti-Black mind.

Whether their anti-Black monsters live or die, Black horror fiction featuring human monsters insist that we do not know, as Nyong'o puts it, "what a human outside an anti-black world could be, do, or look like" (26); therefore, to acquire such knowledge requires the elimination of anti-Blackness. That goal is one of the main reasons why I believe that it is important to read and study Black horror fiction—it reminds us that there is more than one way to be human. Denying that fact, according to the short stories and novels examined in this book, is what leads to the production of human monsters. Thus, anti-Blackness is not only a rejection of the fact that there are multiple ways to be human, but it also presumes that Black people do not fully fit in its limited conception of the human. Indeed, the anti-Blackness definition of the human underscores what Alexander Weheliye calls "Man," which is "the modern, secular, and western version of the human that differentiates full humans from not-quite-humans and nonhumans on the basis of biology and economics" (139n3). According to that definition, as Weheliye argues, Man is "synonymous with the heteromasculine, white, propertied, and liberal subject" in which Black people become literal "no-bodies" and "exploitable nonhumans" (135).[7] In this light, to learn what a human in a world absent of anti-Blackness could be, do, or look like, we must begin with acknowledging that Man is just one version of the human founded on the disassociation of *Black human* from *human*. In so doing, we also acknowledge that there are and will be versions of the human that are not defined by anti-Blackness; therefore, we should avoid or stop treating Man as humanity's evolutionary end if we want to end the reproduction of anti-Black monsters.

Although the works of horror examined in this book make a compelling case for why we should discard Man as the dominant version of the human, they also ask us to think about how to transform that goal into a reality. In other words, they ask us to think about what it would take to convince people to end anti-Blackness. Put differently, what rewards do people receive for believing in anti-Blackness? These questions are noteworthy given that

---

7. A similar point is represented in Octavia Butler's *Imago* (1989), the final novel of the *Xenogenesis* trilogy, where it critiques the calls to save or transcend Man because they "exclude the possibility that there is more than one way to be human and, therefore, imply that we must become posthuman to better ourselves" (Jenkins, "Transhumanism" 138). Implicit in this notion that humans must transcend their humanity to be "better" is the misguided assumption that the Western version of the human represents humanity's evolutionary end. Thus, Blackness in that conception of the human "is not a sign of humanity's present nor future, only its past" (141).

several of the texts examined in this book depict instances where White and other non-Black people are oppressed by an ideology of anti-Blackness or are harmed or killed by an anti-Black monster. For instance, even though *Who Fears Death* is set in postapocalyptic Sudan, Okorafor's depiction of Onye's racially and ethnically diverse band of potential monster slayers offers the same message as those Black horror stories that feature human monsters and are set in the US—not all non-Black people benefit from anti-Blackness. Yet, as suggested by the Black monsters discussed herein (e.g., Torch of Burke's "Chocolate Park" and Marc of Boatman's "Our Kind of People"), there are Black people who are "active agents" of anti-Blackness.[8] Thus, if Blackness is devalued and being anti-Black is rewarded, then how do we convince people to eliminate anti-Blackness or prevent them from becoming anti-Black monsters? According to the stories examined in *Anti-Blackness and Human Monstrosity*, we must nullify the ideo-pleasure that an anti-Black person might derive from producing and consuming Black people in pain. Stated more directly, we must protect Black people's right to self-defense, their right to use symbolic or physical violence to defend their beingness. Since the goal of the anti-Black monster is to prevent Black people from enjoying their beingness or being alive, these texts, even the ones where the monster survives, insist that we will see fewer anti-Black monsters if Black people's right to self-defense is protected. Indeed, if that right is protected by the state's citizens, laws, and actions, then we have the first sign of what a world without anti-Blackness would be like, since such protection would represent an anarchical change in the sociality of America and the modern world precisely because it relies on a notion of the human that includes Black people.

---

8. George Lipsitz has noted that "White supremacy is an equal opportunity employer; nonwhite people can become active agents of white supremacy as well as passive participants in its hierarchies and rewards" (viii). I am making a similar claim about anti-Blackness as an equal opportunity employer.

WORKS CITED

Addison, Linda. "Genesis—The First Black Horror Writers/Storytellers." *Black Celebration: Amazing Articles on African American Horror,* edited by Sumiko Saulson, 2019, pp. 12–17.

Adjorlolo, Samuel, and Heng Choon (Oliver) Chan. "The Controversy of Defining Serial Murder: Revisited." *Aggression and Violent Behavior,* vol. 19, no. 5, 2014, pp. 486–91. *ScienceDirect,* https://doi.org/10.1016/j.avb.2014.07.003.

Ahmad, Aalya. "Transgressive Horror and Politics: The Splatterpunks and Extreme Horror." *The Palgrave Handbook to Horror Literature,* edited by Kevin Corstorphine and Laura R. Kremmel, Palgrave MacMillan, 2018, pp. 365–76.

Alexander, Michelle. *The New Jim Crow: Mass Incarceration in the Age of Colorblindness.* The New Press, 2012.

Ali, Lorraine. "Tucker Carlson Hits a Dangerous New Low in His Response to the Buffalo Shooting." *Los Angeles Times,* 16 May 2022, https://www.latimes.com/entertainment-arts/tv/story/2022-05-16/tucker-carlson-tonight-fox-news-buffalo-shooting-response.

Anderson, Carol. *White Rage: The Unspoken Truth of Our Racial Divide.* Bloomsbury, 2016.

Anderson, James, et al. "An Account of a Monster of the Human Species, in Two Letters; One from Baron Reichel to Sir Joseph Banks, Bart. and the Other from Mr. James Anderson to Baron Reichel. Communicated by Sir Joseph Banks, Bart. P.R.S." *Philosophical Transactions of the Royal Society of London,* vol. 79, 1789, pp. 157–59. *JSTOR,* https://www.jstor.org/stable/106689.

Anim-Addo, Joan, and Maria Helena Lima. "The Power of the Neo-Slave Narrative Genre." *Callaloo,* vol. 40, no. 4, 2017, pp. 3–13.

Appiah, Kwame. *Experiments in Ethics.* Harvard UP, 2008.

Asma, Stephen. *On Monsters: An Unnatural History of Our Worst Fears.* Oxford UP, 2009.

Bailey, Moya. *Misogynoir Transformed: Black Women's Digital Resistance.* New York UP, 2021.

Baldwin, James. "The Black Boy Looks at the White Boy Norman Mailer." *Esquire,* May 1961, pp. 102–6. https://classic.esquire.com/article/1961/5/1/the-black-boy-looks-at-the-white-boy-norman-mailer.

Bantinaki, Katerina. "The Paradox of Horror: Fear as a Positive Emotion." *The Journal of Aesthetics and Art Criticism,* vol. 70, no. 4, 2012, pp. 383–92. JSTOR, https://www.jstor.org/stable/43496533.

Bauer, Margaret D. "Alice Walker: Another Southern Writer Criticizing Codes Not Put to 'Everyday Use.'" *Studies in Short Fiction,* vol. 29, no. 2, 1992, pp. 143–51.

Benshoff, Harry. "Blaxploitation Horror Films: Generic Reappropriation or Reinscription?" *Cinema Journal,* vol. 39, no. 2, 2000, pp. 31–50. JSTOR, https://www.jstor.org/stable/1225551.

Berlin, Ira. *The Making of African America: The Four Great Migrations.* Viking, 2010.

Bernal, Martin. "Race in History." *Global Convulsions: Race, Ethnicity, and Nationalism at the End of the Twentieth Century,* edited by Winston Van Horne, State U of New York P, 1997, pp. 75–92.

Bernstein, Patricia. *The First Waco Horror: The Lynching of Jesse Washington and the Rise of the NAACP.* Texas A&M UP, 2005.

Berry, Daina Ramey, and Kali Nicole Gross. *A Black Women's History of the United States.* Beacon, 2020.

Boatman, Michael. "Our Kind of People." *Voices from the Other Side: Dark Dreams II,* edited by Brandon Massey, Dafina, 2006, pp. 123–30.

Brooks, Kinitra D. *Searching for Sycorax: Black Women's Hauntings of Contemporary Horror.* Rutgers UP, 2018.

Bryant, Earle V. "The Sexualization of Racism in Richard Wright's 'The Man Who Killed a Shadow.'" *Black American Literature Forum,* vol. 16, no. 3, 1982, pp. 119–21. JSTOR, https://www.jstor.org/stable/2904350.

Bryce, Jane. "African Futurism: Speculative Fictions and 'Rewriting the Great Book.'" *Research in African Literatures,* vol. 50, no. 1, 2019, pp. 1–19. Project Muse, https://doi.org/10.2979/reseafrilite.50.1.01.

Burke, Chesya. "Chocolate Park." *Let's Play White.* Apex, 2011, pp. 48–71.

Burke, Minyvonne. "Buffalo Shooting Suspect Said He Carried Out Attack 'for the future of the White race,' Federal Complaint Says." *NBC News,* 16 June 2022, https://www.nbcnews.com/news/us-news/buffalo-shooting-suspect-said-carried-attack-future-white-race-federal-rcna33886.

Burnett, Joshua Yu. "The Great Change and the Great Book: Nnedi Okorafor's Postcolonial, Post-Apocalyptic Africa and the Promise of Black Speculative Fiction." *Research in African Literatures,* vol. 46, no. 4, 2015, pp. 133–50. JSTOR, https://www.jstor.org/stable/10.2979/reseafrilite.46.4.133.

Butler, Octavia E. *Kindred.* Beacon, 1988.

Byrd, Merry. "The Sankofa Spirit of Afro-futurisms in *Who Fears Death* and *Riot Baby.*" *Femspec,* vol. 21, no. 1, 2021, pp. 45–71.

Carnegie, Andrew. "The Gospel of Wealth." Carnegie Corporation of New York, 1889, https://www.carnegie.org/about/our-history/gospelofwealth/.

Carroll, Noël. *The Philosophy of Horror, or Paradoxes of the Heart.* Routledge, 1990.

Charlton, Richard Wayne, and Jaco Barkhuizen. "Serial Murder." *The Encyclopedia of Criminology and Criminal Justice,* edited by Jay S. Albanese, Wiley, 2014. Research-Gate, https://doi.org/10.1002/9781118517383.wbeccj266.

Clarke, John Henrik. "Santa Claus Is a White Man." *The Best Short Stories by Black Writers, 1899–1967,* edited by Langston Hughes, Back Bay, 1967, pp. 181–87.

Cohen, Jeffrey Jerome, editor. "Monster Culture (Seven Theses)." *Monster Theory: Reading Culture,* U of Minnesota P, 1996, pp. 3–25.

Coleman, Robin R. Means. *Horror Noire: Blacks in American Horror Films from the 1890s to Present.* Routledge, 2011.

Collins, Patricia Hill. *Black Sexual Politics: African Americans, Gender, and the New Racism.* Routledge, 2009.

Combs, Barbara Harris. *Bodies out of Place: Theorizing Anti-Blackness in U.S. Society.* U of Georgia P, 2022.

Cooper, Brittney C. *Beyond Respectability: The Intellectual Thought of Race Women.* U of Illinois P, 2017.

Cunningham, D. J., and E. H. Bennett. "The Brain and Eyeball of a Human Cyclopian Monster." *The Transactions of the Royal Irish Academy,* vol. 29, 1887–1892, pp. 101–22. *JSTOR,* https://www.jstor.org/stable/30078812.

Curry, Tommy J. "Foreword: Black Maleness as a Deleterious Category." *Appealing Because He Is Appalling: Black Masculinities, Colonialism, and Erotic Racism,* edited by Tamari Kitossa, U of Alberta Press, 2021, pp. xi–xxvi.

———. *The Man-Not: Race, Class, Genre, and the Dilemma of Black Manhood.* Temple UP, 2017.

Davis, Angela Y. "Race and Criminalization: Black Americans and the Punishment Industry." *The House That Race Built,* edited by Wahneema Lubiano, Vintage, 1998, pp. 264–79.

Davis, Lexi. "Are You My Daddy?" *Whispers in the Night,* edited by Brandon Massey, Dafina, 2007, pp. 63–83.

d'Hont, Coco. "Boundary Crossing and Cultural Creation: Transgressive Horror and Politics of the 1990s." *The Palgrave Handbook to Horror Literature,* edited by Kevin Corstorphine and Laura R. Kremmel, Palgrave MacMillan, 2018, pp. 377–89.

Diawara, Manthia, and Phyllis Klotman. "*Ganja and Hess*: Vampires, Sex, and Addictions." *Black American Literature Forum,* vol. 25, no. 2, 1991, pp. 299–314. *JSTOR,* https://www.jstor.org/stable/3041688.

Dillard, Angela. *Guess Who's Coming to Dinner Now?: Multicultural Conservatism in America.* New York UP, 2001.

Du Bois, W. E. B. "Jesus Christ in Texas." *Dark Matter: Reading the Bones,* edited by Sheree Thomas, Warner Books, 2004, pp. 95–104.

———. "The Talented Tenth." *The Future of the Race,* authored by Henry Louis Gates Jr. and Cornel West, Vintage, 1997, pp. 133–57.

———. "The Talented Tenth Memorial Address." *The Future of the Race,* authored by Henry Louis Gates Jr. and Cornel West, Vintage, 1997, pp. 159–77.

duCille, Ann. "The Shirley Temple of My Familiar." *Transition*, no. 73, 1997, pp. 10–32.

Due, Tananarive. *The Between*. HarperPerennial, 1996.

Dukakis, Andrea. "Murder of Colorado Radio Man Alan Berg Still Resonates 30 Years Later." *Colorado Public Radio*, 18 June 2014, https://www.cpr.org/show-segment/murder-of-colorado-radio-man-alan-berg-still-resonates-30-years-later/.

Fanon, Frantz. *Black Skin, White Masks*. Grove Weidenfeld, 1967.

Farley, Anthony Paul. "Toward a General Theory of Antiblackness." *Antiblackness*, edited by Moon-Kie Jung and João H. Costa Vargas, Duke UP, 2021, pp. 82–104.

Farrell, Amanda L., et al. "Testing Existing Classifications of Serial Murder Considering Gender: An Exploratory Analysis of Solo Female Serial Murderers?" *Journal of Investigative Psychology and Offender Profiling*, vol. 10, 2013, pp. 268–88. *Wiley Online Library*, https://doi.org/10.1002/jip.1392.

Federal Bureau of Investigation. *Serial Murder: Multi-Disciplinary Perspectives for Investigators*. Behavioral Analysis Unit, National Center for the Analysis of Violent Crime, US Department of Justice, 2008.

Ferguson, Roderick A. *Aberrations in Black: Toward a Queer of Color Critique*. U of Minnesota P, 2004.

Fleming, Robert. Introduction. *Havoc After Dark: Tales of Terror*. Kensington, 2004, pp. xiii–xiv.

———. "The Ultimate Bad Luck." *Havoc After Dark: Tales of Terror*. Kensington, 2004, pp. 37–49.

Floyd, Carlton D., and Thomas E. Reifer. *The American Dream and Dreams Deferred: A Dialectical Fairytale*. Lexington Books, 2023.

———. "What Happens to a Dream Deferred? W. E. B. Du Bois and the Radical Black Enlightenment/Endarkenment." *Socialism and Democracy*, vol. 32, no. 3, 2018, pp. 52–80.

Francis, Alison. "Contextualizing Escape in the Neo-slave Narratives of Octavia Butler's *Kindred* and Sherley Anne Williams's *Dessa Rose*." *Human Contradictions in Octavia E. Butler's Work*, edited by Martin Japtok and Jerry Rafiki Jenkins, Palgrave, 2020, pp. 13–27.

Franklin, John Hope, and Alfred A. Moss Jr. *From Slavery to Freedom: A History of African Americans*. McGraw-Hill, 1994.

Fredrickson, George. *Racism: A Short History*. Princeton UP, 2002.

Fridel, Emma E., and James Alan Fox. "Too Few Victims: Finding the Optimal Minimum Victim Threshold for Defining Serial Murder." *Psychology of Violence*, vol. 8, no. 4, 2018, pp. 505–14. *APA PsycNet*, http://doi.org/10.1037/vi00000138.

George, Rickey Windell. "Good 'Nough to Eat." *Voices from the Other Side: Dark Dreams II*, edited by Brandon Massey, Dafina, 2006, pp. 209–34.

Gilroy, Paul. *Against Race: Imagining Political Culture Beyond the Color Line*. Belknap-Harvard UP, 2001.

———. "Introduction to the HarperPerennial Edition." *Eight Men*, author by Richard Wright, HarperPerennial, 1996, pp. xi–xxi.

Giroux, Susan Searles. "Sade's Revenge: Racial Neoliberalism and the Sovereignty of Negation." *Patterns of Prejudice*, vol. 44, no. 1, 2010, pp. 1–26.

Glave, Dianne. "'My Characters Are Teaching Me To Be Strong': An Interview with Tananarive Due." *African American Review,* vol. 38, no. 4, 2004, pp. 695–705.

Goldberg, David Theo. "Racial Americanization." *Narrative, Law and Society,* vol. 1, no. 1, 2004, *AmeriQuests,* https://doi.org/10.15695/amqst.v1i1.9.

Gomez, Jewelle. *The Gilda Stories.* Firebrand Books, 2005.

———. "The Second Law of Thermodynamics: Transcription of a Panel at the 1997 Black Speculative Fiction Writers Conference Held at Clark Atlanta University." *Dark Matter: Reading of the Bones,* edited by Sheree R. Thomas, Warner, 2004, pp. 349–68.

———. "Speculative Fiction and Black Lesbians." *Signs,* vol. 18, no. 4, 1993, pp. 948–55.

Gonzalez, Nina. "Reproducing for the Race: Eugenics, 'Race Suicide,' and the Origins of White Replacement Conspiracy Theories, 1882–1924." 2022. UC Davis, MA thesis. *eScholarship,* https://escholarship.org/uc/item/0v38s4hm.

Gorham, Candace. *The Ebony Exodus Project: Why Some Black Women Are Walking Out on Religion—And Others Should Too.* Pitchstone, 2013.

Graham, Lawrence Otis. *Our Kind of People: Inside America's Black Upper Class.* Harper-Perennial, 1999.

Guran, Paula. "Behind the Bates Motel: Robert Bloch." *DarkEcho,* Aug. 1999, http://darkecho.com/darkecho/horroronline/bloch.html.

Halberstam, Jack. *Skin Shows: Gothic Horror and the Technology of Monsters.* Duke UP, 1995.

Hampton, Gregory J. *Changing Bodies in the Fiction of Octavia Butler: Slaves, Aliens, and Vampires.* Lexington Books, 2010.

Harris, Aisha. "Santa Claus Should Not Be a White Man Anymore." *Slate,* 10 Dec. 2013, https://slate.com/human-interest/2013/12/santa-claus-an-old-white-man-not-anymore-meet-santa-the-penguin-a-new-christmas-symbol.html.

Harris, Trudier. "Tiptoeing through Taboo: Incest in 'The Child Who Favored Daughter.'" *Modern Fiction Studies,* vol. 28, no. 3, 1982, pp. 494–505. *JSTOR,* http://www.jstor.org/stable/26281235.

Harrison, Marissa A., Susan M. Hughes, and Adam Jordan Gott. "Sex Differences in Serial Killers." *Evolutionary Behavioral Sciences,* vol. 13, no. 4, 2019, pp. 295–310. *APA PsycNet,* https://doi.org/10.1037/ebs0000157.

Harrison, Marissa A., et al. "Female Serial Killers in the United States: Means, Motives, and Makings." *The Journal of Forensic Psychiatry & Psychology,* vol. 26, no. 3, 2015, pp. 383–406, *Taylor & Francis Online,* https://doi.org/10.1080/14789949.2015.1007516.

Harrison, Sheri-Marie. "Marlon James and the Metafiction of the New Black Gothic." *liquid blackness: Journal of Aesthetics and Black Studies,* vol. 6, no. 2, 2022, pp. 62–85. *Duke UP,* https://doi.org/10.1215/26923874-9930293.

———. "The New Black Gothic." *Los Angeles Review of Books,* 23 June 2018. *LARB,* https://lareviewofbooks.org/article/new-black-gothic/.

Hartman, Saidiya. *Scenes of Subjection: Terror, Slavery, and Self-Making in Nineteenth-Century America.* Oxford UP, 1997.

Hefner, Brooks E. "Rethinking *Blacula*: Ideological Critique at the Intersection of Genres." *Journal of Popular Film & Television,* vol. 40, no. 2, June 2012, pp. 62–74. *Taylor & Francis Online,* https://doi.org/10.1080/01956051.2011.620038.

Herbert, Bob. "Impossible, Ridiculous, Repugnant." *New York Times*, 6 Oct. 2005, https://www.nytimes.com/2005/10/06/opinion/impossible-ridiculous-repugnant.html.

Hine, Darlene Clark, et al. *The African American Odyssey*. 6th ed., Pearson, 2014.

Hochschild, Jennifer L. *Facing Up to the American Dream: Race, Class, and the Soul of the Nation*. Princeton UP, 1995.

hooks, bell. *Killing Rage: Ending Racism*. Owl, 1995.

Humann, Heather Duerre. "Beyond Science Fiction: Genre in *Kindred* and Butler's Short Stories." *Human Contradictions in Octavia E. Butler's Work*, edited by Martin Japtok and Jerry Rafiki Jenkins, Palgrave, 2020, pp. 91–106.

Huntington, Clare. "The Complex First Family." *Family Court Review*, vol. 56, no. 2, 2018, pp. 351–53. *Wiley Online Library*, https://doi.org/10.1111/fcre.12346.

Jakobsen, Janet R. "Religion." *Keywords for American Cultural Studies*, edited by Bruce Burgett and Glenn Hendler, New York UP, 2007, pp. 201–4.

James, Joy. *Transcending the Talented Tenth: Black Leaders and American Intellectuals*. Routledge, 1997.

Japtok, Martin. "African American Literature and the Gothic: Some Critical Usage Considerations." *Journal of Foreign Languages and Cultures*, vol. 2, no. 2, 2018, pp. 1–10.

Japtok, Martin, and Jerry Rafiki Jenkins, editors. "What Does It Mean to Be 'Really' Black?: A Selective History of Authentic Blackness." *Authentic Blackness/"Real Blackness": Essays on the Meaning of Blackness in Literature and Culture*, Peter Lang, 2011, pp. 7–51.

Japtok, Martin, and Winfried Schleiner. "Genetics and 'Race' in *The Merchant of Venice*." *Literature and Medicine*, vol. 18, no. 2, 1999, pp. 155–72.

Jenkins, Candice M. "Family." *Keywords for African American Studies*, edited by Erica R. Edwards et al., New York UP, 2018, pp. 82–85.

Jenkins, Jerry Rafiki. "*Blacula* and the Question of Blackness." *Screening Noir*, vol. 1, no. 1, 2005, pp. 49–79.

———. *The Paradox of Blackness in African American Vampire Fiction*. The Ohio State UP, 2019.

———. "Race, Freedom, and the Black Vampire in Jewelle Gomez's *The Gilda Stories*." *African American Review*, vol. 46, no. 2–3, 2013, pp. 313–28.

———. "Is Religiosity a Black Thing?: Reading the Black None in Octavia E. Butler's 'The Book of Martha.'" *Pacific Coast Philology*, vol. 55, no. 1, 2020, pp. 5–22.

———. "Transhumanism, Posthumanism, and the Human in Octavia Butler's *Xenogenesis*." *Human Contradictions in Octavia E. Butler's Work*, edited by Martin Japtok and Jerry Rafiki Jenkins, Palgrave Macmillan, 2020, pp. 121–45.

Jenkins, Jerry Rafiki, and Katie Sciurba. "Body Knowledge, Reproductive Anxiety, and 'Paying the Rent' in Octavia E. Butler's 'Bloodchild.'" *Science Fiction Studies*, vol. 49, no. 1, 2022, pp. 120–37.

Jordan, Patrick W. *Designing Pleasurable Products*. Taylor and Francis, 2000.

Jones, Miriam. "*The Gilda Stories*: Revealing the Monsters at the Margin." *Blood Read: The Vampire as Metaphor in Contemporary Culture*, edited by Joan Gordon and Veronica Hollinger, U of Pennsylvania P, 1997, pp. 151–67.

Keetley, Dawn, editor. *Jordan Peele's Get Out: Political Horror*. The Ohio State UP, 2020.

Keith, Tamara. "Pro-Trump Group Returns Donation from White Nationalist after Media Inquiry." *NPR,* 25 July 2020, https://www.npr.org/2020/07/25/895196681/pro-trump-group-returns-donation-from-white-nationalist-after-media-inquiry.

Kennedy, Randall. *Interracial Intimacies: Sex, Marriage, Identity, and Adoption.* Vintage, 2004.

King, Debra Walker. *African Americans and the Culture of Pain.* U of Virginia P, 2008.

Kitossa, Tamari, editor. Introduction. *Appealing Because He Is Appalling: Black Masculinities, Colonialism, and Erotic Racism,* U of Alberta Press, 2021, pp. xxxix–xcvii.

Knight, Zelda G. "Some Thoughts on the Psychological Roots of the Behavior of Serial Killers as Narcissists: An Object Relations Perspective." *Social Behavior & Personality: An International Journal,* vol. 34, no. 10, 2006, pp. 1189–206. *APA PsycNet,* https://doi.org/10.2224/sbp.2006.34.10.1189.

Kotecki, Kristine. "Apocalyptic Affect in Nnedi Okorafor's Speculative Futures." *Research in African Literatures,* vol. 51, no. 3, 2020, pp. 164–79. *Project Muse,* https://muse.jhu.edu/article/783601/pdf.

Kristeva, Julia. *Powers of Horror: An Essay on Abjection.* Columbia UP, 1982.

LaValle, Victor. *The Changeling.* Spiegel & Grau, 2018.

Lester, Neal A. "'Not my mother, not my sister, but it's me, O Lord, standing . . .': Alice Walker's 'The Child Who Favored Daughter' as Neo-Slave Narrative." *Studies in Short Fiction,* vol. 34, no. 3, 1997, pp. 289–305.

Lewis, Christopher S. "Queering Personhood in the Neo-Slave Narrative: Jewelle Gomez's *The Gilda Stories.*" *African American Review,* vol. 47, no. 4, 2014, pp. 447–59.

"Lexi Davis." *Goodreads,* https://www.goodreads.com/author/show/742259.Lexi_Davis. Accessed 6 Nov. 2023.

Lindow, Sandra. "Nnedi Okorafor." *Journal of the Fantastic in the Arts,* vol. 28, no. 1, 2017, pp. 46–69. *JSTOR,* https://www.jstor.org/stable/10.2307/26390193.

Lipsitz, George. *The Possessive Investment in Whiteness: How White People Profit from Identity Politics.* Temple UP, 1998.

Long, Lisa A. "A Relative Pain: The Rape of History in Octavia Butler's *Kindred* and Phyllis Alesia Perry's *Stigmata.*" *College English,* vol. 64, no. 4, 2002, pp. 459–83. *JSTOR,* https://www.jstor.org/stable/3250747.

Manning, Patrick. *The African Diaspora: A History through Culture.* Columbia UP, 2009.

Marx, Karl, and Friedrich Engels. *Manifesto of the Communist Party.* Introduced by A. J. P. Taylor, Penguin, 1967, pp. 77–121.

Massey, Brandon, editor. Introduction. *Whispers in the Night,* Dafina, 2007, pp. 1–4.

———. Introduction. *Voices from the Other Side: Dark Dreams II,* Dafina, 2006, pp. 1–2.

———. Introduction. *Dark Dreams: A Collection of Horror and Suspense by Black Writers,* Dafina, 2004, pp. ix–xii.

Maxwell, Angie. "What We Get Wrong about the Southern Strategy." *Washington Post,* 26 July 2019. https://www.washingtonpost.com/outlook/2019/07/26/what-we-get-wrong-about-southern-strategy/.

Mbembe, Achille. *Necropolitics.* Translated by Steven Corcoran, Duke UP, 2019.

McKittrick, Katherine. *Demonic Grounds: Black Women and the Cartographies of Struggle.* U of Minnesota P, 2006.

Mead, Charles H. "A Quantitative Study in Human Teratology." *Human Biology*, vol. 2, no. 1, 1930, pp. 1–33. *JSTOR*, https://www.jstor.org/stable/41447018.

Meaddough, R. J., III. "The Death of Tommy Grimes." *The Best Short Stories by Black Writers, 1899–1967*, edited by Langston Hughes, Back Bay, 1967, pp. 408–13.

Medovoi, Leerom. "Theorizing Historicity, or the Many Meanings of *Blacula*." *Screen*, vol. 39, no. 1, 1998, pp. 1–21.

Miller, Eugene E. "Folkloric Aspects of Wright's "The Man Who Killed a Shadow." *CLA Journal*, vol. 27, no. 2, 1983, pp. 210–23. *JSTOR*, https://www.jstor.org/stable/44321774.

Montgomery, Christine, and Ellen C. Caldwell. "Visualizing Dana and Transhistorical Time Travel on the Covers of Octavia E. Butler's *Kindred*." *The Bloomsbury Handbook to Octavia E. Butler*, edited by Gregory Jerome Hampton and Kendra R. Parker, Bloomsbury, 2020, pp. 151–80.

Morris, Susana M. *Close Kin and Distant Relatives: The Paradox of Respectability in Black Women's Literature*. U of Virginia P, 2014.

Moynihan, Daniel. *The Negro Family: The Case for National Action*. United States Department of Labor, Office of Policy Planning and Research, 1965.

Murphy, Bernice M. "Contemporary Serial Killers." *Twenty-First Century Gothic: An Edinburgh Companion*, edited by Maisha Wester and Xavier Aldana Reyes, Edinburgh UP, 2021, pp. 117–30.

Nelson, Alondra. "Introduction: Future Texts." *Social Text*, vol. 20, no. 2, 2002, pp. 1–15.

Nevins, Jess. *Horror Fiction in the 20th Century: Exploring Literature's Most Chilling Genre*. Praeger, 2020.

Nickel, Philip J. "Horror and the Idea of Everyday Life: On Skeptical Threats in *Psycho* and *The Birds*." *The Philosophy of Horror*, edited by Thomas Fahy, UP of Kentucky, 2010, pp. 14–32.

Nixon, Nicola. "Making Monsters, or Serializing Killers." *American Gothic: New Interventions in a National Narrative*, edited by Robert K. Martin and Eric Savoy, U of Iowa P, 1998, pp. 217–36.

Nyong'o, Tavia. *Afro-Fabulations: The Queer Drama of Black Life*. New York UP, 2019.

Oduwobi, Oluyomi. "Rape Victims and Victimisers in Herbstein's Ama, a Story of the Atlantic Slave Trade." *Tydskrif vir Letterkunde*, vol. 54, no. 2, spring 2017, pp. 100–111. *Gale Literature Resource Center*, http://link.gale.com/apps/doc/A655199366/LitRC?u=cclc_palomar&sid=bookmark-LitRC&xid=5bfc2352.

Okorafor, Nnedi. 's *Who Fears Death*. HarperVoyager, 2018.

———. "Writing Rage, Truth and Consequence." *Journal of the Fantastic in the Arts*, vol. 26, no. 1, 2015, pp. 21–26. *JSTOR*, https://www.jstor.org/stable/26321077.

Pahl, Miriam. "Time, Progress, and Multidirectionality in Nnedi Okorafor's *Who Fears Death*." *Research in African Literatures*, vol. 49, no. 3, 2018, pp. 207–22. *JSTOR*, https://www.jstor.org/stable/10.2979/reseafrilite.49.3.12.

Pass, Michael, et al. "'I Just Be Myself': Contradicting Hyper Masculine and Hyper Sexual Stereotypes among Low-Income Black Men in New York City." *Hyper Sexual, Hyper Masculine?: Gender, Race and Sexuality in the Identities of Contemporary Black Men*, edited by Brittany C. Slatton and Kamesha Spates, Routledge, 2020, pp. 165–81.

Patterson, Orlando. *Slavery and Social Death: A Comparative Study*. 1982. Harvard UP, 2018.

Peaslee, L. D. "A Human Monstrosity." *Science*, vol. 37, no. 965, 1913, p. 982. *JSTOR*, https://www.jstor.org/stable/1637952.

Perry, Pamela. "White." *Keywords for American Cultural Studies*, edited by Bruce Burgett and Glenn Hendler, New York UP, 2007, pp. 242–46.

Pieski, John E. V. "Subnormal Mentality as a Defense in the Criminal Law." *Vanderbilt Law Review*, vol. 15, no. 3, 1962, pp. 769–95. *Scholarship@Vanderbilt Law*, https://scholarship.law.vanderbilt.edu/vlr/vol15/iss3/4.

Poole, W. Scott. *Monsters in America: Our Historical Obsession with the Hideous and the Haunting.* Baylor UP, 2018.

Quashie, Kevin. *Black Aliveness, or A Poetics of Being.* Duke UP, 2021.

Raymond, Claire. "The Crucible of Witnessing: Projects of Identity in Carrie Mae Weems's *From Here I Saw What Happened and I Cried.*" *Meridians*, vol. 13, no. 1, 2015, pp. 26–52. *JSTOR*, https://www.jstor.org/stable/10.2979/meridians.13.1.26.

Reeves, Dia. *Slice of Cherry.* Simon Pulse, 2011.

Renegade Cut. *The Feminine Horror.* 13 Oct. 2018, *Youtube*, https://www.youtube.com/watch?v=EjDwLg2bgTk.

Reyes, Xavier Aldana. "Introduction: What, Why and When Is Horror Fiction?" *Horror: A Literary History*, edited by Reyes, British Library Publishing, 2016, pp. 7–17.

Russell-Brown, Katheryn. *Protecting Our Own: Race, Crime, and African Americans.* Rowan & Littlefield, 2006.

Saini, Angela. *Superior: The Return of Race Science.* Beacon Press, 2019.

Samatar, Sofia. "Toward a Planetary History of Afrofuturism." *Research in African Literatures*, vol. 48, no. 4, 2017, pp. 175–91. *JSTOR*, https://www.jstor.org/stable/10.2979/reseafrilite.48.4.12.

Santilli, Paul. "Culture, Evil, and Horror." *The American Journal of Economics and Sociology*, vol. 66, no. 1, 2007, pp. 173–94. *JSTOR*, https://www.jstor.org/stable/27739626.

Sciurba, Katie, and Jerry Rafiki Jenkins. "*Smoky Night* and the Un-telling of the L.A. Riots." *Journal of Children's Literature*, vol. 45, no. 1, 2019, pp. 4–13.

Scott, Darieck. *Extravagant Abjection: Blackness, Power, and Sexuality in the African American Literary Imagination.* New York UP, 2010.

Sharpe, Christina. *In the Wake: On Blackness and Being.* Duke UP, 2016.

———. *Monstrous Intimacies: Making Post-Slavery Subjects.* Duke UP, 2010.

Slatton, Brittany C. "The Black Box: Constrained Maneuvering of Black Masculine Identity." *Hyper Sexual, Hyper Masculine?: Gender, Race and Sexuality in the Identities of Contemporary Black Men*, edited by Kamesha Spates and Brittany C. Slatton, Routledge, 2020, pp. 33–41.

Smith, Robert C. *Conservatism and Racism, and Why in America They Are the Same.* State U of New York P, 2010.

Spates, Kamesha, and Brittany C. Slatton, editors. "Introduction: Blackness, Maleness, and Sexuality as Interwoven Identities: Toward an Understanding of Contemporary Black Male Identity Formation." *Hyper Sexual, Hyper Masculine?: Gender, Race and Sexuality in the Identities of Contemporary Black Men*, Routledge, 2020, pp. 1–4.

Spillers, Hortense J. "Mama's Baby, Papa's Maybe: An American Grammar Book." *Black, White, and in Color: Essays on American Literature and Culture*, U of Chicago P, 2003, pp. 203–29.

Southern Poverty Law Center. "Council of Conservative Citizens." https://www.splcenter.org/fighting-hate/extremist-files/group/council-conservative-citizens. Accessed 22 Sept. 2023.

Strings, Sabrina. *Fearing the Black Body: The Racial Origins of Fat Phobia.* New York UP, 2019.

"Strom Thurmond: A Featured Biography." United States Senate, https://www.senate.gov/senators/FeaturedBios/Featured_Bio_Thurmond.htm.

Taney, Roger Brooke, and Supreme Court of the United States. *U.S. Reports: Dred Scott v. Sandford, 60 U.S. 19 How. 393.* 1856. Periodical. *Library of Congress,* www.loc.gov/item/usrep060393a/.

Taylor, Leila. *Darkly: Black History and America's Gothic Soul.* Repeater, 2019.

Thernstrom, Stephan, and Abigail Thernstrom. *America in Black and White: One Nation, Indivisible.* Touchstone, 1999.

Thiessen, Mark. "Anchorage Police Investigated in White Privilege Card Photo." *AP News,* 13 July 2022, https://apnews.com/article/police-alaska-social-media-donald-trump-f8778d0f7f7628f665205f69b0537e85.

Tiger, Lionel. *The Pursuit of Pleasure.* Transaction, 2000.

Vargas, João H. Costa, and Moon-Kie Jung. "Introduction: Antiblackness of the Social and the Human." *Antiblackness,* edited by Moon-Kie Jung and João H. Costa Vargas, Duke UP, 2021, pp. 1–14.

Vint, Sherryl. "'Only by Experience': Embodiment and the Limitations of Realism in Neo-Slave Narratives." *Science Fiction Studies,* vol. 34, no. 2, 2007, pp. 241–61. *JSTOR,* https://www.jstor.org/stable/4241524.

Wabuke, Hope. "Afrofuturism, Africanfuturism, and the Language of Black Speculative Literature." *Los Angeles Review of Books,* 27 Aug. 2020, https://lareviewofbooks.org/article/afrofuturism-africanfuturism-and-the-language-of-black-speculative-literature/.

Walker, Alice. "The Child Who Favored Daughter." *In Love & Trouble: Stories of Black Women,* Harcourt Brace, 1973, pp. 35–46.

Ward, Jane. *Not Gay: Sex between Straight White Men.* New York UP, 2015.

Warren, Calvin L. *Ontological Terror: Blackness, Nihilism, and Emancipation.* Duke UP, 2018.

Weheliye, Alexander G. *Habeas Viscus: Racializing Assemblages, Biopolitics, and Black Feminist Theories of the Human.* Duke UP, 2014.

Weinstock, Jeffrey Andrew, editor. "Introduction: A Genealogy of Monster Theory." *The Monster Theory Reader,* U of Minnesota P, 2020, pp. 173–91.

Wells, Ida B. *Southern Horrors: Lynch Law in All Its Phases. Southern Horrors and Other Writings: The Antilynching Campaign of Ida B. Wells, 1892–1900,* edited by Jacqueline Jones Royster, Bedford/St. Martin's, 1997, pp. 49–72.

———. *A Red Record. Southern Horrors and Other Writings: The Antilynching Campaign of Ida B. Wells, 1892–1900,* edited by Jacqueline Jones Royster, Bedford/St. Martin's, 1997, pp. 73–157.

Wester, Maisha. *African American Gothic: Screams from Shadowed Places.* Palgrave Macmillan, 2012.

Wester, Maisha, and Xavier Aldana Reyes, editors. "Introduction: The Gothic in the Twenty-First Century." *Twenty-First Century Gothic: An Edinburgh Companion*, Edinburgh UP, 2021, pp. 1–16.

White, Deborah Gray, et al. *Freedom on My Mind: A History of African Americans with Documents*. Bedford/St. Martin's, 2017.

White, E. Frances. *Dark Continent of Our Bodies: Black Feminism and the Politics of Respectability*. Temple UP, 2001.

Wiegman, Robyn. "The Anatomy of Lynching." *A Question of Manhood: A Reader in U.S. Black Men's History and Masculinity*, edited by Darlene Clark Hine and Earnestine Jenkins, Indiana UP, 2001, pp. 349–69.

Wilderson, Frank B., III. *Afropessimism*. Liveright, 2020.

———. *Red, White, & Black: Cinema and the Structure of U.S. Antagonisms*. Duke UP, 2010.

Wilkerson, Isabel. *Caste: The Origins of Our Discontents*. Random House, 2020.

Wilson, Natalie. *Willful Monstrosity: Gender and Race in 21st Century Horror*. McFarland, 2020.

Winter, Kari. *Subjects of Slavery, Agents of Change: Women and Power in Gothic Novels and Slave Narratives, 1790–1865*. U of Georgia P, 1992.

Withnall, Adam. "Donald Trump's Unsettling Record of Comments about His Daughter Ivanka." *Independent*, 10 Oct. 2016, https://www.independent.co.uk/news/world/americas/us-politics/donald-trump-ivanka-trump-creepiest-most-unsettling-comments-roundup-a7353876.html.

Wright, Alexa. "Monstrous Strangers at the Edge of the World: The Monstrous Races." *The Monster Theory Reader*, edited by Jeffrey Andrew Weinstock, U of Minnesota P, 2020, pp. 173–91.

Wright, Richard. "The Man Who Killed a Shadow." *Eight Men*, introduction by Paul Gilroy, HarperPerennial, 1996, pp. 185–201.

INDEX

horror and, 78–79; hypersexuality and, 51–52; kyriarchy and, 78–79; monstrosity and, 53–79; racism and, 48n15; slavery and, 59–69; in Walker, 55–56

Restoration horror plays, 7–8, 8n7

Reyes, Xavier Aldana, 7

Ridgeway, Gary, 128n5

Roof, Dylann, 48

Rushdy, Ashraf, 59

sadism, 14; anti-Black, 49, 135; moral, 21, 87, 91; racial, 13–14

Saini, Angela, 28n7

salvation, 57–58

sameness, racial, 24–26, 37–38, 141

Santa Claus, 26–27, 26n5, 27

"Santa Claus Is a White Man" (Clarke), 15, 21–24, 24n3, 25–29, 49

Santilli, Paul, 8n7

Sapphire (writer), 56

Saul, John, 6

Scenes of Subjection (Hartman), 140n4

Schleiner, Winfried, 11n9

Schow, David, 94n6

Science (magazine), 1

science fiction, 2n2, 61, 70, 72

Sciurba, Katie, 20n1

Scott, Darieck, 81, 91n4

Scott, Ralph, 32

Searching for Sycorax (Brooks), 8

Second Treatise of Government (Locke), 19

seduction, 66–67

Séjour, Victor, 60

serial killers, 10n8, 16–17; Black elite and, 118–25; Blackness and, 110–13; criminal enterprise motive and, 115–16; defining, 109; female, 125–32; good and bad, 132–34; history of, 109; horror and, 10–12, 108–9, 134; maternal impression and, 11n9; mental illness and, 107–8, 115; motivations of, 109–10, 115–16, 131; victim selection by, 109–10, 116; victim-centered narratives of, 114–15, 118

settler colonialism, 19–20

Sexton, Jared, 137n2

sexual assault, 50–51, 62, 70, 75–76, 80, 82–83

sexuality: hypersexuality, 15–16, 50–52, 54, 78, 80–84, 87, 93–94, 98–99, 101–5, 138; sadism and, 14; serial killers and, 117; subjugation and, 82

Sharpe, Christina, 14, 61, 106, 111, 137

Sing, Unburied, Sing (Ward), 143

Singular, Stephen, 33n10

16th Street Baptist Church bombing (Birmingham), 30

Slatton, Brittany C., 80, 104

slave narratives, 5n4, 59–60, 59n3, 61, 68

slavery: family and, 38, 64; in *Gilda Stories*, 3; horror and, 4–5; in *Kindred*, 59–69; respectability and, 59–69; in Séjour, 60; women and, 63–64

Slavery and Social Death (Patterson), 54

Slice of Cherry (Reeves), 17, 108, 126–34

Snyder, Timothy, 28

social death, 54–56, 59, 61, 64, 67–68, 86, 137

Southern strategy, 31–33, 38, 135

"Speculative Fiction and Black Lesbians" (Gomez), 6n7

Spillers, Hortense J., 38, 47, 137n2

splatterpunk, 94, 94n6, 98

"Spunk" (Hurston), 22

Stigmata (Perry), 60

Strings, Sabrina, 51–52

Talented Tenth, 22–23

"Talented Tenth, The" (Du Bois), 120–21

Talked to Death (Singular), 33n10

Taylor, Leila, 12

teratology, 107–8

territorialization, 64

"This Is America" (Childish Gambino), 143

Thurmond, Strom, 31, 31n9

Tiger, Lionel, 14

Titterington, Victoria B., 126, 128, 130

Toomer, Jean, 22–23

Transaction of the Royal Irish Academy, The, 2

Trump, Donald, 39, 46n14, 47–48

Trump, Ivanka, 39n12

Tubman, Harriet, 66

"Ultimate Bad Luck, The" (Fleming), 16, 82, 84–85, 87–92, 105, 141, 144

NEW SUNS: RACE, GENDER, AND SEXUALITY IN THE SPECULATIVE
Susana M. Morris and Kinitra D. Brooks, Series Editors

Scholarly examinations of speculative fiction have been a burgeoning academic field for more than twenty-five years, but there has been a distinct lack of attention to how attending to nonhegemonic positionalities transforms our understanding of the speculative. New Suns: Race, Gender, and Sexuality in the Speculative addresses this oversight and promotes scholarship at the intersections of race, gender, sexuality, and the speculative, engaging interdisciplinary fields of research across literary, film, and cultural studies that examine multiple pasts, presents, and futures. Of particular interest are studies that offer new avenues into thinking about popular genre fictions and fan communities, including but not limited to the study of Afrofuturism, comics, ethnogothicism, ethnosurrealism, fantasy, film, futurity studies, gaming, horror, literature, science fiction, and visual studies. New Suns particularly encourages submissions that are written in a clear, accessible style that will be read both by scholars in the field as well as by nonspecialists.